WAR

OR WORDS?

OR WORDS?

Interreligious Dialogue
as an Instrument
of Peace

Edited by Donald W. Musser
and D. Dixon Sutherland

THE
PILGRIM
PRESS
Cleveland

The Pilgrim Press
700 Prospect Avenue
Cleveland, Ohio 44115-1100
pilgrimpress.com

Printed in the United States of America on acid-free paper

09 08 07 06 05   5 4 3 2 1

Library of Congress Cataloging-in-Publication Data

War or words? : interreligious dialogue as an instrument of peace / edited
  by Donald W. Musser and D. Dixon Sutherland.
      p.   cm.
    Includes bibliographical references.
    ISBN 0-8298-1683-6 (pbk. : alk. paper)
    1. Religions – Relations. 2. Peace – Religious aspects. I. Musser,
  Donald W., 1942- II. Sutherland, D. Dixon, 1950-
  BL410.W37 2005
  201'.5 – dc22
                                                      2005041929

Contents

Acknowledgments   vii

Introduction   1

Part I
ISSUES IN THE DIALOGUE BETWEEN RELIGIONS

1. Replacing Clashes with Dialogue among Religions and Nations: 7
   Toward a New Paradigm of International Relations
   Hans Küng

2. Ethical Challenges in the "War" on Terrorism   22
   Martin L. Cook

3. Islam and the Problem of Violence   36
   John Kelsay

4. Jewish-Christian Relations: After the *Shoah*   58
   Steven Leonard Jacobs

5. Dangerous Faith: Religion and Foreign Policy in the   75
   Administrations of George W. Bush
   Donald W. Musser, D. Dixon Sutherland,
   and Daniel A. Puchalla

Part II
OBSTACLES TO RELIGIOUS DIALOGUE

6. Absolute Truth Claims: Blockade to Dialogue   105
   Charles A. Kimball

7. Is the Empowered Woman a Warrior or a Dove?   124
   The Enigma of Feminism, Religion, Peace, and Violence
   Valarie H. Ziegler

8. Latin American Liberation Theology and the Dialogue for Peace   144
   Daniel M. Bell Jr.

9. Revitalization Movements and Violence   169
   John Mohawk

Part III

MOVING TOWARD DIALOGUE

10. Reconciliation: An Intrinsic Element of Peace and Justice   185
    Ada María Isasi-Díaz

11. The Justice of God and the Peace of Earth   204
    John Dominic Crossan

Notes   221

Contributors   246

Acknowledgments

The president of Stetson University, H. Douglas Lee, and the university's Values Council are foremost among those to whom we are indebted in bringing this volume to print. They avidly supported our proposal for a yearlong lecture series at Stetson on peace, violence, and religion while America was reeling from both the terrorist attacks of September 11, 2001, and debating the possible invasion of Iraq. Many of those lectures have been edited into essays that appear in this volume. Notable participants in this effort include Mary Ann Rogers, James R. Beasley, Karen Kaivola, Leonard Nance, Cindy Bennington, Emily Mieras, and Lisa Guenther. In addition, Nicole Galinat and Emily Snyder, our student assistants, have helped immeasurably to bring the manuscript to final form.

As always, the congenial collegiality of our colleagues in Religious Studies at Stetson (Mitchell Reddish, Kandy Queen-Sutherland, Phillip C. Lucas, Clyde Fant, and Barry Altman) has provided a working context that has given us ongoing intellectual stimulus.

The support of our marital partners enabled us to keep clear minds for our editing and wet lines for our ichthusiastic break-times on the St. Johns River.

Ulrike Guthrie, our editor, advised and supported us through every stage of our work. She is a marvel!

Introduction

No world peace without peace between the religions. No peace between the religions without dialogue between the religions.

— Hans Küng

Talk is cheap, the saying goes. But talk is only cheap if it is conducted as a monologue. Dialogue, on the other hand, is tremendously costly. It takes extraordinary energy and patience on the part of all those who are talking, if done with integrity. Monologues assume only talking. Dialogue assumes not only talking, but also a great deal of listening. The beginning of change, then, comes with dialogue.

Unfortunately, the events of September 11, 2001, have spawned mainly monologues. The talk has primarily centered on connections between religion and violence, accusations about violent inclinations found in religions, and countering defenses of religious justifications for the use of violence. This book was born out of listening to the morass of monologues about religion, violence, and peace in the aftermath of 9/11 and the subsequent attack by the United States on Iraq. As two university professors teaching undergraduate students about religion, we listened intently, attempting to articulate our own understanding (or lack of it) to our students. Yet, we discussed privately our discontentment with our efforts. Echoing in the background of all our "talk," we kept hearing Hans Küng's dictum that appears above. We began to realize that Küng's epigraph is really a warning — a warning that must be taken seriously if we are earnest about seeking peace in the world. Without peace between the religions of the world, there can be no hope for peace, but only more violence and destruction. And the key to that hope lies in dialogue — not monologue — between religions.

That is the intention of this book. We are asking the questions: If world peace is dependent on peace among the world's religions, and peace among the religions of the world depends on dialogue between them, then what should the dialogue look like now? Who should be at the discussion table? What does it take to get the necessary parties to the table? What are the important issues? What obstacles must be overcome in order to have any meaningful dialogue and outcome?

The essays that follow attempt to address what we consider to be "sea level" topics. They focus on some of the essentials necessary for the dialogue between religions to take place at all. Each essay therefore provides an element of transparency about the conditions necessary for any honest and useful dialogue on violence and peace to take place. They explore the contexts of religious dialogue, the parties participating, the issues that need discussion, the obstacles to meaningful dialogue, and the promise that such discussions will engender a more peaceful world.

One caveat to readers. One of the problems with collected essays is the lack of a progression of thought, so that a disparity exists between the essays. We are well aware that this book is no different. As we reflect on this "problem," however, we are convinced that the representation of issues that follows echoes the reality of dialogue much more than any tight presentation that flows with unity and logical progression. Conversations rarely follow any tight progression of thought, but rather present a give-and-take. Readers should therefore not expect to find an easy symmetry between the essays. Rather, each essay provides sparks that hopefully ignite meaningful instead of trite conversation. In an effort to help readers link important (not all!) connections of thought between authors, we have included a brief introduction to each essay.

The book is divided into three parts. Part I contain essays addressing important challenges to any current dialogue between religions. Martin Cook begins by facing the fact that terrorism has changed the way we must think about going to war. Any dialogue between religions must include a frank discussion about the traditional Christian theory of just war, since American politicians readily use this theory as a benchmark for deciding if military action is justified. Cook asks, "Is the traditional just war theory appropriate in the face of modern-day terrorism?"

John Kelsay then proposes that any dialogue must include an understanding of the traditional Muslim concept of *Shari'a*. *Shari'a* is the approved method for textual and theological interpretation of the Qur'an that is central to any Muslim dialogue. Kelsay critiques the *fatwah* against Western civilization that was written by Usama bin Laden and others on the grounds that it violates accepted methods of understanding the Qur'an, and he calls for a dialogue that reflects authoritative methods of *Shari'a*.

Any meaningful dialogue between Jews and Christians must be done within the historical and theological context of the genocidal violence of the Holocaust. Steven Jacobs insists that Christian complicity in that violence requires an attitude of humility and repentance, instead of typical evangelical triumphalism. The peaceable coexistence of Christians and Jews depends upon this shift in attitude.

Musser, Puchalla, and Sutherland suggest that Christian attitudes toward violence and war can be found in premillennial dispensationalism, a "futurist" interpretation of the Hebrew prophets and other apocalyptic writers. This worldview encourages a passive or even fatalistic attitude among Christians in the face of global violence. It lulls believers into thinking that violence between the state of Israel and its neighbors is inevitable, and that the United States is a chief player for bringing in the kingdom of God by means of violence in the Middle East. These attitudes have a powerful political influence on American foreign policy.

Part II focuses on the main obstacles to religious dialogue about peace and violence. One of the most detrimental barriers to dialogue is dogmatism. Charles Kimball argues that fundamentalism in religions demands that absolute truths are located exclusively in their texts and traditions. As a result, religious fundamentalism militates against serious dialogue in which discussants "hear" each other and are willing to understand empathetically the other parties.

Valarie Ziegler observes that another obstacle to dialogue is sexism. American women have historically provided leadership in peace movements, challenging traditional male power structures that constructed oppressive architectures of domination. Dialogue between religions must honestly address the injustices done to women. At the same time, women must assess the nascent violence (the "warrior" motif) that has also been manifest in their behavior.

Economic injustice is a major obstacle to dialogue for peace. Taking the case of recent Latin America, Daniel Bell points out that unbridled capitalism and the oppressive market control of American corporations is regarded by most in the world as a kind of terrorism. This structural violence "crucifies" the poor in Latin America. Using the interpretive methods of radical orthodoxy, Bell argues for the necessity of the powerful to "crucify" themselves so that a more just society might come to be.

Behind almost every genocidal event is a utopian idea lodged deeply within the religiously based movement. This is true for Nazism, the Crusades, and the efforts of expansionist missionary movements. A group attempting to reclaim what they regard as a utopian past that was taken away from them by some undeserving opponent commits gross violence. John Mohawk argues that any dialogue between religions must confront this reality and demythologize the idea of utopian reality in order to avert the rise of ideologically based aggression between ethnic, religious, and nationalistic groups.

Part III provides two positive steps that would move religions toward possible dialogue about peace instead of violence. Ada María Isasi-Díaz emphasizes the necessity of both oppressed and oppressors having an attitude of reconciliation, and the desire to deal openly with a divisive past in order that dialogue may lead to a common future. John Dominic Crossan provides an assessment of the concept of justice in the Bible as an alternative vision of the world. He proposes that the alternative biblical vision contributes a much different aphorism for peace — an aphorism that the religions of the world should adopt for themselves and promote among nations. It goes: "Not peace through victory, but peace through justice."

Part I

ISSUES IN THE DIALOGUE BETWEEN RELIGIONS

One

Replacing Clashes with Dialogue among Religions and Nations

Toward a New Paradigm of International Relations

HANS KÜNG

Hans Küng's introductory essay attempts to paint in broad strokes the daunting task of working toward peace among the nations of the world. Speaking directly to the political ferment of violence in Israel and Iraq, he calls for a new paradigm of international relations. Küng lays heavy responsibility especially on the governmental leadership of the United States, given its decisive roles in historic opportunities for peace during two world wars and the collapse of Soviet communism in 1989.

Küng's new paradigm maintains that geopolitical clashes between nations must be replaced with dialogue. This is not mere traditional diplomacy, but dialogue between the religions of clashing nations. Only then can a realistic vision of peace begin. Küng pleads for a "politics of peace" based on a series of projections that call for essential shifts in attitudes and approaches initiated by the United States.

Küng's essay is a vision that underlies the thesis of this book: that dialogue must begin among the religions of the world as presupposition to any hope for peace among the nations of the world. The issues he addresses form a framework for all of the essays that follow. Issues of just war (Cook), attitudes toward and by women (Ziegler), and the problems of absolute truth claims (Kimball) play important roles in Küng's call for a new paradigm. Especially pertinent to this vision

7

is the essay by Musser, Sutherland, and Puchalla, which points out specific religious orientations within the Bush administration which spell disaster for any hope of peace. These issues must be addressed transparently for dialogue to be possible.

Provocations for Dialogue

1. *Is honest dialogue possible between the religions of the world? What should the ground rules for such dialogue be?*

2. *Can religious leaders in the United States, without prejudice or self-interest, challenge the theological foundations of political foreign policies of nations that support unfairly one nation or ethnic population over another?*

3. *How can religions begin to focus on the centrality of a theology and ethic of peace as determinative for the future of the world?*

• • •

THREE SYMBOLIC DATES in the history of the West signal the new paradigm in international relations that is slowly and laboriously establishing itself: the paradigm's announcement (1918), its realization (1945), and finally its breakthrough (1989).

The Clashes of Nations

The first opportunity: 1918, the First World War, supported on both sides by the Christian churches, ended with a net result of around 10 million people dead and the collapse of the German empire, the Habsburg empire, the Czarist empire, and the Ottoman empire. The Chinese empire had collapsed earlier. Now for the first time there were American troops on European soil, and on the other side, the Soviet empire was in the making. This marked the beginning of the end of the Eurocentric-imperialistic paradigm of modernity and the dawning of a new paradigm. That new paradigm had not yet been defined, but had been foreseen by farsighted and enlightened thinkers, and was first set forth in the arena of international relations by the United States of America. With his "Fourteen Points," President Woodrow Wilson wanted to achieve a "just peace" and the "self-determination of the nations," without the annexations and demands for reparations that some in Congress wanted. President Wilson has been ignored too much in the United States and was even denigrated by Henry Kissinger, who often polemicized against "Wilsonianism."

The Versailles Treaty of Clémenceau and Lloyd George prevented the immediate realization of the new paradigm. That was "Realpolitik," a term first used first by Bismarck, but whose ideology was developed by Machiavelli and first put into political practice by Cardinal Richelieu. Instead of a just peace, there emerged a dictated peace in which the defeated nations took no part. The consequences of this approach are well known: Fascism and Nazism. Backed up in the Far East by Japanese militarism and not sufficiently opposed by the Christian churches, these were the catastrophic reactionary errors that two decades later led to the Second World War, a war far more devastating than any previous war in world history.

The second opportunity: 1945 saw the end of the Second World War with a net result of around 50 million people dead and many more million exiled. Fascism and Nazism had been defeated, but Soviet Communism appeared stronger and more formidable than ever to the international community, even though internally it was already experiencing a political, economic, and social crisis because of Stalin's policy. Again, the initiative for a new paradigm came from the United States. In 1945 the United Nations was founded in San Francisco, and the Bretton Woods Agreement on the reordering of the global economy was signed (and this became the foundation of the International Monetary Fund and the World Bank). In 1948 came the Universal Declaration of Human Rights, along with American economic aid (Marshall Plan) for the rebuilding of Europe and its incorporation into a free trade system. But Stalinism blocked the implementation of this paradigm in its sphere of influence, which led to the division of the world into East and West.

The third opportunity: 1989 saw the successful peaceful revolution in Eastern Europe and the collapse of Soviet Communism. After the Gulf War it was again an American president who announced a new paradigm, a "new world order," and found enthusiastic acceptance all over the world with this slogan. But in contrast to his predecessor, Woodrow Wilson, President George H. W. Bush felt embarrassed when he had to explain what this "vision thing" for the international order should look like. No change in Iraq, no democracy in Kuwait, no solution for the Israel-Palestine conflict, no democratic change in other Arab states. Likewise now, under President George W. Bush there are increasing doubts even in the United States that the so-called war against terrorism can constitute our vision for the future. So today the question arises: over the last decade, have we again forfeited the opportunity for a "new world order," a new paradigm?

We should not give up hope. And most especially I would say that it is committed Christians, Jews, Muslims, and members of other religions who should not give up hope but work for the new paradigm. After all, despite the wars, massacres, and streams of refugees in the twentieth century, despite the Gulag archipelago, the Holocaust — the most inhuman crime in the history of humanity — and the atomic bomb, we must not overlook some major changes for the better. After 1945, not only has humanity seen numerous astonishing scientific and technological achievements, but many ideas set forth in 1918 that had been pressing for a new, postmodern, and overall global constellation have been better able to establish themselves. The peace movement, the women's rights movement, the environmental movement, and the ecumenical movement all have made considerable progress in this era. There has also emerged in this period a new attitude to war and disarmament, to the partnership of men and women, to the relationship between economy and ecology not only among the Christian churches and the world religions but in society at large. After 1989, following the end of the enforced division of the world into West and East and the definitive demystification of both the evolutionary and the revolutionary ideology of progress, concrete possibilities for a pacific and cooperative world have begun to take shape. In contrast to European modernity, these possibilities are no longer Eurocentric but polycentric. Despite all the monstrous defects and conflicts still plaguing the international community, this new paradigm is in principle postimperialistic and postcolonial, with the ideals of an ecosocial market economy and truly united nations at its core.

So despite the terrors of the twentieth century, we can still see something like a hesitant historical progress. Over the last century, the formerly dominant political orientations have been banished for good. For one, imperialism has no scope in global politics after decolonialization. Moreover, since the end of the South African apartheid regime, racism, a consistent policy of racial privilege and racial discrimination, is no longer the explicit political strategy of any country. Likewise, in the lands of Western Europe from which it originated, nationalism has become a nonword and for many people is being replaced by dialogue, cooperation, and integration.

The Dialogue among Nations and Religions

Instead of the previously mentioned divisive politics, we see many countries moving toward a novel political model of regional coopera-tion and integration, and attempting to peacefully overcome centuries of confrontation. The result, not only between Germany and France first, not only in the European Union, but in the whole area of the OECD (Organization for Economic Cooperation and Development, founded in 1948 and developed in 1960), including all of the industri-alized countries (the European countries, the United States, Canada, Mexico, Australia, New Zealand, and Japan) has been half a cen-tury of democratic peace. That truly is a successful paradigm change! There are wars in Asia, Africa, South America, and in the Islamic world (e.g., El Salvador, Guatemala, Nicaragua, Colombia, Israel-Palestine, Sudan, Yemen, Algeria, the Gulf, Bosnia, and Kosovo), but one simply can no longer imagine a war between Germany and France or the United States and Japan.

So, after this all-too-brief historical tour, I want to move to the fundamental definition of the new paradigm of international relations. I have received much stimulation and support in a small international discussion "group of eminent persons" convened by United Nations Secretary-General Kofi Annan for the United Nations "Year of Dialogue among Civilizations, 2001,"[1] an endeavor that produced a report for the UN General Assembly, "Crossing the Divide: Dialogue among Civilizations."

On the basis of the experiences in the European Union (EU) and the OECD, the new overall political constellation can be sketched briefly as follows. Here, ethical categories cannot be avoided. Basically, the new paradigm entails policies of regional reconciliation, understanding, and cooperation instead of the modern national politics of self-interest, power, and prestige. Specifically, the exercise of political action now calls for reciprocal cooperation, compromise, and integration instead of the former confrontation, aggression, and revenge. This new overall political constellation manifestly presupposes a change of mentality, which goes far beyond the politics of the present day. For this new overall political constellation to hold, new approaches to international politics are needed.

For one, new international organizations are not enough here; what is needed is a new mind-set. National, ethnic, and religious differences must no longer be understood fundamentally as threats but rather as possible sources of enrichment. Whereas the old paradigm always presupposed an enemy, indeed a traditional enemy, the new paradigm no longer envisions or needs such an enemy. Rather, it seeks partners, rivals, and economic opponents for competition instead of military confrontation, and uses "soft" power (diplomatic influence and political persuasion, cultural influence and prestige) instead of "hard" military power (Joseph Nye).

This is possible because it has been proven that in the long run national prosperity is not furthered by war but only by peace, not by opposition or confrontation but by cooperation. And because the different interests that exist can be satisfied through collaboration, it is possible to come up with policies that are no longer a zero-sum game where one party wins at the expense of the other, but a positive-sum game in which all win.

Of course, this does not mean that politics has become easier in the new paradigm. It remains the art of the possible, though it has now become largely nonviolent. If the paradigm is to function, it cannot be based on a random postmodernist pluralism, where anything goes and anything is allowed. Rather, it presupposes a social consensus founded on particular basic values, basic rights, and basic responsibilities. All social groups and all nations must contribute to this basic social consensus, especially religious believers, but also nonbelievers and adherents to the different philosophies or ideologies. In other words, this social consensus, which cannot be imposed by a democratic system but has to be presupposed, envisages not one specific ethical system, but a common minimum of ethical standards, a common ethic, an ethic of humankind. This global ethic is not a new ideology or superstructure, imposed by the West on "the rest," but brings together the common religious and philosophical resources of all of humankind. For instance, the Golden Rule is found both in the Analects of Confucius and in the writings of Rabbi Hillel (before Christ) and of course in Jesus' Sermon on the Mount, but also in Muslim and other traditions: "What you do not wish done to yourself, do not do to others." Furthermore, a few very basic directives are common to all cultures, all humanity, for example, not to murder, not to steal, not to lie, not to abuse sexuality. I shall return to this point.

A global ethic should not be imposed by law but be brought to public awareness. A global ethic is oriented simultaneously to persons, institutions, and results. To this degree, a global ethic does not just focus on collective responsibility, relieving the individual of any responsibility (as if only the social "conditions," "history," and the "system" were to blame for specific abuses and crimes). Instead, it is focused in a particular way on the responsibility of each individual in his or her place in society and specifically on the individual responsibility of political leaders.

A freely made commitment to a common ethic of course does not exclude the support of law but rather includes it, and can in some circumstances even appeal to law. Such circumstances include cases of genocide, crimes against humanity, war crimes, and aggression contrary to international law, as in the former Yugoslavia. Meanwhile, following the ratification by more than sixty nations, the International Criminal Court (ICC) has been established and empowered to receive notice of and judge violations, specifically when a signatory state is unable or unwilling to inflict legal penalties on atrocities committed on its territory.

A Realistic Vision of Peace

Though historically the United States has been in favor of international agreements, especially adjudication through the International Criminal Court, along with Israel it has unfortunately tried to sabotage its current role. The administrations of George W. Bush are notorious for their opposition to other important international agreements, such as the Kyoto agreement to reduce global warming, the Comprehensive Test Ban Treaty, the Anti-Ballistic Missile Treaty, and the implementation of the Biological Weapons Treaty. These are sad facts for all admirers of American democracy: To many people not only in the Islamic world, but also in the Asian and African worlds, as well as in Europe, the Bush administration of the only remaining superpower seems to be disrupting any ability to realize the new paradigm. I cannot avoid, therefore, comparing the new paradigm with the political reality after September 11, 2001, given the fact that the fight against terrorism had to be started and the monstrous crime in New York and Washington and Pennsylvania could not remain unatoned for.

After the war in Afghanistan and the illegal and immoral war in Iraq — two wars that have brought anything but peace to both countries — more than ever the decisive questions are: What international commitment are we to make? And should we simply continue the fight against terrorism in this style? Can armed forces solve the terrorist problem? Can a bigger NATO stop terrorism? And should

European nations now furnish and finance what would amount to a "foreign legion" in the service of the Pentagon? My concern is not the alternatives of the past, but the alternatives of the future. Do we in fact have any alternatives as long as foreign policy consists principally of military policy and billions are being spent on sinfully expensive new weapon systems and transport planes, instead of kindergartens and schools, healthcare and public services at home, and preventing and overcoming poverty, hunger, and misery throughout the world? Do any opportunities exist at all for the new paradigm, particularly beyond the OECD world?

With appropriate caution, I would like to suggest that there might be some such opportunities. I do so in full awareness of all the real uncertainties of the future. These uncertainties often result in fundamental changes, but these changes are not always for the worse — as we have seen in the changed attitude of the Bush administration regarding the United Nations. I shall adopt a realistic anti–Murphy's Law stance: What can go wrong need not always go wrong. As an admirer of the great American tradition of democracy and the demand for human rights, I would plead for a politics of peace — even in the face of the campaign against terrorism, which I believe has to be not only a military struggle, but also a political, economic, and cultural one.

It could be that the present U.S. administration will realize that those who think that they can win the fight against evil throughout the world are self-righteously condemning themselves to eternal war, and that even the sole remaining superpower and the self-designated police force of the world can carry out a successful policy only if it does not act unilaterally and in a high-handed way but instead has real partners and friends, not "security interests." If this could be, then perhaps the United States could begin practicing the humility in dealing with other nations that George W. Bush promised before his election in 2000.

It could be that the United States, more shrewdly than former empires, will not overextend its power and come to grief through megalomania, but will preserve its position of predominance by taking into account not only its own interests but also the interests of its partners. The attempt to organize a messy world to our liking is hubris. Remembering the French, the British, the German, the Japanese, and the Russian empires, we know that pride comes before the fall.

It could be that the Bush administration will recognize that maintaining the peace in Bosnia eight years on continues to depend on twelve thousand foreign troops, and that peace-building in Iraq will be much harder and take much longer. It will mean a long-term occupation and nation-building that cannot be effectively pursued alone or under an exclusively U.S. umbrella. Winning peace is so much more difficult than winning a war.

It could be that the American president, whose recent budget surplus decreased by 4 trillion dollars and who in the future must again reckon with deficits, will once again reorient his budgetary policy and instead of being primarily concerned with military policy and oil will be concerned with a more successful economic policy — an economy that may still have in its future further Enron-style bankruptcies, Arthur Andersen crimes, stock market disasters, a recession, or perhaps even a Wall Street crash.

It could be that the present American administration, because it does not want to alienate the whole Islamic world, will take more interest in the causes of Arab and Muslim resentment toward the West in general and to the United States in particular; that instead of being concerned only with the symptoms, it will be more concerned with healing for the social, economic, and political roots of terror; that instead of spending yet more billions for military and policing purposes it will devote more means to improving the social situation of the masses in its own country and those who lose out all over the world as a result of globalization.

It could be that the superpower USA would also act out of enlightened self-interest to prevent the international sense of law from being shaken, for when the only superpower sets standards for itself that differ from those that apply generally in international law, it actually encourages noncompliance by breakaway powers and results in terrorism and the breakdown of international rules governing the use of force.

It could be that (to say only one word on the Israeli-Palestinian conflict as the main source of terrorism) a new majority of the Israeli people will manage to elect leaders who will provide Israelis peace and security and a viable economy, leaders who themselves are peace-minded and have the vision and ability, without American pressure, to lead the country out of the morass and implement the road map — supported by the United States, the European Union, the United Nations, and Russia — to withdraw from all occupied territories and to gain recognition of the state of Israel by all Arab states, along with normal political and economic relations between them. This would make possible an autonomous and viable (not dismembered) state of Palestine, preferably in an economic union with Israel and Jordan, which could be a real blessing for the whole region and especially for Israel.

Indeed, *it could be that* then even the radical Palestinians, who apply the same logic of violence, will stop their bloody terrorist activities, and that the Palestinians will realistically restrict their "right to return" to symbolic return for some particularly hard cases — in exchange for new settlements and financial compensation. In the long run, only recognition by Israel will lead to a less authoritarian and corrupt and more democratic administration in Palestine.

In light of my memoir, *My Struggle for Freedom* (Grand Rapids: Eerdmans, 2003), in which everybody can read how I struggled for the approval of the epoch-making "Declaration of the Second Vatican Council" in favor of the Jews, I trust no one will accuse me of anti-Semitism. Likewise, in my *Judaism between Yesterday and Tomorrow* (New York: Crossroad, 1992), I presented a comprehensive sympathetic view of Judaism, its history, the challenges of the present, and the possibilities for the future. I therefore felt very proud to receive an honorary degree from Hebrew Union College in Cincinnati in 2000.

My views are confirmed for me by the blistering and encouraging article by the former speaker of the Israeli Parliament, Avraham Burg, published in Israel and translated and republished in *The Forward*, the legendary Yiddish magazine. As a respected Israeli Labor politician of impeccable Orthodox credentials he writes:

> The Jewish people did not survive for two millennia in order to pioneer new weaponry, computer security programmes or anti-missile missiles.... We were supposed to be a light unto the nations. In this we have failed. It turns out that the two-thousand-year struggle for Jewish survival comes down to a state of settlements, run by an amoral clique of corrupt law-breakers who are deaf both to their citizens and their enemies. A state lacking justice cannot survive.... The countdown to the end of Israeli society has begun.[2]

Burg is therefore in favor of two states, which is the only alternative to a racist state. And he thinks that this is not exclusively Israeli or Jewish business:

> Israel's friends abroad — Jewish and non-Jewish, presidents and prime ministers, rabbis and lay people — should choose as well. They must reach out and help Israel to navigate the road map towards our national destiny as a light unto the nations and a society of peace, justice and equality.[3]

To this end, particular demands would be made of the three prophetic religions, Judaism, Christianity, and Islam, not to support uncritically the official politics of their respective governments but to show their prophetic role: "Do not repay anyone evil for evil" (Rom. 12:17, NRSV). This New Testament saying is today addressed to those Christian crusaders in the United States and elsewhere who look for evil only in the other, thinking that a crusade hallows any military means and justifies all humanitarian "collateral damage."

"An eye for an eye, a tooth for a tooth" (Exod. 21:24): this saying from the Hebrew Bible on limiting damage is addressed to those Israeli fanatics who prefer to take two eyes from their opponent instead of just one, and would like to knock out several teeth too, forgetting that the perpetuation of "an eye for an eye makes the world go blind" (Gandhi).

"And if they incline to peace, do thou incline to it" (Surah 8:61): this saying from the Qur'an is addressed to those Palestinian warriors of God who today would still like to blot out the state of Israel from the map and try to sabotage all peace initiatives.

Conclusion

Peace among the religions is a presupposition of peace among the nations. Let me therefore conclude with a few elementary remarks on a global ethic, which in the age of globalization is more urgent than ever. Indeed, the globalization of the economy, technology, and communication also needs the globalization of ethics to cope with global problems. The two fundamental demands of the 1993 Chicago Declaration — confirmed by the Third Parliament of the World's Religions in Cape Town in 1999 and taken up in the manifesto "Crossing the Divide" for the UN Year of Dialogue among Civilizations — are the most elementary ones that can be made in this regard. They are fundamental and bear repeating in the context of this book.

The first fundamental principle is for True Humanity: Now as before, women and men are treated inhumanely all over the world. They are robbed of their opportunities and their freedom; their human rights are trampled underfoot; their dignity is disregarded. But might does not make right! In the face of all inhumanity our religious and ethical convictions demand that every human being must be treated humanly. Every human being — male or female, white or colored, young or old, American or Afghan — must be treated in a truly humane way, not in an inhuman, even bestial manner.

The second fundamental principle is the Golden Rule: There is a principle that is found and has persisted in many religious and ethical traditions of humankind for thousands of years: What you do not wish done to yourself, do not do to others. . . . This should be the irrevocable, unconditional norm for all areas of life, for families and communities, for races, nations, and religions.

On the basis of these two fundamental principles, four ethical directives, found in all the great traditions of humanity, have to be remembered:

- You shall not murder, torture, torment, or wound. Stated in positive terms: have reverence for life; be committed to a culture of nonviolence and reverence for life.

- You shall not lie, deceive, forge, manipulate. Stated in positive terms: speak and act truthfully; be committed to a culture of truthfulness and tolerance.

- You shall not steal, exploit, bribe, or corrupt. Stated in positive terms: deal honestly and fairly; be committed to a culture of fairness and to a just economic order.

- You shall not abuse sexuality, cheat, humiliate, or dishonor. Stated in positive terms: respect and love one another; be committed to a culture of partnership and equal dignity for all.

After 1989 a lack of vision for peace has persisted. I have presented what this vision really *could be*. It is not a vision of war — "Sweet is war only to those who do not know it" (Erasmus of Rotterdam). It is a vision of peace. The four propositions below encapsulate the vision of peace — and the demand for religious dialogue.

There will be no peace among the nations without peace among the religions.
There will be no peace among the religions without dialogue among the religions.
There will be no dialogue among the religions without global ethical standards.
There will therefore be no survival of this globe without a global ethic.

Bibliography

Küng, Hans. *The Catholic Church: A Short History.* New York: Modern Library, and London: Weidenfeld and Nicolson, 2001.
———. *A Global Ethic for Global Politics and Economics.* Trans. John Bowden. London: SCM, 1997; New York: Oxford University Press, 1998.
———. *Global Responsibility: In Search of a New World Ethic.* London: SCM, 1991; New York: Crossroad, 1993.

————. *Tracing the Way: Spiritual Dimensions of the World Religions.* New York and London: Continuum, 2002.

Küng, Hans, ed. *Globale Unternehmen — globales Ethos: Der globale Markt erfordert neue Standards und eine globale Rahmenordnung.* Frankfurt: F.A.Z. Verlagsbereich Buch, 2001.

————. *Yes to a Global Ethic.* New York: Continuum, 1996; London: SCM, 1991.

Küng, Hans, and Helmut Schmidt, eds. *A Global Ethic and Global Responsibilities: Two Declarations.* London: SCM, 1998.

Picco, Giandomenico, Hans Küng, and Richard von Weizsäcker, and others. *Crossing the Divide: Dialogue among Civilizations.* South Orange, N.J.: Seton Hall University, 2001.

Two

Ethical Challenges in the "War" on Terrorism

MARTIN L. COOK

Martin L. Cook provides a basic starting point for a dialogue on peace and war in religious perspective by citing the seminal influence of St. Augustine (fifth century CE) on the arguments about justified violence in Christianity. He then assesses the secularized version of the just war tradition under the rubrics of just cause (jus ad bellum) *and just conduct* (jus in bello) *in warfare.*

He discusses the war on terrorism as a contemporary case and asks how just war theory applies (and is limited) in the engagement of sovereign nations and terrorist organizations. Among his focal questions are: (1) How do we think about the rights of terrorist organizations when current just war theory assumes conflict between sovereign nations? (2) Does modern just war thinking need to include the threat to civilization that transcends a particular sovereign nation or group of nations? and (3) Is terrorism primarily a threat to civilization rather than a nation? (4) Is unilateral action by a nation (e.g., the United States) against a terrorist group (e.g., al Qaeda) covered by contemporary just war theory?

Cook's essay both lays out the traditional criteria for justified violence by nations and probes the limits of war theory in the modern world. He provokes serious thinking by Christians who have in history both eschewed violence and also have engaged in just war.

22

Provocations for Dialogue

1. *What principles of traditional just war theory as discussed by Cook are most heatedly debated in America's war on terrorism? Why?*

2. *For the sake of peace is it necessary for sovereign nations to concede some aspects of their national interests for the sake of a greater, global good?*

3. *Has the war in Iraq been a just war?*

• • •

The Origins of the Just War Idea

T HE EARLIEST Christian church had a strong bias against the use of force and participation in the military function of the government. Grounded both in the teachings of Jesus regarding nonviolence and the practical reality that participation in Roman government would require participation in pagan religious ceremonies, early Christianity maintained a hands-off attitude toward the government. With the conversion of the Emperor Constantine to Christianity in the fourth century, the possibilities of a Christian Roman empire, and an increasing military threat to the stability of the empire itself, the church progressively made its peace with the necessity of government and the use of force.

St. Augustine signified this transition with his pivotal distinction between the City of God and the City of Man. From Augustine's foundation, the church slowly developed an increasingly complex and nuanced just war tradition which allowed it to articulate an intermediate position between the church's historic pacifism on the one hand and the Roman empire's untroubled acceptance of the use of military force on the other.

With the Enlightenment in Western Europe in the eighteenth century, the initially religious tradition became increasingly secularized.

Profound thinkers such as Hugo Grotius felt the need to free the tradition from its religious moorings and to create a moral tradition of just
war that would be valid, as he said, "even if God did not exist." It is the
secular version of the tradition that became the foundation of contemporary secular international law and which formed the moral and legal
framework within which acts of military force are justified and judged.

It is not my intent to rehearse the history of the development of
just war tradition. Rather, I wish to take it in its developed form
and to look at the particular moral and legal challenges raised by the
unusual character of the current war against terrorism.

As we will see, the nature of this conflict raises issues and challenges
that have not been faced by the just war tradition for a number of
centuries. I suggest that international law may prove to be less relevant to guiding our thinking about this challenge than the older and
deeper philosophical and religious roots of the more ancient just war
tradition.

The Existing Just War Tradition

The just war framework divides judgments about war into two essential elements. On the one hand are those judgments that a particular
political circumstance justifies recourse to military force for its redress. This tradition inherits from its Christian roots a strong bias
against the use of force and a presumption that methods short of use
of force are always preferable to military solutions to political problems. But it balances that bias with another; namely, the presumption
that evil should be punished and that stability and order must be
maintained, by force if necessary. These aspects of just war theory attempt to establish standards of judgment and categories to be applied
to determine when, in a particular set of political circumstances, use
of force is justified.

Jus ad Bellum

Collectively, these judgments are referred to by their Latin term *jus
ad bellum*. The main provisions of this requirement are that there

must be a just cause for the war, that the war be authorized by a recognized authority, that there be a reasonable hope of success, that there be a proportionality between the gravity of the cause of the war and the foreseeable destruction redressing that cause will bring about, that the use of force is indeed the last resort, and that the final goal or purpose of war be the securing of a better and more stable peace.

First, the just cause aspect of *jus ad bellum* is meant to establish a threshold of gravity of offense sufficient to justify use of military force. As this tradition developed throughout history, various things have been counted as just causes. For example, in the Middle Ages offended honor was considered a just cause. Because the intent of the tradition is to restrict the use of force, there has been a tendency, as the tradition has developed, to narrow the range of just causes. In its contemporary form, just cause is largely restricted to aggression received. In its simplest form, aggression is manifest when one country's tanks have crossed the border and invaded another country.

Second, the requirement of right authority was initially meant to put a limit on private war or wars not authorized by a legitimate government. This was, of course, a real problem in the Middle Ages, where local aristocracy had private armies at their disposal; it is increasingly becoming a real problem again as organizations such as al Qaeda also possess military power uncoupled from responsible governments.

In the modern context, the United Nations was created to restrict warfare as a normal means of international resolution of disputes, except for absolutely and unambiguously defensive wars. Specifically, the Security Council of the United Nations holds the authority to make determinations that conditions that threaten international peace and stability are worthy of redress by military means. Member states of the United Nations retain the right of self-defense, but only in unambiguous circumstances.

Within the United States, there is an ambiguity about who has the right to authorize the use of military force. The Constitution provides that the president be the commander-in-chief of the armed forces of the United States. It also reserves the power to declare war to the Congress of the United States. For much of American history, this division actually made sense, since the presumption was that there would be no large standing military force, and that the Congress would have to authorize money to raise an army to fight any significant war. Recent circumstances have modified this distinction since the urgency of the Cold War threat required having standing military forces ready to respond promptly. As commander-in-chief, the president has had a standing military force that could be deployed on presidential authorization alone.

Since the Vietnam War, Congress has attempted to restrain this unilateral authority of the president through the War Powers Act, but all presidents have held that the War Powers Act is unconstitutional, and neither the executive branch nor the Congress has chosen to adjudicate this issue before the Supreme Court.

Third, the reasonable hope of success criterion is essentially a commonsense test. Since the use of military force will inevitably involve destruction of property and probably deaths of numerous individuals, any morally serious defense of use of force must be able to convince itself that this means of redressing the issue is likely to be effective. Otherwise, the destruction is purely gratuitous.

Fourth, justification of the recourse to military force also involves a global proportionality assessment. This is a judgment that the issue to be resolved is in some reasonable proportion to the amount of damage anticipated by the use of military means.

Fifth, the requirement that use of force be the last resort is the final criterion of *jus ad bellum*. The essential idea here is that if nonmilitary means of redressing the fundamental issue exist, they should be tried if possible. This is not, of course, a wooden requirement that everything conceivable be tried. Instead, it is a commonsense test that things that show any promise of being successful should be tried. Readers will recall that this was the central debate in anticipation of the Gulf War: Would another trip by the Russians be effective in getting Iraq to withdraw from Kuwait? Was further UN negotiation likely to be effective?

Sixth, a just war must be fought for the purpose of securing a better and more stable peace. Since just war is brought on by necessity, it must be concluded in a changed circumstance in which there is less likelihood that that necessity will arise again in the near future. This requires changes that will render the aggressor less likely to attack again (restrictions on weapons, changes in government policy, perhaps reparations) and also counsels ethical restraint in the means used in war to ensure against abiding hatreds among the parties.

Jus in Bello

The other wing of just war theory is *jus in bello*; that is, making judgments about how war is conducted. The two central moral principles that apply are the principles of discrimination and proportionality. The principle of discrimination distinguishes between legitimate military targets and illegitimate targets. Some individuals and targets may be legitimately attacked, while civilians and civilian objects are immune from deliberate attack. Military planners are morally obligated to choose weapons and tactics that as far as possible allow attack of legitimate military targets while avoiding damage and destruction to nonmilitary targets.

The principle of proportionality requires that the amount of destruction visited on a military target be proportional to the military value of the object. Essentially equivalent to the military principle of economy of force, proportionality requires that military commanders weigh the military value at the time of the target and use only an amount of force (and cause a degree of destruction) in reasonable proportion to that military value. For example, it would (other things being equal) be unjustifiable to use a very large explosive device to eliminate a relatively minor military target in an area surrounded by civilian individuals and civilian objects because the destruction of those civilian persons and objects would not be justified in light of the minimal military value of the target.

Applying Just War Criteria
to the War against Terrorism

While the criteria I have articulated have been the mainstays of just war thinking for many centuries, there are some distinct problems in applying this tradition to the current engagement against terrorist organizations worldwide.

The first and most obvious difficulty is that the just war tradition since the Peace of Westphalia in 1648 has granted only sovereign nation states the legitimate right to wage war. Prior to the Protestant Reformation of the sixteenth century, European nations were autonomous in principle, but in practice nations were often subordinated to a common loyalty to the pope and the ideal of Christendom. After the Reformation and the religious wars that followed, it became obvious that the idea of a unified Christian Europe was no longer possible. After several centuries of wars that attempted to restore that unity in the name of one form of Christianity or another, at Westphalia the states of Europe accepted a new international order, dominated by sovereign states. These new sovereign states would have the twin rights of territorial integrity and political sovereignty. In other words, peace would be gained in Europe by allowing each state to control its own internal affairs. In practice, this meant that Catholic states would persecute Protestants, and Protestant states would persecute Catholics. But international stability was to be bought, as we would say in modern parlance, at the price of human rights.

Since Westphalia, then, only states can legally wage war against one another. This criterion runs into considerable difficulty in the "war" against terrorism. Take the recent case of al Qaeda. In the case of Afghanistan, the fact that the Taliban government of Afghanistan was unwilling to produce the al Qaeda representatives within its territory made it possible to conduct war against the *de facto* government of Afghanistan, as well as against the terrorist groups whom they harbored. But, as engagements with al Qaeda have extended globally, the character of those engagements has changed dramatically with reference to the various states in whose territory they may be found. The Taliban government's alliance with al Qaeda made it a legitimate military target. Some states, such as the Philippines and Georgia, may invite American forces to operate with their own forces to suppress terrorist organizations that they have reasons for wanting to subdue. Other states, such as Pakistan, may have governments willing to act to suppress and locate al Qaeda representatives, but at considerable domestic political risk to their own government's stability. Still other states may be too weak, even if willing, to act against al Qaeda; some may indeed actively support or covertly be willing to tolerate terrorist presence in their territories.

Given this complex picture, how do we begin to think about our relationship to these various situations? The modern theory of state sovereignty would counsel that every state is free to do within its own territory whatever it chooses. Presumably, that freedom includes harboring individuals and groups that are unpalatable to other states. But clearly, the American government's intent to pursue al Qaeda wherever it may be found, if necessary in the face of resistance or noncooperation from the governments in whose territories they may reside, raises serious issues about national sovereignty. In terms of just war, what legitimacy can there be for such interventions?

There are no troubling ethical or legal questions involved with states that choose to cooperate with the American efforts. These nations are clearly acting within the scope of their sovereignty to invite another nation to assist them to locate and defeat terrorist groups internal to their territory. But what about those states that do not cooperate, either from inability or from unwillingness? The standard of Westphalian respect for territorial integrity and sovereignty would argue strongly against granting the United States or even a coalition of nations the authority to intervene in such circumstances — at least in the absence of an authorizing resolution from the UN Security Council.

It may be that the era of Westphalian sovereignty is fading. Recall that the *moral* tradition of just war (as distinct from the specific *legal* tradition) is much older and more robust than its particular instantiation in formal international law in its post-Westphalian form.

St. Augustine is instructive in this regard. In his "Letter to Count Boniface," Augustine urges Roman military commander Boniface to see his military service in resistance to barbarian invasion as a mournful but necessary duty. The necessity of fighting has been imposed by those who have disrupted the relative peace and order of the Roman empire, and not by Boniface's will. Writing from his home in North Africa to this senior military officer after Rome itself has already fallen, Augustine invokes Jesus' saying, "Blessed are the peacemakers" and applies it to the conscientious soldier who, by using arms against the barbarian, is attempting to restore the peace that has been broken by invasion. The temporal peace Augustine urges Boniface to restore is not, by any stretch of the imagination, the perfect peace of the City of God. It is the lesser temporal order of the Human City — a "tranquility of order" in which there are still many who are miserable, but within an overall framework of order. Individuals in that order may be wretched, Augustine grants, but "they would ... be far more wretched if they had not that peace which arises from being in harmony with the natural order of things."[1] Augustine realizes that, in the conflict between the barbarians and the Roman army in his lifetime, the stakes are literally the collapse of civilization as his world had known it for centuries. He realizes that Rome's defeat would not just rearrange the individual miseries of his world. What would follow is the Dark Ages, from which centuries would be required before even a flicker of civilization reappeared in the Western Roman empire.

What is the relevance of this ancient discussion to the current global war against terrorism? Like Augustine, we are now dealing with threats and challenges that do not fit the model of state sovereignty that has defined the Westphalian world for the past four centuries. What is threatened by al Qaeda is not captured in a conceptual model which thinks of wars as conflicts between states, or in which what is at stake is the prospering or survival of a particular state's political order or territory. If al Qaeda's fondest hopes were realized, what would fall is not the United States of America, but rather the entire world order created over centuries by the forces of capitalism, Enlightenment rationality, modern science, and political democracy.

It is fashionable, of course, to criticize the Western nations for the miseries created for many groups and other nations. There are, indeed, many valid and important questions to be raised about the deleterious effects of globalized trade, the World Trade Organization, and the spread of American consumer culture across the planet. But it is no more of the essence of the argument to idealize Western civilization than it was for Augustine to pretend that Rome ruled a world of sweetness and light. Moral seriousness requires, instead, asking, "If this civilization falls, what comes next?"

There is always room for reform and change under an umbrella provided by Augustine's "tranquility of order." A sober assessment of the situation asks not about the perfection of order, but about the cost of its collapse. One intellectual disease of much of modern liberalism and many a modern university is a kind of moral utopianism which one-sidedly dwells on the deficiencies and injustices of existing civilization. Such a perspective neglects to balance moral criticism of imperfections with an equivalent recognition of the value of order. Such thinking is then squeamish about the reality that such order is always maintained by power, often in ways that are less than perfect or ideal. Such moral utopianism fails entirely to provide a moral and conceptual framework within which real-world political decisions can be made. One finds such views, for example, in perspectives that attribute responsibility for the attacks of September 11 exclusively or primarily to elements of American policy and conduct — while not recognizing the absolutely essential role of America and her power in maintaining what passes for "tranquility of order" in the modern world.

When one contemplates a world with an absence of that order, few can improve on Thomas Hobbes's description:

> Whatsoever therefore is consequent to a time of War, where every man is Enemy to every man; the same is consequent to the time, wherein men live without other security, than what their own strength, and their own invention shall furnish them withal. In such condition, there

is no place for Industry; because the fruit thereof is uncertain: and consequently no Culture of the Earth; no Navigation, nor use of the commodities that may be imported by Sea; no commodious Building; no Instruments of moving, and removing such things as require much force; no Knowledge of the face of the Earth; no account of Time; no Arts; no Letters; no Society; and which is worst of all, continual fear, and danger of violent death; and the life of man, solitary, poor, nasty, brutish, and short.[2]

What I am suggesting is that we may well be at one of those historical moments when a real shift in our thinking is required. It is not the just war framework of the post-Reformation Westphalian order that provides the deepest insight to our circumstance — although the fact that black-letter international law presupposes that order makes harmonizing our challenges with that form of the just war tradition necessary. But the terrorist challenges are not fundamentally challenges to particular states, but rather to civilization itself as we know it.

For all the brutality of its foundations and conduct, the *Pax Romana* was, for Augustine, clearly an order worth defending; no less is the defense of the *Pax Americana* in our time and place. Indeed, a striking fact about the early Christian church is, for all its ambivalence about serving in the Roman government, there was never the hint of a doubt that the stability, safety, and ease of travel made possible by Roman power was a gift of God. Similarly, it does not require much imagination to envision the dreadful consequences of a collapse of the complex and interlocking structures of the modern international system. Of course, there is plenty of misery in our world, but it pales to insignificance in comparison to an abrupt break or collapse in the structures that keep it intact.

The most important point of the just war perspective in the Christian church was a firm embrace of the realm of practical politics as a locus of moral seriousness. The temptation to flee the world of moral ambiguity and shades of gray is, of course, a powerful one — a tug no morally serious person can avoid feeling. But it is, from the religious core of the just war perspective, a temptation to be resisted in favor of the hard, messy, and (as Augustine put it) "mournful" work of sustaining relative goods in the face of greater evils.

Just War and Global Civilization

The core of my argument so far has been that the particular form of just war embodied in most international law of the modern period is conceptually ill-equipped to guide us in thinking about the war against terrorism. So far, I have stressed the older core concern of just war: the need to maintain global order and stability as a precondition for any other improvements in the lot of global humanity.

That, of course, was Augustine's argument in support of the moral importance of the Roman empire. But his was an argument that, morally speaking, began and ended with order itself. In the modern context, after centuries of development of traditions of the rights of human individuals and groups, and the self-determination of peoples, we would be remiss if we ended the argument there. Clearly, these traditions provide conceptual means of reaching through even the most stable of orders in the name of principles that transcend the state and the empire. How are those principles to be given sufficient weight, without lapsing back into the kind of moral utopianism I have so roundly criticized?

Here, it is important to remember what questions we were debating before September 11. For many years, since the end of the Cold War, the debate had been about the diminishing character of national sovereignty. The possibility that, now that all questions were not run through the filter of Cold War politics, the world would really evolve toward more cooperative international relations and genuine guarantees of human rights dominated the discourse.

The conflict in Kosovo, whatever one thinks of its wisdom, was (morally speaking) a genuinely new thing: use of military force in defense of human rights, where the national interests of the interveners were minimal. To Secretary of State Madeline Albright, this represented moral progress: finally the United States and the world would put some teeth into the Genocide Convention and other human rights treaties. No longer would state sovereignty provide cover for states that fall below an acceptable international standard of conduct.

Of course, harmonizing such an internationalist perspective with state sovereignty was complex — witness the unwillingness of China and Russia to authorize such action in the UN Security Council. Honest advocates of the Kosovo intervention grant that, in terms of existing international law, the intervention was at best necessary and desirable, if illegal. Witness also the deep ambivalence of the United States to commit its military forces to nation building or to subordinate them to United Nations or coalition command.

Ironically, the war on terrorism raises a similar debate with regard to internationalism. It is the debate that is swirling around all the questions of where that war goes next — most clearly, but hardly only, regarding Iraq. Unlike the Roman empire, the United States has to contend with the reality of world opinion, of international institutions and nongovernmental agencies, and of the world press.

The Bush administration has been talking as if the realities of American power made absolute unilateralism about how to proceed next a real possibility. But as a practical — never mind moral — matter, that is very difficult. Military operations on any large scale face enormous difficulties without international cooperation in granting such things as the rights to conduct military operation on foreign soil, overflight privileges, and intelligence sharing.

But just as the pre–September 11 issues raised the question of whether, in the words of George H. W. Bush, a "new world order" might arise from the end of the Cold War, so does the war against terrorism. In the long run, a global or coalition effort against terrorism will only be possible if the world community can come together on shared definitions of conduct of what will and will not be acceptable behavior. If thresholds of what constitutes unacceptable terrorism, just like thresholds of what constitutes genocide, can emerge as a global consensus, a new understanding of the meaning of sovereignty will emerge.

If that is possible — and it is a complex and subtle diplomatic task, to be sure, to sustain that consensus — then unlike Rome, which faced its barbarian invasions alone, the United States can lead a united civilized world against the new barbarians. If that consensus can be built and maintained, the tranquility of order will be built on more than power — although the importance of power should never be neglected. It will be a new world order based on shared values, sustained and defended by power wielded in the name of, and with the support of, a united world defending its common civilization.

The views expressed in this article are those of the author and do not necessarily reflect the official policy or position of the U.S. Air Force, the Department of Defense, or the U.S. government.

Three

Islam and the Problem of Violence

JOHN KELSAY

John Kelsay's essay provides a case study of the question of just cause that Martin Cook raised in the previous article. It also serves as a primer to Islamic views of religious violence (jihad) *and the logic of Usama bin Laden's terrorist campaign against the United States.*

Kelsay particularly studies the legitimacy of the so-called fatwa *(authoritative opinion) that bin Laden and others cite as justification for their violent actions against the United States and its allies. He outlines the basic features of* Shari'a, *a traditional mode of interpreting the Qur'an, and asks if the Declaration (the so-called* fatwa) *is in keeping with Islamic belief and practice. In his discussion he unpacks the various meanings of* jihad, *so important for Islamic understanding of justified violence. He also introduces the internal debates between al Qaeda and other fundamentalist Muslims.*

Kelsay exposes two pressing issues within Islam that bear upon the question of just and unjust sovereign states. In particular, he asks, (1) Must an Islamic state be justly governed by laws and policies that derive exclusively from the Qur'an? and (2) In what sense can a nation be just if its policies are derived from non-Qur'an traditions?

This essay provides outsiders with insight into the conceptual workings of Islamic thinkers and provides perspective on the ways in which violence is debated.

Provocations for Dialogue

1. *What problems are involved in deciding who is a legitimate interpreter of a religious text? In Islam? In Christianity?*

2. *Under what circumstances (emergency situations) can the guidelines for justified war be modified or revised?*

3. *What problems exist with regard to who is a "civilian" or a "noncombatant"? Can violence against civilians or noncombatants ever be justified in warfare?*

• • •

THE TWOFOLD PREMISE of this volume is that attention to religion is a necessary part of comprehending violence, and that dialogue between religions is a necessary step in reducing violence. I certainly agree with this premise, with the reminder that "necessary" is always less than "sufficient," and with the caveat that an important aspect of religious approaches to violence includes the claim that armed force is, under certain conditions, necessary to the pursuit of justice. This means that for many religious traditions, "the problem of violence" is perhaps better stated as "the problem of illegitimate force." This is certainly true for Islam, and correspondingly, jihad, in the sense that fighting directed by legitimate public authorities and governed by the norms of right conduct is a necessary response to violence.

With this in mind, this essay seeks to answer the question: what does the involvement of Muslims in the attacks of September 11, 2001, tell us about Islamic approaches to violence? I shall proceed as follows. First, I want to examine the (so-called) *fatwa* or "authoritative opinion" issued in February 1998 by Usama bin Laden and others held most responsible for the September 11 attacks. This document is best understood in the context of the longstanding tradition of Islamic law, called *Shari'a*. Understood from this tradition, it becomes apparent that bin Laden's opinion contains several important weaknesses, in the sense that the reasoning of the document is out of line with important aspects of the *Shari'a* tradition.

Following this analysis, I discuss Muslim responses to the tactics advocated by bin Laden and his colleagues, which are most decisively illustrated in the September 11 attacks. I focus on a series of exchanges that occurred between "fundamentalist" or "radical" Muslims between June and December 2002. I consider these important because they indicate ways in which even those who may be considered natural allies of bin Laden are troubled by his departure from *Shari'a* precedents. I conclude by reflecting briefly on the implications of the debate within Islam inspired by bin Laden, as well as by the tactics of al Qaeda for an understanding of the relations between Islam and violence.

The *Declaration* of 1998

On February 23, 1998, a London paper, *al-Quds al-Arabi*, published a document under the headline "Text of a Declaration by the World Islamic Front with respect to Jihad against the Jews and the Crusaders." Five people are associated with the document. All are known from movements involved with armed resistance. One is Usama bin Laden. None of the signers is a recognized scholar of Islam, though Ayman al-Zawahiri, an Egyptian physician, is from a family with scholarly credentials.[1] This lack of credentials is important. As one often hears, Islam has no formal clergy. Nevertheless, from a very early period the Islamic community recognized a class of religious specialists. The issuing of authoritative opinions regarding Islamic practice was the duty of certain members of this class. However, the development of modern Islam illustrates some change in this historic practice, with the end result that, on occasion, "ordinary" Muslims give opinions. If these opinions gain authority, the reasons are tied to personal charisma rather than to any connection to an authoritative class of religious experts.

Despite this deficiency, the *Declaration* speaks in authoritative terms. It identifies norms relevant to the behavior of Muslims, particularly with respect to fighting the United States and its allies. The language suggests that sincere Muslims should read, discuss, and follow its directives.

The *Declaration* begins with a pious recitation:

> Praise be to God, who revealed the Book, controls the clouds, defeats factionalism, and says in His Book: "But when the forbidden months are past, then fight and slay the pagans where you find them, seize them, beleaguer them, and lie in wait for them in every stratagem" [Qur'an 9:5]; and peace be upon our Prophet, Muhammad Bin 'Abdallah, who said: "I have been sent with the sword between my hands to ensure that no one but God is worshiped, God who put my livelihood under the shadow of my spear and who inflicts humiliation and scorn on those who disobey my orders."[2]

In the normative tradition of Islam, the goal of *Shari'a* — which is the form of this *Declaration* — is to comprehend divine guidance. That is the meaning of the term *Shari'a*, which is more popularly translated "Islamic religious law." The term implies the belief that there is an ideal way to live that will make for happiness in this world and the next.[3] This belief is crucial to Islam.

God, the merciful and compassionate Creator and Lord of all, provides his creatures with guidance pertaining to this ideal way of life. The world is filled with "signs" that indicate such guidance. But the surest of the signs of God, the best sources for those who would walk the straight path that God favors, are the Qur'an and the example of the Prophet. Thus, the authors of the *Declaration* begin with the invocation of the two basic sources of *Shari'a*, the Book of God "wherein is no doubt" and the example of the Prophet, given as mercy to humankind.

They then continue:

> The Arabian Peninsula has never — since God made it flat, created its desert, and encircled it with seas — been stormed by any forces like the crusader armies spreading in it like locusts, eating its riches and wiping out its plantations. All this is happening at a time in which nations are attacking Muslims like people fighting over a plate of food.[4] In the light of the grave situation and the lack of support, we and you are obliged to discuss current events, and we should all agree on how to settle the matter.

Here, the authors further establish the connection of their *Declaration* with Islamic tradition. One who reads traditional biographies of Muhammad will be struck by the emphasis on Divine Providence in preparing the way for the last prophet. In such books, the Arabian Peninsula is the site of many of the most important events in world history. Abraham journeys there; with his son, Ishmael, he builds the Ka'ba as the first house of worship. Through his descendants, Ishmael becomes the father of a great nation, his descendants ultimately attaining status as progenitors of the various tribes of the Peninsula. When the tribes come under stress during the sixth century CE, leaders of the Quraysh, the most prominent tribe and guardians of the Ka'ba, sponsor initiatives aimed at emphasizing the unity of the sons of Ishmael. They thus prepare the way for the Arab Prophet, who comes to reemphasize the message of submission — that there is one God, that human beings are responsible to a moral law, and that divine judgment is a reality. By the end of the Prophet's career, he will say that "Arabia is now solidly for Islam." The Peninsula, the location of the two holy places (Mecca and Medina), will forever be considered by Muslims as an inviolable trust, given to Muslims as a sign and seal of their devotion to the Prophet's message. No land is more holy, no trust more sacred.[5]

This passage is important as a historical reference, yet it speaks to contemporary Muslims. There have been times of crisis in which the inviolability of Arabia was threatened. None of these has been more serious than the current crisis, however, in which the lives and wealth of Muslims are the direct target of a war of annihilation. Greedy and rapacious nations attack Muslims all over the world, but Arabia, with its treasure trove of natural resources, is the grand prize. The next few paragraphs of the *Declaration* are devoted to delineating how that is so, and to identifying the nation most responsible for the international campaign against Muslims.

The authors cite "three facts that are known to everyone": the "occupation" of the Arabian Peninsula by the United States, the ongoing misery of the people of Iraq, and the struggles between Palestinians and Israelis. Of these, the first claim is the most important, in terms of the overall direction of the *Declaration*. The continuing presence of foreign, especially U.S., troops on Arabian soil since the end of the Gulf War provides a means for plundering the riches of the Arabian Peninsula. Their presence is "dictating to its rulers, humiliating its people, terrorizing its neighbors, and turning bases in the Peninsula into a spearhead through which to fight the neighboring Islamic peoples." The authors note that some people have in the past argued about this — probably a reference to criticisms made of the 1996 "Epistle." But now they write, "All the people of the Peninsula have now acknowledged it."

Establishing the fact of occupation is critical to the argument of the *Declaration*. In this connection, it is useful to recall that *Shari'a* reasoning is best understood as a kind of case or response law. One is always trying to find guidance for the present by connecting the Qur'an, the example of the Prophet, and the wisdom of previous generations of scholars to current situations. In this, the assessment of facts is crucial. One set of facts suggests a certain kind of normative judgment; another set of facts leads in a different direction.

Thus, in 1996, bin Laden's *Epistle* argued that the facts at that time indicated that the United States and its allies had declared war on God, his messenger, and the Muslims, and that this made it obligatory for Muslims as a community to put aside their differences and contribute to the resistance as they were able.

The 1998 *Declaration* sees things a bit differently. The war against Islam is further along, and thus it becomes obligatory for every Muslim to participate in the defense of Islam. This is a very important development. A brief excursus into the Islamic law of war helps clarify why this shift is so important for understanding the Muslim justification of the use of violence against the United States.

Islamic Law of War

The term *jihad* means "struggle" or "effort." In the Qur'an, it is always joined with the phrase *fi sabil Allah*, which means "in the path of God." Every Muslim is called to "command good and forbid evil," to defend and establish justice.

One struggles in a variety of ways. Preaching, for example, spreads the word of Islam and calls people to practice justice. If people do not heed the preaching of the word, and in particular if they respond with discrimination or persecution of believers, one continues to struggle in ways that exhibit "steadfastness." The example of the Prophet and his companions in Mecca, in the years between 610 and 622, is quite apt. Faced with continual and sometimes violent persecution, they remained nonviolent. It was only when things reached the point that God, as a means of protecting the small community of believers, ordered the Prophet to migrate to Medina that this nonviolent posture changed. At that time, we are told, Muhammad received Qur'an 22:39–40:

> Permission for fighting is given to those who are victims of aggression. God is powerful in assisting them. These are people wrongly driven from their land for saying "God is our Lord." If God did not deter one group of people by means of another, then monasteries, churches, synagogues, and mosques where the name of God is abundantly mentioned would be destroyed.[6]

In Medina, the Islamic struggle took on a military cast, although this was always accompanied by diplomatic, economic, and religious initiatives as well. The point was to create an alliance of tribes in Arabia to secure the freedom of Muslims to worship God.

Following Muhammad's death the Arab tribes, now united under the banner of Islam, pushed out of the Arabian Peninsula and conquered most of the Middle East and North Africa. There are many questions not only about how they accomplished this, but also about "why?"[7] For our purposes, the more significant development was a set of judgments developed by a scholarly class of religious specialists about the justification of violence. In many respects this mode of thinking is parallel to Christian thinking and more generally what Westerners know as the just war tradition.[8]

The important point in relation to the 1998 *Declaration* is that, historically, the scholars who developed the judgments associated with *jihad* did so in the context of an Islamic empire. In that context, they said, the military aspect of *jihad* can be understood in two ways. First, there is a kind of armed struggle in which Muslim troops, under the leadership of an established Muslim ruler, try to secure the borders of an Islamic state. In this kind of struggle, the duty of Muslims is technically described as *fard kifaya*, or a *collective* duty, which means that the ruler of the Muslims must have a standing army at his disposal, and the community as a whole should provide support. Some Muslims will join the army, while others will pay taxes to support it. Each person is to do his/her part, but the obligation of defense rests with the community as a whole.

A second kind of struggle is different. In this case, we have to imagine that an enemy has invaded the territory of Islam. The enemy's forces are damaging Muslim property. Citizens who have every right to believe that their ruler can and will protect them from attack are being injured or killed. The enemy is violating the rights of Muslims, carrying the campaign into the heart of Islamic territory. The end result is that Islam itself is in danger in the sense that the Muslim community's capacity to carry out its mission is radically delimited. In the most extreme case, one might fear that this capacity will be eliminated.

In this second kind of struggle, the scholars said that fighting is *fard 'ayn*, an *individual* duty. This means that every Muslim must fight to defend Islam. The idea is that an emergency exists. The scholars went further, saying that in a true emergency, "necessity makes the forbidden things permitted." Under this rubric, they talked about the ordinary lines of authority that make society work, and they argued that these lines did not hold in an emergency situation. Their primary emphasis was on emergency conditions that allowed or even required the authorities in neighboring territories to ignore the usual boundaries between "spheres of influence" and to come to the aid of suffering Muslims. Some texts might be taken to imply something more radical, however: that the emergency justifies action by individual Muslims. Under this reading a woman can fight without obtaining permission from her father or husband and a young person can fight without obtaining permission from the parents. While this was not much discussed, one might entertain the possibility that an emergency would justify groups of ordinary Muslims in organizing a militia for the protection of Muslims. In the absence of an effective central authority, the duty to defend Islam against an invader devolves to the people. In just war terms, one would say that authority to make war devolves to the people, to each and to all.

This kind of emergency provision is obviously open to abuse. Most Islamic reflection has been concerned with the possibility that the emergency provision might be used as a cover for revolutionary or even criminal activity. Islamic scholars were quite realistic about the ways religious motivations can, under certain circumstances, lend themselves to the justification of actions that do more harm than good. Muslim authorities usually spoke of this through the symbol of the Kharijites, a group that stood as a prime example of religious zeal leading to excess during the early period of Islamic development. Muslim authorities thus knew the problems associated with the emergency provision. But they left it on the books, for the obvious reason that one cannot rule out the possibility that such situations might exist.

The language of armed struggle as an individual duty stands behind the 1998 *Declaration*. The "facts" no longer support the judgment that armed resistance to the United States and its allies is a communal obligation. Rather, resistance is now an individual duty, in which every Muslim must understand the emergency and do his or her part. The degree of intensity is supported by the authors with a citation from the law books: "As for fighting to repel, it is aimed at defending sanctity and religion, and all agree it is a duty. Nothing, with the exception of faith itself, is more sacred than repulsing an enemy who is attacking faith and life."[9]

This leads to the heart of the *Declaration*, which is the ruling that killing (or one could also translate, "fighting") Americans and their allies, or as the authors write a few lines down, killing (fighting) them and plundering their money, is a matter of individual duty for every Muslim who can, in any country where it is possible. The goal is to move the invading forces "out of all the lands of Islam, defeated and unable to threaten any Muslim." This last phrase catches the sentiment that motivates the authors; they believe that fighting the United States and its allies constitutes a just response to American attacks on Islam. They further believe that the American attacks have gone so far that Islam is under an emergency condition. Muslims should fight to defend justice: "And why should you not fight in the cause of God and of those who, being weak, are ill treated? [Men,] Women and children, whose cry is 'Our Lord, rescue us from this town, whose people are oppressors; and raise for us one who will help!'" (4:75). Fighters, in other words, are the guardians of the weak against the forces of oppression.

Violations of *Shari'a* Precedent?

Some have criticized the ruling of the *Declaration* as exceeding the bounds of Islamic law, even with respect to the emergency provision. Some critics focus on issues of authority, others on the scope of armed struggle in Islam, still others on the fact that the document calls for indiscriminate or total war. All of these reflect legitimate questions.

With respect to authority, I have already mentioned that the authors of the *Declaration* lack the credentials to qualify as members of the class of religious specialists. How, then, do they justify issuing a normative statement regarding the duty of Muslims? I think there are two possibilities — and these are not mutually exclusive. The first possibility is that the authors believe that the emergency condition justifies their assumption of the role of a religious specialist. Remember that in the emergency situation, the ordinary lines of authority are suspended. If that is the case in the family and in political life, perhaps it is so in matters of *Shari'a* discourse as well.

The second possibility has to do with basic democratic tendencies of Islam. It is commonly held that Islam has no clergy. The implication is that nearness to God, and the authority that flows from that, is not the province of any special class of people. The authority of religious specialists was historically supported by a habit of deference.

But there is nothing to suggest that such authority is anything more than habitual. Further, according to some legal texts, the criteria for exercising "independent judgment," and thus for making normative pronouncements, are really quite minimal. Indeed, some even suggest that a person or group of persons can have competence within one area of *Shari'a* reasoning — for example, the law of war — without obtaining the right to make pronouncements more generally.[10] At most, the question of authority seems to be of this nature: One can argue that bin Laden and his colleagues "ought not" make pronouncements like this, but one would be hard-pressed to say that they "cannot" do so. The issue is whether anyone listens.[11]

With respect to the scope of armed struggle in Islam, the *Declaration* calls for attacks in any country where it is possible. This is not a direct violation of Islamic norms, but it is unusual. Recall that the crucial point of the emergency provision has to do with the defense of Islamic territory, which is under attack. Most of those who invoke the emergency provision focus on what we might call "homeland defense." That is true, even for most of the radical groups, which have invoked the emergency provision in the last several decades. Egyptian Islamic Jihad and Hamas, for example, speak of their campaigns in terms of establishing a just and effective Islamic authority in their homelands.[12] In recent history, there is one prominent example of a Muslim force carrying out "emergency" defense activities far beyond its homeland. This is Shaykh Umar Abd al-Rahman and the Islamic Group (a kind of splinter from Egyptian Islamic Jihad) who wanted to attack American interests signified by the World Trade Center. This resulted in the 1993 bombing of the towers, for which Shaykh Umar and others remain in American prisons. The idea then and also in the 1998 *Declaration* is that the experience of homeland defense shows that Muslim fighters will have to strike not only at oppression close to home, but also at distant powers that support oppression. In particular, they will have to strike at the home front of those powers.

Again, this is not a violation of Islamic norms, but it is unusual. Recalling the worries Muslim scholars express about abuses of the emergency provision, one might now consider a new nuance; namely, the possibility exists that an overzealous group dedicated to armed resistance might strike at targets far from the homeland, and thus bring down on Muslim lands the wrath of a foreign power — for example, the action of the United States against the Taliban regime in Afghanistan.

The more direct violation of Islamic norms in the 1998 *Declaration* has to do with the call for direct and intentional strikes at civilian targets — that is, for indiscriminate or total warfare. Let there be no mistake about this; Islam is very clear on the matter. The Prophet said, "Do not cheat or commit treachery, do not mutilate or kill women, children, or old men."[13] In other sayings attributed to the Prophet, these directives are reiterated. The presupposition is that soldiers fight soldiers. How then do devout Muslims like the authors of the *Declaration* justify calling on Muslims to target American civilians? Readers of a just war text like Michael Walzer's *Just and Unjust Wars* no doubt already have thought about his famous discussion of "supreme emergency." Walzer argues that in a context where defeat is imminent and where defeat suggests the possibility of annihilation of a people or of a way of life, the ordinary limitations on fighters are temporarily suspended, and moral reasoning is limited to "utilitarianism of extremes."[14] Perhaps Muslims who, like the authors of the *Declaration*, are convinced that the United States is engaged in a war intended to annihilate Islam might believe that they are justified in attacking civilians under a similar kind of provision. As already indicated, the language of the *Declaration*, and indeed, the very concept of armed struggle as an individual duty, suggests emergency conditions. Those who fight should understand themselves to be "repulsing an enemy who is attacking religion and life."

Further, the reasoning associated with armed struggle as *fard 'ayn* carries with it the notion that "necessity makes the forbidden things permitted." One might reason that, if direct and intentional attacks on civilians are among the forbidden things (which they are), the necessity imposed by emergency conditions permits such attacks.

There is a major problem with such reasoning, however, given the way Islamic tradition typically thinks about the emergency condition.

That is, the maxim by which "necessity makes the forbidden things permitted" is not taken as an excuse for murder.[15] As mentioned previously, the emergency condition permits action outside normal lines of authority, but none of the examples include permission to commit murder.

This is a major obstacle to the kind of attacks the authors of the *Declaration* want to encourage. I find it most interesting that they do not cite any precedents for an exception that would cover such attacks. Indeed, when bin Laden has been questioned about such matters, he typically answers in two ways. First, he says that the United States has attacked civilians, too. Second, he argues that since all Americans benefit from the oppressive policies of their government (for example, cheap oil prices), they thus deserve what they get; one who readily accepts gains won by the immoral actions of others can scarcely claim to be guiltless.[16]

In either case, the argument is hardly something that the *Shari'a* tradition of judgments about *jihad* using armed force would recognize as compelling. Indeed, it seems the authors of the *Declaration* have no ground upon which to stand in terms of Islamic practical reasoning. The idea that there can be an individual duty for every Muslim to participate in armed struggle to defend Islamic territory or values makes good Islamic sense. But the idea that there can be an individual duty for every Muslim who is able to directly and intentionally kill American or any other civilians does not.

Muslim Responses to Bin Laden

That al Qaeda's advocacy of indiscriminate killing is highly problematic is indicated by significant Muslim response. Following the events of September 11, 2001, a number of prominent spokespersons condemned the attacks, precisely on the grounds that direct and intentional targeting of civilians violates *Shari'a*. That Muslims living in the United States, or more generally that moderate or liberal Muslims would do so, is significant, although unsurprising. It is surprising, however, that a number of Muslims, whose opposition to the United States and its allies is well known, also expressed concern that bin Laden and his colleagues were calling Muslims to act in violation of Islamic tradition. As an example, consider four "moments" in an extended "conversation" between representatives of al Qaeda and other "fundamentalist" Muslims during the last half of 2002.

Moment One

On June 7, 2002, an al Qaeda spokesperson named Sulayman abu Ghayth published an article entitled "In the Shadow of the Lances" on the Internet.[17] Abu Ghayth (who had become well-known for several statements following 9/11 and the beginning of U.S.-led action in Afghanistan) addressed the Muslim community to make sure it understands al Qaeda's arguments:

> Perhaps the Islamic community is waiting for one al-Qa'ida man to come out and clear up the many questions that accompany any communiqué, message, or picture [concerning 9/11], to know the truth, the motives, and the goals behind conflict with the Great Idol of our generation.

Abu Ghayth's article developed a defense of al Qaeda's program of fighting against the United States and its allies. He listed a number of reasons that justify such fighting. For example:

> America is the head of heresy in our modern world, and it leads an infidel democratic regime that is based upon separation of religion and state and on ruling the people by the people via legislating laws that contradict the way of God and permit that which God has prohibited. This compels the other countries to act in accordance with the same laws in the same ways...and punishes any country [that resists] by besieging it, and then by boycotting it. In so doing, [America] seeks to impose on the world a religion that is not God's.

The United States, then, is a prime example of an unjust state, since divine law does not govern it. Its injustice is compounded by the fact that it seeks to export this form of government. And, as we come to understand, the injustice of the United States is expressed by its willingness to use or to support the use of military force against those who would choose another model for political order. Abu Ghayth lists various places in which this is so: Palestine, Iraq, Afghanistan, Somalia, Sudan, the Philippines, Indonesia, Kashmir, and others. In many of the cases he cites a number indicating (as he takes it) the number of innocents killed. This is critical to the argument, for abu Ghayth wants ultimately to justify not only armed resistance to the United States and its allies, but the kind of armed resistance advocated by the leaders of al Qaeda and related groups in the 1998 *Declaration*. Abu Ghayth thus offers *Shari'a* justifications for attacks on civilians. God said, "one who attacks you, attack as he attacked you," and also, "The reward of evil is a similar evil," and also "When you are punished, punish as you have been punished."

These Qur'anic citations, as interpreted by recognized religious scholars, establish a right of reciprocal justice. According to this notion, victims of injustice have the right to inflict damage on those responsible for their suffering, in a manner proportionate to the harm suffered. According to this line of thought, the numbers of innocents killed by the United States suggests that we [Muslims] have not reached parity with them. We have the right to kill 4 million Americans, 2 million of them children, and to exile twice as many and wound and cripple hundreds of thousands.

It is important to note that abu Ghayth stipulates that the damage inflicted by the United States and its allies is both "direct and indirect." For his purposes, the distinction does not matter. Those who suffer have the right to inflict damage proportionate to their losses. And this, he writes, is the only way to deal with the United States:

> America knows only the language of force. This is the only way to stop it and make it take its hands off the Muslims and their affairs. America does not know the language of dialogue or the language of peaceful coexistence! America is kept at bay by blood alone.

Moment Two

Abu Ghayth's article provides an important defense of al Qaeda tactics. Other Muslims are not persuaded, however. And thus on July 10, 2002, the television network al-Jazeera interviewed a well-known Saudi religious scholar and dissident, Shaykh Muhsin al-'Awaji.[18]

Two other dissidents joined by telephone. All three served time in Saudi prisons for criticism of the royal family and its policies of cooperation with the United States during and especially following Operation Desert Shield and Desert Storm in 1990–91. None of the three is friendly to American policies with respect to historically Muslim states. Indeed, they are in favor of armed resistance to American aggression, and they approve the use of martyrdom operations.

This conversation then turned to Usama bin Laden. Since the three scholars agree with al Qaeda on the necessity of government by divine law and on the justice of resistance to the United States and its allies, it is most interesting that they indicate that, after initial approval of bin Laden, they and many others have changed their opinion. Shaykh al-'Awaji says:

> In the past, when he was fighting the Russians in Afghanistan, bin Laden was the greatest of *jihad* warriors, in the eyes of the Saudi people and in the eyes of the Saudi government. He and the others went to Afghanistan with official support, and the support of the learned [the "ulama" or religious scholars.]

In some ways, this positive assessment of bin Laden still holds.

> What the Saudis like best about bin Laden is his asceticism. When the Saudi compares bin Laden to any child of wealthy parents, he sees that bin Laden left behind the pleasures of the hotels for the foxholes of *jihad*, while others compete among themselves for the wealth and palaces of this world.

Nevertheless, this positive judgment must now be qualified, because of al Qaeda's tactics. Bin Laden is guilty of spreading discord among Muslims. He labels people as heretics when he has no proof, and some al Qaeda operations bring harm to Muslims. Bin Laden and his colleagues also violate Islamic norms of honorable combat, and this is an important reason for qualifying earlier, positive assessments. Shaykh al-'Awaji accuses bin Laden in these words: "He and those with him target innocent people, and I refer to the innocents on the face of the entire earth, of every religion and color, and in every region." Recalling Islamic tradition on these matters, one cannot help but think of the saying of the Prophet: "Do not cheat or commit treachery. Do not mutilate anyone or kill children [or other noncombatants]." Shaykh al-'Awaji is far from approving of abu Ghayth's (or al Qaeda's) notion of reciprocal justice. For him, and for those joining him in this interview, Muslims are to fight with honor, which means, among other things, that they are not to engage in direct attacks on noncombatants.

Moment Three

We should not forget that Shaykh al-'Awaji and his colleagues agree with much of al Qaeda's program. As I have said, they are not favorably disposed to American policies in the Middle East and elsewhere, but they want to see Muslims fight according to traditional norms.

A different kind of criticism was articulated a few months later by Shaykh 'Umar Bakri Muhammad of al-Muhajiroun ("The Emigres"), a fundamentalist group based in the United Kingdom. Shaykh 'Umar's tract, *Jihad: The Method for Khilafah?* appeared at www .almuhajiroun.com in September 2002. While hardly an elegant piece of work, and thus difficult to read, this tract tries to evaluate the place of armed struggle in the attempt to establish a state governed by divine law. The author also discusses the nature and place of armed resistance in contemporary contexts.

According to Shaykh 'Umar, *jihad*, in the sense of "armed struggle," is a term reserved for fighting authorized by an established Islamic government. This is the sense of the reference to *khilafah* in his title. Literally, the term suggests "succession" to the Prophet Muhammad. Shaykh 'Umar uses the term as a designation for Islamic government. His discussion reiterates one of the great themes of Islamic political thought — that is, the necessity that justice be embodied in a political order. And, as he indicates, when this political order is in place, it should seek to extend its influence by appropriate means. These means can and should include honorable combat.

For the last eighty years, the kind of authority indicated by the term *khilafah* has been absent from political life. This fact sets the context for the rest of Shaykh 'Umar's argument. Muslims are required to work to change this situation, and to establish *khilafah*. To that end, may they or should they engage in *jihad?* The answer is no. First, the nature of the concept of *Jihad* designates fighting that occurs under the auspices of an established government. By definition, then, fighting that takes place apart from such a government's authorization cannot be *jihad*. To this definitional no, Shaykh 'Umar adds a second reason: Islamic political thought requires that authority be legitimate. It must be established through a process of consultation and assent. The submission of Muslims to an authority thus ought not be compelled. Islamic government should be established through persuasion.

Shaykh 'Umar indicates that the process of consultation and assent may be conducted in a number of ways. He then moves to a discussion of contemporary resistance among Muslims. In his view, the Muslim community is in a kind of political twilight zone. Without a duly constituted *khilafah*, there can be no fighting worthy of the title *jihad*. Yet Muslims are in need of defense, in Chechnya, Kashmir, and other locations. What are they to do?

As Shaykh 'Umar views it, Islam recognizes a right of extended self-defense. Each person has the right to defend his/her own life, liberty, and property. Everyone also has the right, and in some sense the duty to defend the lives, liberties, and properties of others who are victims of aggression. This kind of fighting is called *qital*, a word that quite literally indicates "fighting" or "killing." Where Muslims are under attack, their coreligionists around the globe may and should come to their defense. When they do, however, they should understand that fighting is delimited, first in terms of its goals. *Qital* is not *jihad*. As such, it is not a proper means of establishing Islamic government. Second, *qital* is limited in its means. Interestingly, *qital* and *jihad* are similar in this respect, since both are governed by norms of honorable combat, or as Shaykh 'Umar puts it, by the "pro-life" values of the Prophet Muhammad: "not killing women and children, not killing the elderly or monks, not targeting the trees or animals. . . . Foreign forces occupying Muslim lands are legitimate targets and we are obliged to liberate Muslim land from such occupation and to cooperate with each other in the process, and can even target their embassies and military bases." Tactics that involve direct attacks on noncombatants are ruled out, however.

Moment Four

Shaykh 'Umar's argument challenges al Qaeda's approach at a number of points. Most important for our purposes, however, is the stipulation that even defensive fighting, which almost by definition involves coming to the aid of Muslims in emergency or near emergency conditions, should be governed by norms of honorable combat. It is not surprising, given arguments like this, that the leadership of al Qaeda would respond. Thus, in November 2002, Usama bin Laden, or someone writing in his name, published a "Letter to America" responding to Muslim and non-Muslim criticisms of al Qaeda.[19]

The first part of the "Letter" is a list of reasons for fighting against the United States and its allies. The "Letter" restates and extends grievances outlined in earlier documents, including Sulayman abu Ghayth's Internet article.

The second part of the text moves to the question of tactics. "You may then dispute that all the above does not justify aggression against civilians, for crimes they did not commit and offenses in which they did not partake." The concern here is clearly with arguments that al Qaeda tactics violate norms of honorable combat. The author of the "Letter" does not accept these arguments. Two counterarguments are cited in justification of a policy of attacking civilians as well as soldiers. First, the United States claims to be a democracy:

> Therefore, the American people are the ones who choose their government by way of their own free will; a choice that stems from their agreement to its policies. . . . The American people have the ability and choice to refuse the policies of their government and even to change it if they want.

Second (and in a way reminiscent of abu Ghayth's argument), the author cites the *lex talionis* (the law of justified retaliation):

> God, the Almighty, legislated the permission and the option to take revenge. Thus, if we are attacked, then we have the right to attack back. Whoever has destroyed our villages and towns, then we have

the right to destroy their villages and towns. Whoever has stolen our wealth, then we have the right to destroy their economy. And whoever has killed our civilians, then we have the right to kill theirs.

Harm suffered may be avenged by the infliction of damage proportionate to the original harm. Muslims have the right to kill Americans and other "enemy" civilians, because the United States and its allies engage in actions that kill civilians on the Muslim side.

Conclusion

Over the course of its fourteen centuries, Islamic political thought has centered on two great themes. The first theme emphasizes the importance of establishing a just public order, while the second focuses on notions of honorable combat. Both may be construed as responses to indiscriminate or illegitimate violence. In particular, the establishment of just public order involves procedures intended to limit the need for and recourse to private vengeance, while notions of honorable combat indicate the conditions under which representatives of a just public order may utilize armed force to maintain order.

For the last eighty years, the tradition of Islamic political thought has been under stress or under dispute. Such disputes are frequent. Religious traditions are always susceptible of dispute, as long as they are *living* traditions. One generation bequeaths to the next a framework for discussion. The new generation then tries to establish a fit between that which is handed down and its own set of circumstances. When people stop arguing about a tradition, that is a sign it is no longer viable.

Thus, Muslim argument about justice, or about the requirements of the *Shari'a*, is nothing new. Nevertheless, one could say that the last eighty years mark a period of particular stress, in which the most contentious point has been the question, "What constitutes a just public order?" In 1924, the new Turkish Republic withdrew support for the Ottoman ruler, and thus effectively abolished the last remaining symbol of the great empires of Islamic history. For much of the last century, Muslim intellectuals argued about the shape a modern political order ought to take. One part of that argument focused on the sort of legal regime such an order should have. The debate has engaged two questions: (1) Does justice require that a state be governed by divine law only, in the sense that its laws and policies are derived directly from the Qur'an and other acknowledged sources of the *Shari'a?* or (2) Can a political order be just when its legal regime is derived from a more diverse set of sources?

Those holding that a just public order must be governed by divine law only are usually characterized as fundamentalists or radicals. Usama bin Laden and others associated with al Qaeda are only the most visible example of this trend. They hold that power is currently in the hands of secularists who do not acknowledge the priority of divine law, and who are thereby illegitimate tyrants. Those arguing for a more diverse set of sources are typically called moderate or liberal Muslims. These may agree that certain policies of the United States or governments allied with it are unjust. They do not hold, however, that the system of government of the United States is itself unjust or tyrannical.

In the last twenty years or so Islamic political thought has increasingly turned attention to the theme of honorable combat. The question might be posed like this: "When one is faced with injustice, is it proper to take up arms?" Perhaps reflecting the view that injustice relates to particular policies rather than to the world system as a whole, moderates have tended to focus on shaping public opinion, fostering diplomacy, and other means as preferable to the use of armed force. This is so, even though they find it hard to say that people struggling with oppression — as, for example, the Palestinians — do not have the right to take up arms. Fundamentalists, by contrast, have tended to move more quickly to the notion that armed force might be justified, and thus to advocate fighting as a proper response to the injustice of existing conditions.

In this essay, I have tried to indicate the ways those Muslims advocating armed force — in particular, fundamentalists — argue the case. Since September 11, 2001, discussion of Islam and armed combat has tended to swing between two assertions: Either Islam has nothing to do with fighting of this type, or it has everything to do with it. Neither of these assertions is accurate. Neither catches the sense of Islamic tradition as a living reality in which people try to discern God's will in particular circumstances by reading agreed-upon texts and reasoning according to established rules. In that light, it is important to understand the conversations Muslims have about political justice and honorable combat. The evidence presented in this essay indicates that these include conversations between allied groups of fundamentalists and radicals, as well as arguments between fundamentalists and moderates. Among other things, internal conversations after September 11 between Muslims about al Qaeda tactics suggest the power of a central thesis: there are limits on what one can do, even when one is fighting for justice. In this sense, the Muslim conversation goes back to the Qur'an itself, which at 2:190 indicates:

> Fight against those who are fighting you
> But do not violate the limits.
> God does not approve those who violate the limits.

Four

Jewish-Christian Relations

After the *Shoah*

STEVEN LEONARD JACOBS

Steven Jacobs addresses head-on the problems and prospects for a meaningful Jewish-Christian dialogue. For discourse that promotes peace, the following issues are central: charges of anti-Semitism in the New Testament; the reality of the Shoah vis-à-vis the Jewish notion of God and the Christian notion of a redeeming Christ as the Son of God; the mission of the church toward Jews; and the complex historical and theological relationship between Judaism and Christianity as a foundation for a post-Shoah relationship. Jacobs deals critically with each of these challenges, forging his way through their complexities to find viable criteria for mutually respectful acceptance. Not that the path will be forged easily. Jacobs adeptly projects very difficult issues on both sides of the discourse. Both religious traditions will need to search their own souls for humility and repentance, learning from each other. Yet, Judaism and Christianity could provide a model for how religions must deal with tremendously hurtful histories to create a promising future that would together work in the name of their God for peace in the world.

Provocations for Dialogue

1. *Can Christians reevaluate exclusivist claims to have the only means to God's salvation? Are such claims historically and scripturally valid? Do alternatives exist?*

2. *Is it valid for evangelical Christians to continue to convert Jews as if they do not understand the God of Israel and the church? Do such efforts aid or detract from promoting peaceful ends around the world?*

3. *Can Jews reclaim their historic acceptance that the righteousness of God may come by way of non-Jews? If so, what are the implications for peace?*

4. *Jews and Christians must come out of their theological ghettoes to reconsider their historic relationship within the intentions of their common understanding of God.*

• • •

The Possibility of a Jewish-Christian Dialogue?

AMONG THE MOST DIFFICULT and problematic theological topics in the aftermath of the *Shoah* for both Jews and Christians is that of authentic dialogue with one another. Even now, half a century after the closure of World War II, there are sincere, devout, and committed religious Jews (and Christians) who reject interreligious dialogue as unnecessary, unproductive, and unworthy of time, energy, and/or intellectual resources. To cite but one relatively recent example: In an article entitled " 'No' to a Jewish-Christian 'Theological Dialogue'!" Dr. Manfred R. Lehmann, a Jewish scholar and businessman from Miami Beach, writes:

> ...you have only to read the unbelievably hateful statements made against Judaism in Rome during Vatican II discussions, which, therefore, led to the greatly watered down Declaration, or the tortuous discussions and reservations which Protestant clergymen have among themselves even to recognize that Jews exist "theologically."
>
> At the recently-held Catholic-Jewish Collegium in Baltimore, the idea of theological dialogue was firmly rejected by the Jewish participants. Mindful of the longstanding "issur" [Jewish legal prohibition] against such a dialogue, the Jewish participants stated that contact with the Church should be limited to political, social, environmental, and similar topics, but not to theology.[1]

Lehmann goes on to cite Israeli philosopher and professor Yeshayahu Leibowitz in his book *Judaism, Human Values, and the Jewish State*: "For Jews who regard Judaism as embodied in Torah and Mitzvot, there can be no coexistence of ideas between Judaism and Christianity and no place for 'Judeo-Christian dialogue.'" He then concludes, "A theological dialogue with Christians must not be on the Jewish agenda!"

A more serious challenge to the concept of Jewish-Christian dialogue is that posed by prolific Jewish scholar Professor Jacob Neusner in his article, "There Has Never Been a Judaeo-Christian Dialogue—But There Can Be One." Neusner posits three criteria by which authentic dialogue takes place:

1. Each party proposes to take seriously the position of the other.
2. Each party concedes the integrity of the other.
3. Each party accepts responsibility for the outcome of the discussion—that is, remains open to the possibility of conceding the legitimacy of the other's viewpoint.

Neusner argues that these criteria have not been met by either side, and therefore no real dialogue has yet taken place. He says:

> ...in the dialogue between Judaism and Christianity surface chatter covers over profound mutual incomprehension. The Judaeo-Christian dialogue has floundered because each side finds it difficult to address the most deeply held convictions of the other: Judaism cannot cope with the conception of God Incarnate in a human being; Christianity finds difficult the conception of the uniqueness and holiness of Israel.[2]

While I take issue with his conclusion that "the only way for a Judaic believer to understand Christianity is *within Judaic terms*, and the only way for a Christian believer to understand Judaism is *within Christian* terms," I fully appreciate the criteria he enumerates. He does hold out, however, the possibility of such dialogue existing at some point in the future.

The critiques of Lehmann and Neusner appear to diminish any promise of a fruitful Jewish-Christian dialogue. In addition to their arguments, we are confronted starkly with Christian culpability and responsibility for what transpired in the *Shoah* during those dark years, 1933–45. To assess Christian attitudes during 1939–45 is even more devastating. To be sure, all serious students of the *Shoah* recognize the powerful implications of the demonization of the Jew from earliest Christianity on, and the prolonged otherness of Jews throughout much of European civilization for the last two thousand years as a resource from which Nazi ideologues could construct the "Final Solution to the Jewish Question/Problem." Then there are the inherent difficulties in coming to grips religiously and theologically with specific historical examples of active complicity and/or active neutrality on the part of supposedly committed Christians of various denominational stripes, who either assisted the Nazis in their genocidal tasks, remained bystanders during those years, and/or failed to aid Jewish men, women, and children in their moment of greatest need.

Yet, despite all of this, serious dialogue between Jews and Christians after the *Shoah* — or, perhaps, because of the *Shoah* — must continue for at least four reasons: (1) Jews and Christians are inextricably bound to each other, historically and contemporarily, whether some among us would wish it were not so, and can mutually benefit from continuing contact with each other; (2) the historical reality of the *Shoah* as a watershed event in Western Christian history, and a genocidal tragedy for Jews the world over, demands dialogue in order to prevent its repetition; (3) the ongoing threat of global destruction equally demands Jewish-Christian dialogue as we join together to harness our collective energies, together with others of goodwill, to stave off the demise of our planet; and (4) as people of faith, Jews and Christians are in a unique position to combat the evils of anti-Semitism as expressed, for example, by the so-called Holocaust revisionists [better "Holocaust deniers"].

The question before us remains: what criteria, in light of the *Shoah*, must be reexamined for there to be *any* meaningful attempt at Jewish-Christian dialogue as we move into this twenty-first century? Corollary to this question are two others. First, does not Christianity weaken its own theological integrity as a religious tradition of contemporary meaning by its hesitancy and ambivalence to confront its

own moral and religious lapses during the years 1933–45, as well
as the presence/absence of God during those years as well? Second,
can any dialogue whatsoever between Jews and Christians take place
which excludes discussion of the theological import of the *Shoah* as
well as the rebirth of the state of Israel in 1948?

I believe there are five issues that require examination in light of
the *Shoah* to move this "new" dialogue forward:

1. The supposed anti-Semitism of the New Testament;

2. The entire notion of God the Father and His Son Jesus the Redeeming
   Christ in an unredeemed world which could and did countenance the
   Shoah;

3. The very "mission" of the church, specifically toward the Jewish people
   and generally toward all non-Christian peoples in the aftermath of the
   Shoah, as well as toward each other;

4. The proper relationship between the "parent" Judaism and the "child"
   Christianity, between Jews and Christians, given the long, sad, and
   tragic history of that relationship, or, rather, nonrelationship; and

5. A serious look at the historical realities and implications of the nonrelationship between Jews and Christians, beginning with the pre–New
   Testament birth of Christianity and the person of Paul, until the rise
   of Nazism.

This essay, therefore, attempts to reexamine these five issues from
the perspective of one child of a survivor-escapee, now deceased, as
well as one ordained to the liberal rabbinate, and now a full-time
academic, who continues to interact with members of the Christian
community in various academic, congregational, and communal contexts. What I believe will emerge from this study are a series of
signposts and directions for those who will continue to engage in
Jewish-Christian dialogue, both now and in the future.

Dialogue Post-*Shoah*: Five Obstacles

Anti-Semitism and the New Testament[3]

It has long been my view that to condemn the New Testament as
anti-Semitic misunderstands the intention and the historical context

of the anti-Judaic portrait painted therein. A much more accurate understanding of that negative depiction would be to see the controversy as an "in-house, intra-family Jewish debate." The exceptions to this might be the Gospel of John, which attacks Jews from outside the family, and later Gentile successors to Paul who, in their burgeoning desire both to separate themselves from their Jewish beginnings and further to create a new and distinct religious response to the times, lost sight of the original meaning of the debate, with disastrous future results.[4]

James H. Charlesworth of Princeton Theological Seminary likewise understands the anti-Semitism of the New Testament as a misunderstanding of the authors themselves:

> In the end it is important to stress that the New Testament authors would have been horrified by the claim that anything they wrote was anti-Jewish. Far from supporting the hatred of the Jews or any movement that produced the Holocaust [or better the *Shoah*], most of the Jews in the Palestinian Jesus Movement would have been gassed at Auschwitz. Almost all of the authors of the New Testament documents were Jews. I am convinced that the Jews who authored the New Testament would want to affirm that they not only were born Jews but continued to be faithful Jews.[5]

Craig A. Evans also sees the anti-Semitism of the New Testament text as the result of divorcing it from its own historical context:

> First of all, there appears to be a lack of awareness of the polemic within the Jewish Scriptures themselves. Secondly, many Jews and Christians read the New Testament writings in the context of medieval and/or modern non-Jewish Christianity.... New Testament polemic should be viewed as part of the intra-Jewish polemic that took place in the first and early second centuries. Finally, the New Testament can be read, and, tragically, has been read in an Anti-Semitic manner.... But divorced from their original context, these expressions do readily lend themselves to Anti-Semitic ideas. Yes, the New Testament can be understood as Anti-Semitic if it is taken out of its early Jewish context. But if it is interpreted in context, as it should be, the New Testament is not Anti-Semitic.[6]

My position, as well as those of both Charlesworth and Evans, are widely accepted by biblical scholars. But what of the person in the pew who has not been enlightened by this fresh reading of the New Testament in context? Or, what of the pastor or rabbi who has not kept current in the literature of such thinking but wishes to engage in dialogue? As Krister Stendahl, emeritus Dean of Harvard Divinity School and former bishop of Stockholm, succinctly puts it: "So there is anti-Semitism in the New Testament. But that is not the issue. The question is what to do about it."[7] Indeed, how can the dialogue begin? I have two proposals to get conversation started.

First, following Evans, the place to begin for Christians after the *Shoah* is with a far deeper and more profound knowledge of the New Testament which, I believe, can only come about by rereading it and understanding it in the context of its own historical milieu.[8] Once this is done, three questions emerge that direct any serious dialogue post-*Shoah*: (1) The fact that the New Testament *does* contain statements which are negatively prejudicial toward Jews and which have been used and could continue to be used for further and future anti-Semitic agendas — *How will Christianity deal with these texts?* (2) The fact that these statements occur within the sacred literature of Christianity — *How does this affect the self-understanding of Christianity?* (3) The fact that among the principal messages of this literature is the call to conversion, including the Jews — *How does this impact the mission of Christianity?*

The first task, then, after realizing the necessity of rethinking one's whole approach to the New Testament as sacred literature, not only to be venerated within the context of religious tradition, but critically examined by accepted scholarly methods, is an educational one: how to translate that new knowledge into the minds and hearts of those "out there" in the pews and communities who will take such knowledge with them into new Jewish-Christian dialogues? Curricula at all levels must be updated — in the seminaries, religiously affiliated colleges and universities, secondary schools, and congregations.[9]

At the same time, Jews also, if we are to engage in serious dialogue, must become conversant in the literature of the New Testament. Not only graduates of the Hebrew Union College–Jewish Institute of Religion, where I personally was first exposed to studying the New

Testament dispassionately as a required course in the rabbinical ordination program, but all Jewish institutions of higher learning, as well as congregational and communal Jewish institutional learning programs must objectively engage in the study of the New Testament. (Groundless is the fear that currently exists within certain segments of the Jewish community that the taste of such "forbidden fruits" will result in the conversion of the Jews. My own study and teaching of the sacred literatures of other faith traditions has only enhanced the appreciation of my own.)[10]

Second, the educational tasks required by this appreciation and understanding of the New Testament are complemented by the new liturgical responsibilities involved in those Christian churches where the Bible is central to worship. How does one "preach the Word" through the lens of this more accurate historical understanding of the New Testament, and, in doing so, draw the worshiper's attention to those painfully problematic passages which raise questions about traditional interpretation and understanding? Does one simply "share scriptures" without commentary? Does one reconstruct the lectionary of one's own religious tradition to exclude those passages which raise these issues, concentrating, instead, on those passages which reflect the highest moral, spiritual, and religious values? Indeed, how does one incorporate this understanding liturgically?

Having now raised these initial concerns and suggestions vis-à-vis the New Testament text, we turn to the second of the five issues, that of God and the Christ.

The Redeeming Christ?

It is my understanding that at the very heart of Christianity is the understanding that, whatever else we may say of Jesus the Christ, his atoning death on the cross, his willingness to offer up his own life in place of pitiable and pitiful humanity spared it further degradation in the sight of God and redeemed it from sin and death forever and all time. In other words, the world and humanity have, somehow, mysteriously, been forever and irrevocably "changed" by this singularly unique act by a singularly unique individual who represented in his person the merging of both the divine and the human in a way never before offered to humanity or ever again to be replicated.

Yet, I would pose the following questions from a Jewish perspective: Where or how is the world redeemed after the Christ? How has the world changed after the Christ, given two thousand years of, at times, Christian oppression of Jews through expulsion, ghettoization, forced conversion, and extermination-annihilation? How does the Christ's redemption of the world square with a *Shoah* which saw the deaths of 6 million Jews, 1 million innocent children below the age of twelve, and an additional half million young people if we raise the age to eighteen? Not to mention 5 million non-Jews, Christians included?

Theologically, is it logical to say that the world was, indeed, "redeemed" by the death of the Christ, but that the world, humanity, continues to ignore its own redemption? Or, is it more logical to say that the world was *potentially* redeemed by the death of the Christ on the cross, a potential that continues to exist for the world, which, up to now, has refused to welcome that potential into its midst? A corollary to this alternative is that the Christ represents, for those who choose him, the paradigmatic model of the very best of which humanity is capable. To surrender one's life out of love for another is an act which is also found among "righteous gentiles" and Jews of the *Shoah*. From my perspective, the actual death of the Christ did not, either at that moment, or up to this moment, redeem our world, but only opened the door to that possibility. But it was not then, nor is it now, the only possibility.[11]

This understanding between Jew and Christian avoids what, historically, have been three of the most tragically difficult obstacles to such dialogue: (1) A rank ordering of the death of the Christ as the supreme event in all human history, all other deaths being of far less significance; (2) a kind of arrogant triumphalism which gives credence to this death and this death alone; and (3) a Jewish difficulty, given Jewish history, equating this death with world redemption and the realities of the Jewish experience.

To maintain the potentially redemptive death of the Christ allows for two possibilities essential to any fruitful Jewish-Christian dialogue: (1) that those who wish to consider themselves Christians are now free to draw from this moment that which gives meaning to their own lives, and (2) that those who do not wish to draw from this moment, in particular the Jewish people, are equally free not to do so.

Greek Orthodox scholar Thomas A. Idinopulous of Miami University (Ohio) would, perhaps, go even further, regarding the "Christ event" not as success but as failure. He has written:

> ...if history shows anything, it shows that Christ did not win but rather lost the decisive battle, not once, but over and over again. It is reasonable to ask, "What would remain distinctive of Christian belief if somehow incontestable proof were provided in history that Christ's cross did not defeat sin, but rather led to more crosses, more sin?" From a Jewish point of view, this is precisely what happened in Jewish-Christian relations. Nevertheless, one must acknowledge that Christian redemption is a matter of faith which, as a religious faith, strengthens, not weakens, in adversity. The Christian is bidden to draw closer to Christ precisely in response to the worsening corruption of the world.[12]

Regarding the death of the Christ as failure, it seems to me, may be accurate historically, but one over which wrestling will take place exclusively within the Christian community and will not serve to build dialogical bridges to the Jewish community. That such comment comes from one within the Christian community merits that it be addressed subsequent to the *Shoah;* its resolution, however, I leave to others.

At bottom, however, is a series of theological questions that must be addressed post-*Shoah.* They are the following:

- Is Jesus the Christ, the one and only begotten son of God, only for those who accept him as such?

- Or, is Jesus the Christ, the one and only begotten son of God, for all humanity — including those who do not accept him as such?

- What, then, about those who neither accept him as such, nor reject him outright, nor stand in ignorance of him?

- What then is the proper Christian response, first to the Jews and also to the Buddhists, Hindus, Muslims, and others?

Again, the potentially redemptive possibilities of the "Christ event" would seem best to address these questions for both Jews and Christians, as well as others. For those who accept Jesus as the Christ, there is no problem; for those who choose not to accept him as such, there is, equally, no problem. For those whose experience does not include even the most limited of encounters with Christianity and Christians, there is no problem.

Morally and ethically, post-*Shoah*, it is one thing to accept the limited and limiting experience of the Christ, letting it serve as a bridge to dialogue. It is quite another to profess the universality of the Christ for all humanity and the "arrogant triumphalism" noted earlier which, all-too-readily, historically (and contemporarily) has accompanied it and act in accord with that understanding — all of which leads us to the third criterion of a new Jewish-Christian dialogue.

The "Mission" of the Church Today?

The so-called Great Commission of the gospel tradition[13] is an obligation incumbent upon all Christians to share the "good news" of Jesus the Christ with all those who are not Christians. Christians need to understand that such an evangelistic outreach to Jews after the *Shoah*, the very same persons who have struggled to rebuild shattered lives and recover their religious identity, is a great offense. A part of that struggle for Jews includes rebuilding the Third Jewish Commonwealth in the state of Israel. Thus, aggressive Christian evangelism remains offensive to the point of repugnance.[14]

Having suffered so much because we were Jews, having called into question so much of previously accepted Jewish religious faith, heritage, and tradition because of the *Shoah*, the answer to our pain is not to surrender to another religious tradition. Indeed, this form of Christian mission terminates dialogue for many Jews, since they perceive it as furthering the work of the Nazis. After all, Hitler and his minions refused to accept religious conversion, even of the previous two generations, as valid exemptions from the "Final Solution."

Presbyterian scholar and pastor Douglas K. Huneke further emphasizes this last point when he writes:

> No Christian who stands in the presence of burning children would dare to seek the conversion of the Jews.[15] Such a Christian must struggle with the contradictions implicit in speaking of a God of love whose followers were the architects of mass murder and genocide; of a covenantal God who did not save the covenantal people, who did not extinguish the flames or dispel the gas or vanquish the adversaries. These irresolvable contradictions will quench the evangelistic fervor and humble the triumphalist spirit of any believer who stands before the Shoah.[16]

Thus, religiously sensitive and knowledgeable Christians, morally and ethically aware of the *Shoah* and its effect upon Jews, must rethink and, ultimately, reject any form of missionizing whatsoever toward Jews. If the experience of the Christ, as previously stated, is potentially redemptive for all humanity, then Christianity is potentially available to all those who would choose to elect it, willing to explore its possibilities and come to it without coercion. To aggressively promote its proselytizing and conversionary activities as the only and exclusive way to experience the Divine-human encounter, however understood and interpreted, is to express no love or caring for Jews, to build no bridges between the two.[17]

From this new awareness, therefore, Christian scholars and preachers must rethink and reject those New Testament passages that charge them to go forth and share their faith with Jews. After the *Shoah*, the time has now come for Christians to admit that there are, indeed, passages in their New Testament which command them to convert the Jews (and others). Now, because of the changed historical circumstance of the *Shoah*, they must reject them as contemporarily meaningful. Christians must read the New Testament in light of the *Shoah*.

The question, therefore, logically arises as to whether or not there are any legitimate avenues for the sharing of such "Good News" with

Jews. The answer: only if requested by Jews themselves. Better, now, to live positive Christian lives by word and example, letting non-Christians observe the evidence of such commitments rather than verbalize them. Those drawn to Christianity and Christians will seek more; those not so drawn, will not.

By extension, post-*Shoah*, what has been written relevant to Jews is equally relevant to all non-Christians, whether or not already ensconced in a religious tradition or not so identified. Conversion to Christianity, other than involuntary and coercive, always remains a possibility, but not the only possibility. Because of the *Shoah*, Christians, too, will now have to live with this inherent religious contradiction: As much as they themselves perceive their way to God through the Christ as the *only* way for humanity to experience God, it remains true only should they elect to do so, despite their understanding of both God and the Christ desiring it. It is better now to accept the fact that individuals and families and groups in a post-Auschwitz world must be free to pursue their own destinies, religious and other, as they perceive them, provided these destinies do not impinge on their neighbors nor do violence or injustice to them.

The Relationship of Christianity to Judaism

Having examined the New Testament and the Christ from a post-*Shoah* Jewish perspective, the next criterion in the quest for a meaningful and relevant Jewish-Christian dialogue is to ask about that association directly: What kind of relationship can be constructed in the aftermath of the Second World War, given the long, sad, and tragic history of what, essentially, has been negative and injurious to both Jews and Christians? How then, now, to move forward?

First, Christians for whom dialogue with Jews is important and primary must be willing to admit that Christianity *does* bear a measure of responsibility and culpability for the *Shoah;* that the "demonization" of the Jews subsequent both to the death of the Christ and the destruction of the Second Temple (70 CE) ultimately played directly into the hands of the Nazis. The perpetuation of these negative, stereotypical myths does continual harm to Jews. It should also be considered by Christians an affront to and stain upon Christianity.

(Having recognized a "bad history" does not mean that it must continue; admission of guilt and/or wrongdoing in the past does not negate future relationships; and serious, open, and honest confrontation with the past can open the door to a positive present and future.)

Second, both Jews and Christians must recognize that Christianity itself, coming out of the very loins of Judaism, remains eternally indebted to Judaism, and must, therefore, be respectful of and appreciative of its parent faith. The recognition by scholars that a proper historical understanding of the origins of Christianity within the matrix of first- and second-century Judaism enhances one's own appreciation of Christianity is still in its infancy. As noted earlier, what must now happen is the translation of that appreciation into the church and the pew so that all who would engage in post-*Shoah* Jewish-Christian dialogue do so with far more knowledge than has characterized such conversations in the past.

Third, Jews in particular must accept as fact that, despite this long, sad, and tragic history, contemporary Christianity and contemporary Christians are not the enemies of the Jewish people; that the *Shoah* revealed to Jews "good Christians" capable of the most affirmatively human (and humane) acts of selflessness on behalf of Jews; and that, up to and including today, there are Christians who continue to take their place with Jews in the face of continuing anti-Semitism, and who regard such hatred and prejudice as a violation of their own sacred religious tradition and an affront to their Christ. It is, therefore, appropriate for Jews to acknowledge with thanks all such efforts and to continue to network with all those who would network with us.[18]

Fourth, Jews must accept in reality, post-*Shoah*, the Talmudic dictum that "the righteous of all nations have a share in the world to come," and interact with our neighbors with this mind-set uppermost in our consciousness. Without question, it is difficult to do so post-*Shoah*, but to withdraw into our own ghettos — intellectually, religiously, spiritually, as well as physically — is equally to deny the instances of righteous conduct that took place throughout the entire Jewish experience, especially during World War II.

Therefore, to further enable a Jewish-Christian dialogue to go forward in the aftermath of World War II, Jews need to rethink our overall understanding of Christianity itself and our own relationship to it: what Christianity is and why Christianity is. Jewish theologians need to begin postulating a positive Jewish theological understanding of Christianity, one that accounts for its diversity as well as its problematic history.

One such possibility would be to understand Christianity as a midrashic interpretation of religious Judaism, one whose roots remain deep within the Jewish religious tradition, and one whose activist appeal to those not born into the Jewish community remains strong and powerful. Its theological messages, as well as its ethical positions, likewise find their origins within Judaism. Initially resentful of its parent, Christianity continues to evolve toward a maturing relationship with Judaism, not yet there, but moving forward. Such movement must continue, and Jews must be prepared to meet Christians in dialogue.

Historical Realities and Implications

The English theologian and historian James W. Parkes remarked, "Bad history does not make good theology." Recognition of this difficult history of the relationship between Jews and Christians is the beginning point from which present and future Jewish-Christian relations move forward. To ignore the past is to do disservice to both present and future.

The uniqueness of Nazi anti-Semitism is its "biological" basis; it is the "end" of an anti-Semitic journey that begins in pre-Christian Egypt, Greece, and Rome with a cultural-social manifestation of anti-Semitism through Christian religious and theological anti-Semitism to a European Enlightenment and post-Enlightenment political anti-Semitism to the biological anti-Semitism of National Socialism. During the so-called Christian period, from the birth of Christianity to the Enlightenment, the relationship between Jews and Christians, in the main — most pointedly after Christianity allied itself with the political machinations of the "Holy" Roman Empire and beyond — took one or more of four possible forms: (1) expulsion — the removal of Jews from the physical environs where we had lived for hundreds if not thousands of years; (2) ghettoization — being allowed to remain but in restricted settlement areas; (3) forced conversion — being allowed to remain but only upon surrendering our Jewish identity and the adoption of Christian identity; or (4) extermination-annihilation — being put to death because we were Jews with no recourse to escape through bribery or whatever.[19]

Additionally, as has been previously addressed, part of this look into history is a renewed look at the person of Paul, his comments about Jews and Judaism in the New Testament, and his own seeming ambivalence in dealing with his Jewish people and faith, heritage, and tradition. Central to this analysis and understanding would be most particularly, but not exclusively, Romans 9–11. Appropriate in this context is Joseph A. Fitzmyer's comment, applicable throughout:

> The reader of Romans 9–11 encounters difficulty in reading these chapters because of three things: [1] Paul's habit of isolating and discussing one aspect of a problem without worrying about ramifications that arise in the mind of the reader [especially the modern reader since the Holocaust]. [2] Paul introduces an unparalleled number of OT texts into his discussion. [3] Paul has a tendency to generalize, when speaking of the election and predestination of Israel.[20]

Again, the New Testament text is the place to start, carefully plumbing its depths and examining closely — historically, theologically, and linguistically — all those passages, Paul's and others, especially those of the four Gospel writers, which directly and indirectly address Jews and Judaism. Having done so, the "story" of the resulting relationship must now, after the *Shoah*, be taught in churches and seminaries, in colleges and universities, if we are to build the kinds of bridges appropriate in a post-Auschwitz world between our two faith communities.

What must, therefore, come from a renewed intensive exploration of this history of Jewish-Christian relationships and study of the New

Testament literature is the solemn commitment not to repeat the horrendous mistakes of the past. After the *Shoah*, both communities must commit themselves to a dialogue of equals, theologically and humanly.

The Past Is Prologue

A meditation found in *The New Union Prayerbook* of the liberal movement of American Reform Judaism is relevant to this discussion:

> The universe whispers that all things are intertwined. Yet at times we hear the loud cry of discord. To which voice shall we listen? Although we long for harmony, we cannot close our ears to the noise of war, the rasp of hate. How dare we speak of concord, when the fact and symbol of our age is Auschwitz.
>
> The intelligent heart does not deny reality. We must not forget the grief of yesterday, nor ignore the pain of today. But yesterday is past. It cannot tell us what tomorrow will bring. If there is goodness at the heart of life, then its power, like the power of evil, is real. Which shall prevail? Moment by moment we choose between them. If we choose rightly and often enough, the broken fragments of our world will be restored to wholeness.
>
> For this we need strength and help. We turn in hope, therefore, to a Power beyond us. He has many names, but He is One. He creates; He sustains; He loves; He inspires us with the hope that we can make ourselves one as He is one....
>
> O God, help us to build Your kingdom, one human world united in heart and soul![21]

In terms of a Jewish-Christian dialogue, the time has now come to move forward, recognizing continually all of the inherent difficulties that the *Shoah* has further imposed upon what has always and already been an enormously difficult and pain-filled process of learning and growing. In tribute to the memories of the Jewish victims of the *Shoah* and those righteous Christians who sought to save them, together, we must go forward.

Five

Dangerous Faith

Religion and Foreign Policy in the
Administrations of George W. Bush

DONALD W. MUSSER, D. DIXON SUTHERLAND,
AND DANIEL A. PUCHALLA

The friendly association of President George W. Bush with evangelical Protestants of a dispensational outlook on history and the future (especially Billy Graham, Franklin Graham, Jerry Falwell, and Pat Robertson) has not only advanced the domestic political agenda of the Christian Right, it also has provided a powerful influence on the Bush foreign policy, especially in the Middle East and the war on terrorism.

Musser, Sutherland, and Puchalla outline the main features of Protestant dispensationalism, emphasizing its script for "God's plan" for the world's future, especially Israel and the Middle East. Elements of dispensationalism that are of interest include the idea that world history follows a predetermined plan, that global conflict is inevitable, and that Christians are active participants in implementing the divine plan.

The essay points to five orientations of the Bush foreign policy that indicate its sympathy for these dispensational premises: (1) avid support of the state of Israel, (2) contempt for militant Muslims, (3) suspicion of global peacemakers, (4) disdain for nuclear disarmament, and (5) trivializing global threats to the environment.

Many of the essays in this volume illumine the issues and implications of the current study. For example, with regard to the

75

*application of just war theory to the war on terror as discussed by
Martin Cook, is violent global conflict inevitable because of a divine
plan? Also, in consideration of Stephen Jacobs's agenda for a vigorous
Jewish-Christian dialogue, what if the future of Israel and Judaism
are "prophesied" in the minds of some Christian conversationalists?
Further, in the light of John Kelsay's attention to legitimate and illegitimate religious authorities, are the Christians to whom George W.
Bush listens legitimate interpreters of Christianity and its vision of
the global future?*

*The following essay by Charles Kimball raises further questions
with regard to the possibility of peace in a world choked with violence; can authoritarian religions enter into fruitful dialogue when
they are absolutely certain about their claims to truth?*

Provocations for Dialogue

1. *What role should religious convictions have on American domestic or foreign policy?*

2. *Does God have a "plan for the future"? Or, are people free to
   make the future by their actions? Can humans in any way thwart
   the "plan of God"?*

3. *Is history predetermined? What are the implications of both
   positive and negative answers to the question? for our understanding of God? and ourselves?*

• • •

THIS STUDY EXPLORES the influence of religion on the foreign policy of George W. Bush in the American government's response
to the trauma that the nation experienced on September 11, 2001.
Although we find no compelling evidence to support an overt religious ideology behind the war on terrorism, we find ample reason to
conclude that President Bush and some of the most pivotal leaders in

his administrations have more than a passing sympathy with the theology of many evangelical, dispensational Protestants. We may refer to these Christians generally as "evangelical Protestants."[1]

In wake of Bush's victory over Al Gore in the November 2000 presidential election, Jerry Falwell said, "I want to stop here and now and say thanks and congratulations to Bible-believing Christians nationwide. You, more than any other voting bloc in this nation, determined the outcome of this presidential election."[2] Although a large majority of Americans would count themselves as "Bible-believing Christians," Reverend Falwell more specifically refers to Christians on the religious and Republican Right. Voting patterns after the election confirmed this claim. About 80 percent of voters describing themselves as on the religious Right voted for Bush.[3]

George W. Bush's affinity with evangelical Protestants is well documented. In his earlier years he had associated with mainline Protestants. As a child, his family attended the Episcopal church in Kennebunkport, Maine, and the Presbyterian church in Midland, Texas, as they traveled between their estates. After marrying Laura Welch in 1977, he began attending the United Methodist church in Midland, where the couple had settled. Bush became active in his congregation, teaching Sunday school and serving on the building committee.[4]

A shift toward the religious Right occurred when Bush became acquainted with Don Evans (Bush's appointee as secretary of commerce). Evans began attending meetings of the local Community Bible Study, a group of evangelical men who took a year at a time to study intensely one book of the Bible.[5] Evans convinced his friend George to come along with him and their mutual friend Don Jones. Bush developed a new appreciation for scripture during these meetings, leading to greater "confidence and understanding" in his own faith.[6]

In 1985 at Kennebunkport, George W. had a renewing religious experience when he heard evangelist Billy Graham preach and subsequently talked with Reverend Graham. He wrote in reflection, "I was humbled to learn that God sent His Son to die for a sinner like me. I was comforted to know that through the Son, I could find God's amazing grace, a grace that crosses every border, every barrier, and is open to everyone. Through the love of Christ's life, I could understand the life-changing powers of faith."[7] With these comments Mr. Bush cites many theological themes central to evangelical Christianity: the substitutionary atonement of Jesus' crucifixion, the centrality of the grace of Jesus Christ for salvation, and the universal extent of the gospel message. Since George W. Bush's religious rebirth was a result of an evangelical Bible study and an evangelical preacher, it should not be surprising to find him using evangelical language and ideas.[8]

After his religious awakening, Bush became associated with numbers of evangelical Protestants with political interests. One was Doug Wead, an Assemblies of God minister and former associate of televangelist Jim Bakker. Another was Michael Gerson, who was instrumental in providing the candidate — and subsequently president — with the rhetoric needed to signal to the Christian Right that Bush was still one of them, while at the same time selling the rationality of compassionate conservatism to secularists and non-Christians.[9] Billy Graham continued as a spiritual advisor and inspiration. Graham's son and heir apparent, Franklin, delivered a decidedly Christian prayer at George W. Bush's inauguration, imploring God to lead the new president to "seek the larger vision of Your will for our nation."[10] The president's "larger vision" for America bears a remarkable similarity to the theology of the future of leading evangelical Protestants such as Graham. He still refers to the Grahams, father and son, as his spiritual mentors. In short, the Bush foreign policy, especially formulated post-9/11, has dispensational overtones.

The association of George W. Bush with evangelical Protestants is both a decidedly personal preference and a politically valuable association. While he has gained enormous political capital from this orientation, painting him as a pragmatist who panders to the conservative Right for purely political reasons is false. Bush and the leading figures in his administrations share in common with evangelical Protestants both domestic and foreign policies, which are born of particular readings of the Bible. Many observers are aware of the religious impulses that form conservative positions on stem-cell research, abortion, evolution, capital punishment, crime, guns, gays, and religious expression in the public sector. But few know or comprehend the comprehensive vision of human history and the future of the world that pervades the religious world that George W. Bush and many of his advisors inhabit. These views are not inconsequential as a subtext for informing and inspiring the administrations' response to terror, especially al Qaeda and the threat of Saddam Hussein, as well as the continuing Israeli-Palestinian crisis.

It should be said that we are not pursuing the thesis that George W. Bush's policies derive *directly* from the religious views of the future we are about to unfold. Nor are we inferring that because Protestant leaders with these theological orientations hold these views, and further, are Bush's strongest supporters, that the president agrees with them on all of these points. Just because Bush is surrounded by advisors and supporters with these views, he is not guilty by association. However, it is also foolish to conclude naively that because Bush has been associated with mainstream (Episcopal, Presbyterian, and Methodist) Christianity, he holds centrist rather than rightist Christian positions. His habits and speech in religious matters tend toward dispensational views. Our approach, then, is to paint a broad picture of the dispensationalist vision of the future and argue that the rhetoric and policies of the Bush "war on terror" and the crisis in Israel is commensurate with a dangerous religious vision.

Dispensational Vision of Human History

Broadly speaking, eschatology entails Christian beliefs about the future of individuals (e.g., life after death)[11] and human history, especially the dynamics of history and the destiny of humanity.[12] The former is individual while the latter is social. Many evangelical Protestants hold to a social eschatology called dispensationalism, which holds that we are in the seventh, and last, period of human history.[13] Its influence spreads far beyond evangelical Protestants.

The modern history of dispensationalism took shape during the meetings of the Plymouth Brethren, which were held throughout the United Kingdom between 1825 and 1832. John Nelson Derby, a former Anglican priest and prominent leader in the Plymouth Brethren, organized dispensationalism into a workable structure of biblical interpretation. Darby was also essential to the propagation of dispensationalism, writing volumes and preaching to a multitude of congregations. He visited the United States several times and was instrumental in spawning the growth of dispensationalism in this country.[14]

Central to dispensationalism is the "millennium," a thousand-year period when Jesus Christ will rule over the earth. Dispensational eschatology outlines the events that bring about this wondrous time of peace and prosperity. This expectation is not merely a pleasant prospect for dispensationalists; it is a "fact" that will occur because it is prophesied in the Bible. The millennium is preceded by the Rapture and Tribulation. Seven years before his triumphal return to earth (his "second coming"), Christ comes to earth secretly to snatch away his followers in an event known as the Rapture. Once the influence of the church is gone from the world, a seven-year period known as the Tribulation will begin.[15]

The details of the Tribulation vary, but six events are commonly expected to occur. The first is the rise of the Antichrist, a servant of Satan, who will gain immense power, build an empire, and eventually rule the whole world. Second, Israel will be invaded by a northern nation called Magog — an invasion she will repel by the intervention of God. Third, the Antichrist will posture himself as friend of Israel and will make it possible for her to rebuild the Jerusalem Temple. Fourth, the Antichrist will eventually set up his own image in the Temple, but the Jews will refuse to worship him as divine. Fifth, the Antichrist will persecute the Jews and many will suffer and die. Sixth, the Antichrist will eventually gather all the armies of the world to crush Israel, and it is when the armies reach the place called Armageddon that Christ will return in his glory to crush the Antichrist's armies. Observing this, remaining Jews will convert to Christianity and acknowledge Jesus as their messiah.

Dispensationalism is not a denomination of Christianity. The influence of its philosophy and theology of history has instead spread across denominational lines into mainline Protestantism, of which Bush is a part. Three evangelical Protestant dispensationalists are especially important as spokespersons of this theological worldview: Billy Graham, Jerry Falwell, and Pat Robertson. These three men are arguably among the most influential religious leaders in the United States today. As we have already seen, Billy Graham and his son and successor Franklin are important influences in George W. Bush's faith. Jerry Falwell and Pat Robertson are very vocal supporters of President Bush and have sizable followings.

Although it can clearly be seen that President Bush has strong personal and political ties to dispensationalist individuals and groups, and that there is a strong evangelical presence in the White House, it is impossible to prove that it is out of this worldview that policy decisions are made. It cannot even be proven that George W. Bush is himself a dispensationalist. Nevertheless, the foreign and domestic policies of the Bush administration from its outset are conducive to most of the essential components of premillennialist dispensationalism. Dispensational Christian leaders certainly find in President Bush a political partner who matches their worldview. Not so certain is to what extent President Bush is guided by dispensational models of the world and human destiny.

At issue in this essay is the practical and potential effect that this eschatology may have — consciously or not — on the decision-making process of George W. Bush and members of his administrations. On the one hand, the president may make a decision out of his religious convictions or based on perceptions colored by dispensationalism. On the other hand, given the immense political power of the Christian Right, the Bush administration may pursue policies consistent with dispensationalist mentalities in order to shore up political support. Either way, the results can be dangerous.

Dispensationalism and the Policies of George W. Bush

Scripted Future

A nation's foreign policy intends at least to stabilize its relation to other nations for the present and to promote peaceful coexistence between nations in the future. Dispensational eschatology is a theology of the future. It ponders over and even predicts states of affairs in the foreseeable future. A divinely foreordained destiny for the world is one of the major precepts of dispensationalism. In order for the events purportedly outlined in biblical prophecy to occur exactly as predicted, God must be directing the course of human history. The world will be subjected to great evil, but only because God has willed it. Furthermore, God will bring a greater good from it. This is not only true of the future, but for the whole story of the universe. All of biblical history, including everything from Eden to the final battle of Armageddon, leads to the return of Christ and the eventual creation of the New Heaven and New Earth. All of history is understood to proceed according to this one purpose. The world for the dispensationalist is not random or chaotic; it is ordered and meaningful.[16]

Dispensationalists uphold human free will, at least with regard to individual persons. At the same time, they hold the seemingly contradictory position that God controls the future and outcome of human history. Dispensational thinkers are caught on the horns of a classic conundrum, claiming both that humans are free to act and thereby affect future events and, at the same time, declaring that a Sovereign God has the future secured.

While those secure in a God-ordained future declare in bumper-sticker theology, "Relax! God is in Control," dispensational leaders such as Jerry Falwell and Pat Robertson have placed themselves into the thick of national politics in order to affect policy that fits prophecy. Yet, if humans can thwart God's plans, then God does not have control over human history, a dangerous theological catch-22, especially for the president of the United States. President Bush believes in free will and also that God is in control: "I could not be governor if I did not believe in a divine plan that supersedes all human plans," said Bush in his autobiography. Within the same paragraph, however, he states: "My faith frees me. Frees me to make decisions that others might not like. Frees me to try to do the right thing, even though it may not poll well. Frees me to enjoy life and not worry about what comes next. I've never plotted the various steps of my life."[17] The implications of Bush's thinking are important. He believes: (1) his religious convictions are directly connected to his political decision making; (2) he should have no fear of the consequences of his decisions because as long as God is in control, all will be alright. David Frum, a former speechwriter for the Bush administration, indicates that this is, in fact, the case: "There is a fatalistic element [about Bush]. If you are confident that there is a God that rules the world, you do your best, and things will work out."[18] There is some indication that Bush takes seriously the divine drive behind his own presidency to the point that his decisions are a part of a larger divine plan, and in the final analysis, they should not be questioned.[19]

Bush's personal strong sense of divine direction expands into the national and global levels. In his 2003 State of the Union address, the president said, "As our Nation moves troops and builds alliances to make our world safer, we must remember our calling, as a blessed country, to make this world better."[20] Further explaining his idea of religious calling, Bush declared in a speech to the National Religious Broadcasters, "We're called to extend the promise of this country into the lives of every citizen who lives here. We're called to defend our nation and to lead the world to peace, and we will meet both challenges with courage and with confidence."

Bush perceives that the United States has a crucial role to play in world affairs, not just because it is a global superpower, but also because the United States is chosen by God as an instrument of God's "plan" for the future, with himself at the helm.

Cosmic and Global Conflict

Dispensationalists have an apocalyptic view of the future. A central theme is a cosmic battle between the forces of good and the forces of evil. In the words of Billy Graham, in his study of the book of Revelation, *Approaching Hoofbeats*, "A worldwide battle rages between forces of God and Satan, between light and darkness, between good and evil. Every man, woman, boy or girl who lived, who lives, or who will live is caught in the crossfire. Evil stalks the earth to dominate and to destroy God's creation."[21] This coming cosmic battle has its counterpart in human history. Graham and other dispensationalists portend apocalyptic conflagration between godly nations and evil nations.

This dichotomy emerges clearly in President Bush's language. In his address to Congress nine days after September 11, he made the absolute distinction: "Either you are with us, or you are with the terrorists."[22] In other speeches, Bush equates being a terrorist with being on the side of evil. In an effort to assure an audience in California that the United States is not fighting against the religion of Islam, he said, "We're taking action against evil people. Because this great nation of many religions understands, our war is not against Islam, or against faith practiced by the Muslim people. Our war is a war against evil. This is clearly a case of good versus evil, and make no mistake about it—good will prevail."[23] In his 2002 State of the Union address, he grouped Iraq, Iran, and North Korea as an "axis of evil, arming to threaten the peace of the world.... They could attack our allies or attempt to blackmail the United States." While the president does speak of protecting the peace of the world, he also further defines an evil regime in terms of its threats to the United States and her allies.

This rhetoric can have nothing but a deleterious effect on American foreign policy. First, when the president puts a "good" America against "evil" terrorists and "evil" empires he feeds the views of terrorists, also apocalyptic in their thinking, who view themselves as "good" and America as "evil." As Mark Juergensmeyer shows, nearly all religious terrorists think in the same terms as dispensationalists:

all the world is a battleground between the forces of good and the forces of evil. This "cosmic war," as Juergensmeyer calls it, gives such zealots a sense of higher purpose and pacifies any fears of death because they know their heavenly reward will be great, and that they will be ultimately victorious because God is on their side. By speaking in these same cosmic war terms, the president is only confirming and reinforcing the dualistic beliefs of the terrorists, and he makes it that much more unlikely that they will stop their violence.[24]

The second concern reiterates a danger that we have already hinted at: putting one's enemies in the corner of evil naturally places oneself in the corner of good. As Elaine H. Pagels puts it, "The language of good and evil is used naturally to interpret specific events like September 11. What is dangerous . . . is to use it to characterize countries and whole people."[25] By calling a country evil, one's own country is by contrast self-designated as good. This unfairly characterizes Iraq, Iran, and North Korea, and automatically dismisses any legitimate arguments that these regimes may have against the United States and her allies, thereby precluding any possibility of diplomatic solutions. Moreover, Bush's rhetoric makes the United States something of a divine entity itself. It is on the side of good; therefore its motives and actions are infallible. Although it is doubtful that Bush would use such a descriptor for this country, it is clear that the president does not want to consider the evils this country may have done to these countries or to terrorists that would have caused them to resort to violence and hatred against America. Furthermore, statements by a military leader such as Lieutenant General William G. "Jerry" Boykin in full uniform addressing evangelical Protestant audiences intensify the apocalyptic mood of the war against terrorism. Boykin exemplifies the dispensational approach: He refers to the United States as a "Christian nation," speaks of the Christian God as "bigger than" Islam's God, the Christian God as "real," the Muslim god as an "idol"; Bush is in the White House, "because God put him there"; the real enemy is "not Usama bin Laden, but a guy named Satan." The allusions to the cosmic and global nature of the war in Iraq and the war on terrorism in general are haunting and should cause great alarm. While the Pentagon "investigated" Boykin, it is significant that President Bush never reprimanded him, much less repudiated his views.

A third concern is that the dualistic rhetoric of good-versus-evil mitigates dialogue with the perceived evildoers and blinds the "good" nation to its flaws, which very well may be a part of the problem. Bush, since his first statements after the September 11 attacks, has seemed uninterested in analyzing alternative reasons for discontent among the countries that produced the hijackers. Instead, he has opted for disappointing, yet characteristic, oversimplified explanations: "Why do they hate us?" he asked in his address to Congress after the attacks. He answered, "They hate what we see right here in this chamber — a democratically elected government. Their leaders are self-appointed. They hate our freedoms — our freedom of religion, our freedom of speech, our freedom to vote and assemble and disagree with each other."[26] Similar tendencies can still be seen in Bush's rhetoric. Rather than engage in a serious debate about whether a preemptive war in Iraq would have been just according to standards established by years of Christian tradition, the president decided that Saddam Hussein was an evil man and based his actions on that premise.[27] Hussein was for Bush a chief example of evil forces in the world, and good must prevail.

Religious Activism

Earlier dispensationalist thinkers like Cyrus Scofield, Hal Lindsey, and John Walvoord were decidedly pessimistic about the prospect for peace in the human future. Their hope and intent was to save souls for an optimistic future in the heavenly hereafter. As a result, evangelical Christians typically were not politically active. That has changed dramatically. John Ashcroft is an example of this change. The son of a very influential Pentecostal minister and himself very devout, Ashcroft sought entry into American politics in order to influence the morality of this country. He brought with him a strong dispensationalist theology, which sees the world in black and white, history at its end, and clear-cut right and wrong answers to complex moral issues. Christianity and Islam are not equal ways to God.

A prominent reason among dispensationalists for political activism is that they believe that God may stay the hand of judgment if the people repent and cleanse themselves of their evil ways. If Christians spread the gospel message to this end, then it is possible that God will delay the coming Tribulation. Billy Graham makes several references to this idea in *Hoofbeats*:

> We must not feel that we are to sit back and do nothing to fight evil just because some day they [the four horsemen] will come with full and final force upon the earth. Yes, God's judgment is inevitable — but He alone knows [when] it is, and until that time we are to learn the lessons of the four horsemen and act in such a way that God may be pleased to delay his judgment and allow our world more time to hear His Word and turn to Him.[28]

Again, the focus here seems to be on the importance of evangelization. God will delay the divine plan so that more people may come to accept Christ.

The Foreign Policy of the Bush Administrations

At issue in our study is not whether George W. Bush personally espouses a formal premillennial dispensational theology associated with most fundamentalists and many evangelical Protestants. We contend, rather, that President Bush has brought an attitude to his foreign policy which bears significant similarities to positions of Billy Graham, Jerry Falwell, Hal Lindsey, James Robison, and Pat Robertson, among many others, all prominent dispensationalists. We believe that Bush and some of his chief advisors hold dispensationalist views about God and the world, and these views function unquestioned as part of their political psyche. As a result, Bush's foreign policy either panders to politically or embraces zealously his chief constituency, evangelical Protestants. The administration is politically in debt to and beholden to the religious Right for his political success. This is not in small part due to their shared religious views, which are decidedly dispensational.

Five orientations support our contention: (1) avid support of Israel, (2) contempt for militant Muslims, (3) suspicion of global peacemakers, (4) disdain for nuclear disarmament, and (5) trivializing environmental threats. Each of these attitudes is manifest in Bush's rhetoric and policies.

1. Avid Support of Israel

Although President Bush's proposed roadmap to peace has included a balanced approach that seeks the coexistence of both the state of Israel and a Palestinian state, the prophetic theology of evangelical Protestants mitigates the implementation of the Bush peace process. While President Bush seeks a peaceful coexistence of the combatants, the pro-Israel and anti-Muslim stance of the religious Right has thwarted and, we predict, will thwart its success. The reasons are rooted in dispensational theology.

One of the central claims of John Nelson Darby, the most influential dispensationalist, is that Israel is, and always has been, "chosen," as opposed to Palestinians (mostly Muslim), who are *not* chosen. From the call of Abraham in Genesis 12 to the consummation of God's purposes for humanity in Revelation, the Jewish people are central to the futurist script.[29] For dispensationalism there has never been an event to more powerfully or with more finality confirm the dispensationalist interpretation of biblical prophecy than the post–World War II creation of the modern state of Israel in 1948. Ever since, the modern state of Israel has been the beneficiary of consistent and often uncritical support of evangelical Christians in the United States. This affirmation has spread widely in the United States and is almost taken for granted among evangelical Protestantism. Dispensationalists take very seriously God's admonishment in Genesis 12:3 ("I will bless those who bless you, and the one who curses you I will curse; and in you all the families of the earth shall be blessed"). Anything but full support of Israel will, it is feared, incur the wrath of God. Pat Robertson, for example, gave this warning after the proposal of the Bush administration's "Road Map to Middle East Peace" in 2003: "If the United States takes a role in ripping half of Jerusalem away from Israel and giving it to Yasser Arafat and a group of terrorists, we are going to see the wrath of God fall on this nation that will make tornadoes look like a Sunday school picnic."[30] Such an attitude will weaken support for any "peace" that the religious Right views as granting Palestinians concessions to Israel's status.

The dispensational reading of scripture also gives the Jewish people the land of Israel. According to Genesis 15:18, Israel owns everything from "the river of Egypt to the great river, the river Euphrates." By today's geography, dispensationalists argue that Israel has rightful claim to the countries of Jordan, Iraq and half of Egypt (if the river in Egypt is taken to mean the Nile).

In 1967, when Israel gained control of the Sinai Peninsula, the Gaza Strip, the Golan Heights, and . . . most importantly . . . the West Bank, including East Jerusalem, dispensational prophecy watchers were ecstatic. In their view, Israel's military victories fulfilled prophecies predicting the return of Christ. The Jews needed to be in control of this territory as a prerequisite for the Tribulation events.[31] This land, however, does not belong to Israel, at least by international law. UN Security Council Resolution 242 states that these areas are classified as occupied territories and therefore Israel must eventually withdraw. Jews have nonetheless settled in these areas illegally, not without enthusiastic emotional and financial help of evangelical Protestants. John Hagee, a dispensationalist pastor in San Antonio, who raised 1 million dollars to help resettle Jews from the Soviet Union in Palestinian territories, said, "I am a Bible scholar and a theologian and from my perspective, the law of God transcends the law of the United States government and the U.S. State Department."[32] Dispensational thinkers appeal consistently to a divine right of Israel to this land. Any international opinion or tribunal, such as the United Nations, who favors the claims of Palestinians in the matter of land, is viewed as evil, in opposition to the divine intentions, even "anti-Christ."

In dispensational theology, therefore, the land is central. It belongs to the Jewish people based on the biblical promises to Abraham. Of particular significance is the area known by Muslims as Haram al-Sharif, but known by Jewish and Christian Zionists as the Temple Mount. It is here that Judaism's Second Temple is believed to have stood before the Romans destroyed it in 70 CE. Today, on this site stand two mosques, one of which houses the rock outcropping from which the Prophet Muhammad is believed to have ascended into heaven. Both fundamentalist Christians and ultraorthodox Jews believe, according to biblical prophecy, that a Third Temple must be built on this site in connection with the coming (Jewish) or coming again (Christian) of the messiah. And make no mistake: a Third Temple will be constructed, because this is God's plan.

For this to occur, the destruction of these mosques is necessary. This presents a disastrous threat to any prospect of peaceful coexistence of Jews and Muslims in the region. Most dispensationalists downplay this prospect. Nevertheless, Grace Halsell documents groups of extremist dispensationalists who are funding efforts to destroy Haram al-Sharif in a terrorist attack.[33] This sort of overt attempt to speed up the prophetic timeline is not necessarily characteristic of most dispensationalists. Richard Land from the Southern Baptist Convention has said, "The idea that evangelicals support Israel because they want to hasten the Second Coming is absolute nonsense. No human being can do anything to hasten or retard that."[34] That being said, we fear that a spirit of hostile complacency will desensitize the religious Right and make it difficult to intervene. The expectation is that Jews *will* rebuild their temple, and so there is no reason for dispensationalists to object to the destruction of Haram al-Sharif or to ensure that East Jerusalem is returned to the Palestinians. Jerry Falwell admits to the violence that would attend this venture:

> The Muslims revere the Dome of the Rock as a holy shrine to commemorate the place where Muhammad supposedly ascended into heaven. There is no way they will ever willingly give up this place. It is sacred to Islam. The only reasonable options would seem to be that it is destroyed by warfare, terrorism, or a natural disaster, like an earthquake.

Only then could the Jews presume to rebuild the temple on that spot. But such an attempt would certainly be met with armed resistance throughout the Muslim World. The current interest in rebuilding the Temple, the first of its kind in the last 1,400 years, is of significant merit. Something momentous is happening in the Middle East today that will soon affect the destiny of our entire planet. This event is the rebuilding of the Jewish Temple in Jerusalem.[35]

No wonder the conservative Likud party in Israel and the religious Right in the United States have been political bedfellows ever since the Camp David Peace Treaty. When Benjamin Netanyahu visited Washington in 1998, his first meeting was not with President Clinton but with Jerry Falwell and more than a thousand dispensational Christians. Today extreme dispensationalists believe that Prime Minister Ariel Sharon is providentially fulfilling the prophecies of the end time, based on their application of Proverbs 24:16 to his return to power, after falling into disfavor.[36]

All of this is bad news for the Bush peace process. Since the first Camp David Peace Treaty of 1979, the agreed-upon procedure for attaining peace between Israel and her Arab neighbors has been to exchange land for security — that is, Israel agrees to withdraw from an occupied area in exchange for an end to hostilities against her.[37] Such a strategy is unthinkable to a dispensationalist. God gave that land to Israel, plain and simple. Peace cannot be bought with it.

Any proposed peace is a moot point anyway. There can never be a solution to the Israeli-Palestinian conflict because dispensationalists contend that this struggle is an essential element in the Tribulation events. In reaction to the 1979 peace treaty, Jerry Falwell said, "In spite of the rosy and utterly unrealistic expectations by our government, this treaty will not be a lasting treaty. You and I know that there's not going to be any real peace in the Middle East until the Lord Jesus sits down up on the throne of David in Jerusalem."[38] This, like all other major problems in the world, will be solved once Christ comes back.

Of course, any argument that George W. Bush's religious convictions preclude him taking an evenhanded part in Middle Eastern diplomacy must answer to this administration's recent attempts to restore the peace process between the Israelis and the Palestinians. Departing radically from dispensationalist mentality, the president has publicly supported the creation of a Palestinian state, both before the American people in his January 2003 State of the Union address and before the leaders of the Arab world in June 2003. In this latter engagement, Bush emphatically stated, "I'm the kind of person who, when I say something, I mean it. I mean that the world needs to have a Palestinian state that is free and at peace."[39] These qualifiers seem to soften what the president said on this issue in his 2003 State of the Union speech: "In the Middle East, we will continue to seek peace between a secure Israel and a democratic Palestine."[40] By this statement, President Bush put the onus for a solution to the problem entirely on the Palestinians. Peace will only come when the Palestinians are no longer threatening Israel and when the Palestinians establish for themselves a democratic government.

The roadmap is based on the principle of land-for-peace obligations on both parties in the three phases of the process, with the final result being an independent Palestinian state at peace with its neighbor Israel. Nevertheless, some of the language of this proposal echoes the sentiment expressed in the 2003 State of the Union address.

> A two-state solution to the Israeli-Palestinian conflict will only be achieved through an end to violence and terrorism, when the Palestinian people have a leadership acting decisively against terror and willing and able to build a practicing democracy based on tolerance and liberty, and through Israel's readiness to do what is necessary for a democratic Palestinian state to be established, and a clear, unambiguous acceptance by both parties of the goal of a negotiated settlement.[41]

Stressed again in the introduction to phase two of the roadmap to peace, the creation of a Palestinian state "can be achieved when the Palestinian people have a leadership acting decisively against terror, willing and able to build a practicing democracy based on tolerance and liberty." Such an attitude may have just as easily endorsed the September 11 terrorist attacks as any religiously inspired affinity for Israel. At this point, nothing may go forward until terrorism is stopped, at least from Bush's perspective. Additionally, it is highly significant that Bush is the first American president to support the creation of a Palestinian state.[42]

The Bush administration may believe that it has the latitude to support a Palestinian state both because of its heretofore aggressive foreign policy, and perhaps because of letters like the one sent by several evangelical leaders to President Bush in July 2002. This letter called for an "evenhanded United States policy towards Israelis and Palestinians." The signatories — which included Clive Calver, president of World Relief; Richard Mouw, president of Fuller Theological Seminary; and David Neff, editor of *Christianity Today* — go on to remind the president that,

> The American evangelical community is not a monolithic bloc in full and firm support of present Israeli policy. Significant numbers of American evangelicals reject the way some have distorted biblical passages as their rationale for uncritical support for every policy and action of the Israeli government instead of judging all actions . . . of both Israelis and Palestinians . . . on the basis of biblical standards of justice.[43]

These leaders, however, represent a more moderate wing of evangelical Protestants than activist dispensationalists. The Bush administration will most likely listen to Jerry Falwell should he begin to criticize this move; and we have already noted Pat Robertson's reticence on the peace initiative.

2. Contempt for Islam

President Bush has repeatedly praised the religion of Islam as peaceful and noble.[44] Prominent evangelical Protestants, however, believe Islam is an unauthentic, inherently violent, and evil religion. Jerry Falwell, Franklin Graham, Pat Robertson, and Jerry Vines (former president of the Southern Baptist Convention and pastor of a megachurch in Jacksonville, Florida), have publicly denounced Islam as an "evil and wicked religion,"[45] Allah as a god who "tells people to die for him in order to get salvation,"[46] and Muhammad as "a demon-possessed pedophile."[47] Jerry Falwell has characterized the violence of the Palestinians as "Satan's opposition" to God's plan for the Jews and for the land of Palestine.[48] These views of prominent proponents of the religious Right fit with their dispensational theology. These views also make it difficult to envision any rapprochement between America and Muslim nations. They even make it difficult to spend time and resources trying.

The animosity of dispensationalists for Islam coexists with a convenient casting of Muslim nations as pawns of the Antichrist in the end-time drama. Jerry Falwell envisions a Muslim army from united Arab nations that will threaten to invade Israel.[49]

The conflict will come to a head at Armageddon, the battle at which Christian supporters of Israel will kill all the enemies of Israel. Jerry Falwell takes on an almost surreal tone as he describes how one-third of the world's population will die:

> While some prefer to view this invading horde as demons, I believe they are an actual army. The battles that follow involve killing men, and the attackers are described as men. The weapons with "breastplates of fire" could well be modern weapons. The "breastplates of fire" and the "fire and smoke" that shot out of both ends of these vehicles certainly sounds like tanks, airplanes, or some modern weaponry.... Tanks, guns, flame-throwers, and laser beams all fit these possible designations. While the horde of demons is unleashed to torture and afflict men, the horde of soldiers is unleashed to attack them as well.[50]

Violence with Islam appears to be an inevitable scenario in the dispensational vision of the future. Peace with Palestinian Muslims, the Iraqi people, and other Muslims, including American Muslims, appears fleeting or futile. Dispensational theology not only distrusts Islam and Muslim people, it associates them with an evil that must be obliterated.

3. Suspicion of Global Peacemakers

Once again, "the plan" determines humanity's destiny for dispensationalists. Jerry Falwell's comments are typical:

> While the desire for peace clings to the deepest crevice of the human heart, the prospects for global destruction are far greater than the prospects for global peace. Undoubtedly, men will continue to strive

for peaceful solutions. But, except for those persons who know Christ, believe the Bible, and understand Bible prophecy, there is no diplomatic or military solution to the world's dilemma. Only those followers of Christ who know God's plan for the ages have any real hope for the future. Apart from Christ, the picture is hopeless and terrible.[51]

The plan Falwell speaks of is, of course, the return of Christ, which will usher in the millennial peace. Billy Graham asserts the same point:

We are aware of the shuffling of the stage in preparation for the greatest battle of all time that will certainly take place in the years ahead. The crisis of the present hour should shatter the optimism concerning human nature of every person listening to my voice. The only reliable hope for the future must be bound up in a living faith in Jesus Christ as Savior and Lord.[52]

These words do not exactly inspire evangelical Protestants toward action that would diminish global violence and engender peace. Despite claims from dispensationalists that they do not teach that believers should do nothing to work for social, political, or economic justice, the words of Falwell and Graham send a clear message that any endeavors to improve the world will ultimately prove futile. Any hope for global peace is even bleaker. Within the context of global politics, peace efforts are regarded with skepticism if not outright suspicion. If peace will only be realized once Christ has returned, then a person, country, or organization that proclaims to seek world peace is to be taken either as a fool or a demon. "Any teaching of peace prior to [Christ's] return is heresy," said popular television preacher James Robison. "It's against the Word of God; it's Antichrist."[53]

For dispensationalists, any movement toward international cooperation portends the coming of a European Antichrist who will appear as a pseudosavior and unite Europe. Millions have read the thinly veiled dispensational fiction of Tim LaHaye and Jerry Jenkins, who speak of a man of Roman descent who rises to become the secretary-general of the United Nations. He is charming, attractive, and a compelling speaker. He tells the world that he can bring peace and unity.[54] The religious Right has long been suspicious of the European Union and the United Nations. Any peacemaking efforts with strong European leadership are subject to suspicion of the president's dispensational supporters.

4. Disdain for Disarmament

The consuming fire of judgment is an element that occurs often in biblical accounts of divine wrath. In Genesis, God "rained on Sodom and Gomorrah sulfur and fire,"[55] Isaiah describes God sending "tongues of fire" for the iniquitous;[56] Amos saw a "shower of fire" coming to burn up Israel;[57] and Ezekiel says that God "will send fire on Magog."[58] In Christian scriptures, 2 Peter says "the day of the Lord will come like a thief, and then the heavens will pass away with a loud noise, and the elements will be dissolved with fire, and the earth and everything that is done on it will be burned up,"[59] and Revelation describes "hail and fire, mixed with blood" falling to the earth and "something like a great mountain, burning with fire, was thrown into the sea."[60] Before 1945, dispensationalists could only imagine what such scenes would look like. When reading passages that described the judgment yet to come, they explained the form of such terrible power either as some great natural disaster or simply a divine energy unknown to science. Hiroshima and Nagasaki, however, showed dispensationalists, and the whole world, that humanity had found the means to destroy itself in the awesome blazes described in scripture.[61]

With several references to fiery judgments in prophetic works, nuclear weapons have proven versatile tools for dispensationalist expositors. When the world falls into the unimaginable world wars of the Great Tribulation culminating at Armageddon, exchanges of nuclear missiles and bombs will cause the global chaos, loss of human life, and ecological disasters seemingly described in Revelation. And, at the end of the millennium, God will destroy all of creation in a great storm of nuclear energy.

Nuclear disaster is then an unavoidable reality for the world — but not for the believer. With the assurance that in the Rapture Jesus will remove all Christians from the world before the Tribulation even begins, the dispensationalist need not fear dying in, or perhaps worse, surviving a nuclear holocaust. As Halsell notes: "They describe its horror as graphically as any antinuclear activist, but not as a *possible* historical outcome to be avoided at all costs. The only way to avoid it is to not be around when it happens, or, to be raptured. Thus, Jerry Falwell could say, 'You know why I'm not worried? I ain't gonna be here.' "[62]

This expectation of nuclear war, combined with this escapist mentality, distrust for peace talks, and pessimism about international cooperation, lead dispensationalists to regard nuclear weapons control and disarmament with scorn and disinterest.

They have consistently been skeptics of international peace efforts. In the 1940s they scoffed at the Acheson-Lilenthal plan for controlling atomic energy, claiming the international agency it proposed would become an instrument of Antichrist.[63] In the 1980s dispensationalists praised Reagan's military and nuclear arsenal expansions as the fulfillment of God's plan. Falwell, along with other prominent evangelists of the 1970s and 1980s such as Hal Lindsey and James Robison, denounced calls for disarmament as suicidal, subversive, and KGB-inspired.[64]

In 1986 Ed Dodson and Ed Hindson, associates of Jerry Falwell, wrote in an issue of the journal *Policy Review* that there is no policy implication from dispensationalism because biblical prophecy cannot be altered. God, they claimed, is responsible for fulfilling prophecy, not humans.[65] But this is not a convincing argument. The future imagined by dispensationalists is played out in political and military scenarios conducted by the actions of human beings. Therefore, persons who wish to encourage nuclear armament — or, at a minimum, resist or ignore disarmament efforts — would not believe they are altering prophecy. They would believe they are playing a part in it. Jerry Falwell's view of nuclear warfare speaks for dispensationalists: "As the nuclear clock ticks on, it is only a matter of time until the inevitable disaster strikes."[66]

Dispensationalism spawns two attitudes about nuclear war within a believer: (1) It is inevitable; (2) It is an event not to be feared.

Given the office Bush holds and the incredible destructive power he wields, any uncritical acceptance of dispensational attitudes by President Bush or members of his administration should elicit immense concern.

5. Disinterest in the Environment

Moving from one way to destroy the world to another, the final policy implication of dispensationalism in the Bush administration is with regard to a disinterest in protection of the environment. For dispensationalists the world situation is destined to grow worse, and since God will do away with it eventually anyway, any effort to clean up or protect the environment is a waste of time and shows a misunderstanding about the future of the world. Furthermore, characteristic of prophecy watchers to adopt and adapt to contemporary issues, growing concerns in the 1970s and 1980s about depletion of the ozone layer, global warming, pollution, and the collapse of ecological networks were interpreted as fulfillments of prophesy. In a recent work, *Planet Earth...2000 A.D.*, Hal Lindsey sees the effects of the increased ultraviolet radiation that would result from a thinned ozone layer as a possible explanation for Revelation 16:9: "The fourth angel poured his bowl on the sun, and it was allowed to scorch people with fire; they were scorched by the fierce heat."[67] In describing the state of the world during the Tribulation, Jerry Falwell implies that the earth's environment is already being prepared for its dismal fate: "Students of global trends paint a bleak and dark picture for the future of the world...a natural environment that will struggle to sustain life, with the air and water polluted, the food supply poisoned; plagues."[68] Members of Congress who score high with the Christian Coalition on issues such as abortion, the death penalty, and pornography often score very low with the League of Conservation Voters on issues of environmental protection. Of the forty-four senators who received an 80 to 100 percent approval rating from the Christian Coalition, the average rating from the League of Conservation Voters was below 10 percent.[69]

As for George W. Bush, he has tried to play the part of the market-conscious environmentalist, or the environmentally friendly businessman. In his 2003 State of the Union address, Bush outlined plans to reduce air pollution from power plants, prevent forest fires, and develop hydrogen-powered cars.[70] Yet, this rhetoric contradicts his actions on other occasions. In September 2002, a committee in the Department of Health and Human Services that studies the effects on human health of low-level exposure to environmental chemicals was restructured and committee officials replaced with members of the chemical industry. The Bush administration has also granted drilling permits to petroleum corporations for such protected areas as Yellowstone National Park, Canyonlands National Park, the Powder River Basin, and the Canyons of the Ancients National Monument, in addition to continued plans to open the Arctic National Wildlife Refuge for drilling. Finally, the Bush administration has taken away from the U.S. Forest Service the function of monitoring wildlife populations in America's forests and assessing the impact that logging and other projects have on wildlife populations.[71] This attitude presumes that the world is a "stage" on which the divine-human drama is played out. No need ultimately exists to preserve the stage, which is destined to end with the return of Christ.

Plundering and not protecting nature makes perfect sense if global history is winding toward a climax that will bring an end to humanity and the earth, both dispensational expectations. Both George W. Bush and Jerry Falwell may be heavily influenced by economic concerns on this issue, but Falwell and dispensationalists are also influenced by a religious vision of the future. "Why save the earth?" they ask, for the end approaches. Once again, Bush policies receive much-needed support from these very dispensationalist adherents.

Conclusion

George W. Bush became president of the United States in 2000 by a very narrow margin of electoral votes. No one disputes that an activist block of conservative Protestant voters tilted the election to

Bush. Few would quarrel with the claim that President Bush's policies have been shaped to fall in line with the political agenda of political conservatives, including evangelical Protestants.

Many observers may be astonished at what we claim in this essay. Some will emphatically deny our conclusions. Others cannot (or will not) comprehend that a theology they have scarcely heard of could be the tail that wags much of the foreign-policy dog of the United States, particularly with reference to the war on terror and the Israeli-Palestinian conflict.

Ignoring our claims about the dispensational theology of the future as it informs the political agenda of the religious Right is fraught with danger. That theology is dangerous, even fatal, because it adheres to a predetermined future, the outcome of which is assured in the minds of its proponents. Their reading of the Bible, which we believe is flawed, assures them that they see the future with absolute certainty. That future entails an apocalyptic scenario in which Christians (especially evangelical Protestants with a dispensational theology) are the earthly agents of the divine plan to bring to our globe a millennium of peace where Jesus rules followed by the end of history. The Jewish people unknowingly are pawns in this drama. Many Jews will die at the hands of anti-Christian evildoers. A remnant of Jews will convert to Christianity. The state of Israel, and especially the Temple Mount (Haram al-Sharif), is the center of these events.

Beneath the rhetoric of the politics of evangelical Protestants lies this dangerous theology. Whenever the president aligns his foreign policy with this constituency, whether consciously or unconsciously, he affirms their script for the future. George W. Bush may be another pawn in this cosmic chess game in which Jesus will return, capture and destroy evil, take the Redeemed to heaven, and destroy the earth. In this scenario, America plays the role of God's blessed nation, representing divine interests for Good. This is why it is important for dispensationalists to believe that America was founded and is a "Christian nation."

Evangelical Protestants agree with the president that an "axis of evil" threatens the world, especially the security of God's America.

Moreover, these evildoers — terrorists who hurt Americans, Israelis, and their allies — are both anti-Christian and anti-American. Many terrorists act in the name of Allah and Islam. Thus, Islam and Muslims are aligned with evil.

Given this theological drama of a scripted future, the influence of dispensationalism on the Bush foreign policy presently results in the following stances:

- The unyielding support of Israel.
- The venomous, though nonpublic contempt for Islam.
- The suspicion of international peace efforts.
- The hesitancy to disarm.
- The pillaging of natural resources with little consideration for future generations.

Evangelical Protestants of a dispensational bent typically condemn Islam as a religion of violence. They are blinded by the log in their eye that keeps them from seeing the violence in their script of the future. Their position makes authentic dialogue impossible and peace improbable. George W. Bush's religious convictions are saturated with the perspectives of dispensational Christianity. Unwittingly or not, his religious faith undergirds his blind confidence in America's place in world affairs, and could lead us into a real Apocalypse.

Part II

OBSTACLES TO
RELIGIOUS DIALOGUE

Six

Absolute Truth Claims

Blockade to Dialogue

CHARLES A. KIMBALL

Charles Kimball gives issues of interpretation and authority raised by Kelsay and Jacobs a more specific theological assessment. Kelsay raises questions about the interpretative methods and authority of Usama bin Laden, who speaks without any formal Islamic authority, and employs the fatwah *in an untraditionally Islamic way. Jacobs questions Christian motivations to evangelize Jews, using biblical texts for missionary purposes. Now Kimball sharpens the issues theologically, asserting that absolute religious truth claims block any real possibility for dialogue between religions.*

Religious dialogue must first and foremost give up making absolute claims to truth, or we are destined to point out our differences and condemn each other (Kelsay's essay), or attempt to "save" other "lost" religions (Jacobs's essay). Kimball suggests that we should instead leave absolute truth to God, and focus on human understandings of religious truths. He uses an example from his own childhood experience. Raised in a very conservative Baptist church, Kimball shows that when the demand for ownership of absolute truth claims are set aside, the result allows for peace instead of violence. It leads us toward inclusion instead of exclusion, accepting different understandings of salvation and of the way God deals with human beings. This would stimulate talk of peaceful coexistence between religions and a common goal within this *world. In the next world, we leave judgments of each other's credibility to God.*

Provocations for Dialogue

1. Do *absolute truth claims among religions further or hinder religious witness for peace in the world?*

2. *Can absolute claims about scripture be supported by the rules of hermeneutics that characterize the history of religions? Do such claims support peace among religions or condone violence?*

3. *Should any religion stake out exclusive rights to geography or assume divinely sanctioned governmental structure? What would be the result if religions of the world abdicated such claims?*

• • •

A POPULAR BUMPER STICKER boldly proclaims a widespread approach to religion: "The Bible says it. I believe it. That settles it." Change the language, substitute "Qur'an" for "Bible," and the declaration would be just as popular in some predominantly Muslim countries. While key elements of religion are affirmed — the centrality of faith, the importance of sacred scriptures, and the desire for clarity and certainty amid the vicissitudes of life — the formula is dangerously simplistic. It belies the rich complexity of religion and erects a formidable barrier between people who are not of one mind. Such rigidity can easily block people of faith and goodwill from exploring ways to move forward toward a more healthy future in our religiously diverse communities, countries, and world. How? Why? What are the alternatives?

In every major religion that has stood the test of time, truth claims constitute the bases upon which the structure rests. These include understandings about God or Ultimate Reality; the nature of the human predicament and how to overcome it; and the origin, meaning, purpose, and ultimate goal of human existence. Religious truth claims are based invariably on the authoritative teachings of inspired or sagelike charismatic leaders or upon the interpretations of sacred texts connected to such gifted leaders. When particular interpretations of foundational truth claims become propositions requiring uniform assent — a phenomenon visible in fundamentalist movements worldwide — rigid doctrines can become absolute truth claims.[1] Emboldened by the certainty of God's truth, history reveals that zealous adherents can and do justify almost any type of behavior. One has only to ponder the recent history of Lebanon, the former Yugoslavia, Nigeria, Israel/Palestine, or the Kashmir region in northern India to recognize how easily zealous individuals and groups within religious communities can justify violent and destructive behavior directed toward others. While the patterns are familiar in all the major religions, they are particularly acute and dangerous today within the two largest religious traditions: Christianity and Islam.[2]

Respective understandings of monotheism have frequently led Christians and Muslims to advocate a narrow exclusivist theology. The propensity toward absolutist views is also connected to the strong missionary impulse in both Christianity and Islam. Both traditions have long histories of conflict and fragmentation as various individuals and sects within each tradition propagated a particular understanding of God's message to the world. Today, the perils of absolute truth claims are magnified in unprecedented ways. In our increasingly interdependent world community, we know there are many weapons of mass destruction and small groups of extremists can wreak havoc on a global scale.

Christians and Muslims compose well over 40 percent of the world's population with some 1.8 billion and 1.3 billion adherents, respectively. Both religions are global in scope. And both Christianity and Islam connect with political structures more readily than do other major religions. Muslims constitute the majority community in more than fifty countries today. Many of those lands are in turmoil or transition as political movements challenge unrepresentative governments, massive economic disparity, and systematic violations of human rights. Numerous revolutionary leaders and groups take inspiration from Islam. Contemporary developments within Israel and the roles and perceptions about the United States figure prominently into an increasingly volatile mix.

Understanding that every religious tradition includes elements that tend toward rigidity and exposing the dangers and fallacies of absolutist claims are important steps in identifying healthy alternatives. Religious truth claims about God or the Transcendent necessarily rely on language. When the language stiffens into unyielding doctrines, sincere and devout people often assume the task of defending God — or their understanding of what God desires or requires. Frequently, the path leading toward a defensive, inflexible position begins with the appropriation of sacred texts.

The Use and Abuse of Sacred Texts

Sacred texts provide a rich source of wisdom and guidance for people and communities of faith. In many traditions, they grow in importance as the community of faith becomes further and further removed from the gifted authority figures whose wisdom, insights, or revelation compose the central teachings.[3] Preserving eyewitness accounts of Jesus' teachings or the poetic words of revelation uttered by Muhammad as well as the non-Qur'anic sayings and actions by Muhammad (*hadith*) and the insights of Jesus' closest disciples were essential steps toward establishing the authoritative written texts in the respective religions.

Because of their status, sacred texts are the most easily abused component of religion. Selective reading and interpretation frequently support absolute truth claims. One has to look no further than daily news reports to find contemporary examples of religious and political leaders quoting selected verses or phrases from the Bible or Qur'an in support of positions that affect the lives of millions. Sacred texts can be powerful tools for promoting an agenda or justifying behavior that might otherwise appear to contradict central teachings within the religious tradition. Shakespeare's poignant observation pointed to this phenomenon: "The devil can cite scripture for his purpose." Today, as in centuries past, substantial numbers of people are guided by absolute truth claims connected to proof texts. While absolutist

claims are found across the theological spectrum — unwavering pacifists and advocates of holy war, for example, can and do cite what
they consider definitive biblical texts — grave dangers arise when the
exploitation of revered texts supports violent zealotry. Contemporary
examples from both religions illustrate the point.

Suicide bombing by Muslims took root in Lebanon two decades
ago. It has become an increasingly common tactic in Israel/Palestine,
Iraq, and Afghanistan in early years of the twenty-first century. The
foundation for this exceedingly powerful and destructive practice is
found in a highly selective reading and interpretation of the Qur'an.
Absolute truth claims are established and propagated to recruit volunteers for suicide missions. More than four hundred individual
Muslims, including those who hijacked the four commercial airplanes
on September 11, 2001, willingly gave up their lives, certain that a
heavenly reward awaited them. The Qur'an includes many references
to the Day of Judgment and eternal bliss for the faithful at the end
of time. The Qur'an suggests that those who die "striving in the way
of God"[4] do not wait for the final judgment, but go immediately to
paradise: "Say not of those who die in the path of God that they are
dead. Nay rather they live" (2:154). Muslims have understood this
and other texts (e.g., 3:169–71) as a promise for martyrs. It is widely
believed that martyrs have a special place along with prophets in
the highest (seventh) heaven. Even so, key questions require answers:
What constitutes martyrdom? Who makes the determination? Ultimately, Muslims agree that such matters are in the hands of God. In
the meantime, a number of religious and political leaders apparently
feel certain they can for speak for God.

In the immediate aftermath of the September 11 attacks, many
Muslim leaders clearly and directly denounced the assaults as un-
Islamic. Suicide is strictly forbidden in Islam. Although the Qur'an
says little, possibly nothing, about suicide, there are numerous, specific prohibitions throughout the *hadith* materials. Suicide is a virtual
one-way ticket to hell. Moreover, Muslims must not harm or kill
civilians even in war. Suicide bombings appear clearly to violate both

central tenets. Religious and political leaders who sanction and champion suicidal attacks base their arguments on selected texts, ignoring fundamental teachings that invalidate their position. They speak only of martyrs who are defending Islam from those who are attacking it. Those who are killed are not innocent people but "infidels" (*kuffar*, "those who reject or say no to God"). Such generic references were evident in some of the famous videotapes released by Usama bin Laden after September 11. The Qur'an includes passages that some interpreters cite to justify attacks on Jews and Christians in particular.

> Fight in the cause of God those who fight you, but do not begin hostilities; for God does not love such injustice. And kill them wherever you find them, and drive them out from the places where they drove you out; for persecution is worse than slaughter; but fight them not at the sacred mosque, unless they (first) fight you there; but if they fight you, slay them. Such is the reward of infidels. (2:190–91)

As with some passages in the Bible, the verses above are harsh and require interpretation. As with the Bible, there is a long history of interpretation for the entire Qur'an. I have discussed the verses above and a wide range of passages with many Muslim leaders over the past thirty years. They often frame their interpretations by reference to the particular setting or circumstances surrounding a verse or verses. They may refer to various well-known commentaries or reflect on a given passage in the context of other passages where similar themes are addressed. While Muslims affirm the Qur'an as the revealed word of God, they still must do what people in all traditions must do with sacred texts, namely, interpret their meaning and significance.

In the case of the passage quoted above, many Muslims focus on the sanction to fight back and kill infidels in the context of being attacked.[5] While this is certainly not a message to love one's enemy or turn the other cheek, it is also not an unqualified statement about fighting and killing Jews, Christians, and others. On the contrary, the Qur'an has numerous passages that embrace Jews and Christians as "people of the book" (*ahl al-kitab*); it affirms the revelation received through various prophets and messengers known in the Bible. Along with Abraham, Moses, David, and others, Jesus is exalted in the Qur'an. Jesus is mentioned by name in ninety-three different verses scattered in fifteen chapters. He is called a prophet, a messenger, a servant of God, a Word from God, the Messiah, and one inspired by the Spirit of God.

The Qur'an venerates Jesus, but warns Christians against dangerous doctrines that are an affront to God. Most notably, the divinity of Christ and the doctrine of the Trinity are rejected explicitly. Both are seen as compromising the monotheistic understanding of God. But this is not the whole picture. The Qur'an also speaks of a heavenly reward for people in some religions:

> Behold! Those who have faith, and those who are Jews, Christians and Sabaeans — those who trust in God and the Last Day, and do what is righteous, they shall have their reward; no fear shall come upon them, neither shall they grieve. (Qur'an 2:62 and 5:69)

The Qur'an sets forth principles to guide Muslims in their relationships with other communities of faith. The communities should exist in freedom. A well-known verse asserts that "There shall be no compulsion in religious matters" (Qur'an 2:256). In other words, there are many ways Muslims have understood various parts of the Qur'an and applied the authoritative teachings in the *hadith* as these relate to interactions with Christians and Jews. Not surprisingly, the various interpretations are often linked with specific circumstances. Decidedly different perspectives can be discerned among Muslims in Spain, for instance, depending on the century. Relationships among "people of the book" are framed rather differently in the context of prosperity and communal harmony under Islamic rule than during horrific times of Christian Inquisition. The same holds true, of course, for Jews and Christians living together with Muslims in varied circumstances.

Suicide attacks by Muslims illustrate clearly the fallacy of absolute truth claims tied to particular verses. It also highlights an increasingly popular approach to the Qur'an among Islamist leaders and groups — reading the text from the perspective of particular, contemporary political circumstances without awareness of or regard for the centuries of interpretation provided by thoughtful Muslim scholars and thinkers.

However marginal these interpretations and calls to action may be in the wider Islamic community, no one can doubt the danger such absolutism poses to peace. We live in an increasingly interdependent and interconnected world community where there are many ways small numbers of people can do great harm. Nineteen men, some or all of whom were expecting "to meet God," hijacked the four commercial airliners on September 11, 2001. Their weapons of mass destruction included box knives and airplanes turned into bombs.

Absolute truth claims linked to violent extremism are present among Christians as well. Contemporary examples of fundamentalist Christians attacking, sometimes murdering, doctors and others who work at abortion or family planning clinics illustrate the point. The absolute truth claims uniting the extremists' agenda is clear: Abortion is legalized murder; abortion is an abomination to God; true Christians must engage in direct action to stop what they see as a slaughter of innocents. On the contrary, the Bible says nothing specific about the highly emotional and controversial issue of abortion. Some might argue that the sixth of the Ten Commandments — "You shall not murder" (Exod. 20:13) — is a basis for opposing abortion. Passionate debates about when life begins and what constitutes human life immediately arise. Among the millions of Christians who strongly oppose abortion on religious grounds, only a small, extremist fringe embraces the absolute truth claims noted above. The vast majority accepts the practice of abortion in cases of rape, incest, or a threat to the life of the mother. Not the extremists. Blinded by the light of absolute truth, these zealots miss the sad irony that they are violating the Sixth Commandment, not to murder, in order to stop those they consider guilty of murder.

An absolute truth claim about the Bible itself confuses or misleads large numbers of contemporary Christians. Without much thought, millions of Christians insist that the Bible is the inerrant Word of God and that it must be interpreted literally. People who approach the Bible as sacred scripture understand the nature of God's inspiration in different ways. However this is done, one still must interpret the materials. The problem with the version of the bumper sticker theology noted above can be stated directly: No one actually interprets the Bible literally. It is simply not possible to make any sense of the Bible if one tries to take everything literally. Hundreds of examples could be cited; three will suffice to make the point.

Who interprets the Song of Songs literally? How does one do this? It is an erotic poem focused on the love between a man and a woman. God is not mentioned in the Song of Songs. Throughout history, Jewish and Christian interpreters have read this majestic poetry as a metaphor of God's love for Israel or the church, but this is hardly a literal reading. The book of Leviticus includes page after page of requirements for proper priestly attire, different ritual practices, and correct behavior by the people. Various penalties are imposed, including death, for violating the laws, for disobeying parents, for not following proper priestly dress codes, and so on. Does anyone take this literally today? Jews and Christians have various explanations for the different circumstances that now occur. Fair enough, but such explanations are different than taking those many chapters literally. When Jesus says, "I am a door..." (John 10:7) or "I am the good shepherd..." (John 10:11), is he referring to himself as a wooden door, a sliding glass door, a screen door? Is he literally a shepherd and his followers literally sheep?

Dispelling the simplistic truth claim about literal interpretation of the Bible is important for two reasons. First, such claims are unworthy of the wealth of wisdom and inspiration contained within the Bible.[6] Second, insisting on a literal interpretation makes it easy to pull out selected verses in order to construct or validate a theological perspective. As with the examples from the Qur'an above, Christians, too, must be very wary of efforts to build a theology based on the presumed meaning of a verse here and a verse there. Shakespeare's insightful observation remains apropos.

Another type of absolute truth claim is readily discernable among many evangelical and fundamentalist Christians today. In the first three years following the September 11 attacks, a number of prominent, often self-appointed Christian leaders seized the media spotlight in order to speak for God. At different times and in slightly different ways, Jerry Falwell, Pat Robertson, Franklin Graham (the son of evangelist Billy Graham), and many others publicly denounced Islam as an evil religion and declared Allah a false god. With cocksure certainty, these leaders boldly declared that Allah is not the God of the Bible and Christians and Muslims are not talking about the same God.[7]

While such absolutist claims are not as directly linked to violent extremism, they are irresponsible and dangerously inflammatory.[8] These declarations go well beyond individual opinion or personal theological understanding. They play publicly to ignorance and fear precisely at a time when Muslim extremists seek to portray conflicts around the world as war between Christians (and Jews in Israel) and Islam. At the very least, the pronouncements are engaging in irresponsible behavior. Religious leaders who smugly proffer these kinds of absolute truth claims are disingenuous or ignorant or, in some cases, both.

In the first place, *Allah* is simply the Arabic word for God. Just as people who speak German pray to *Gott* and French-speaking people pray to *Dieu*, people who speak Arabic pray to *Allah*. This applies not only to Muslims, but also to the more than 15 million indigenous, Arabic-speaking Christians who live and worship in the Middle East today. To say that Christians and Muslims are not talking about the same God reveals woeful ignorance. In more than a decade of work with Middle Eastern Christians, I have never met one who would say that Christians and Muslims are not talking about the same God. Muslim self-understanding could not be clearer. Muslims understand Islam as the same religion revealed by God through many prophets and messengers, most notably a long list of biblical figures such as Noah, Abraham, Moses, David, Jesus, and John the Baptist. Obviously, most Jews and Christians have not understood Islam in the same way as Muslims. That, however, is a different issue than declaring the spiritual descendants of Abraham are not even talking about the same God.

One argument often advanced at this point centers on the divinity of Jesus. Several of the aforementioned Christian leaders — and many others who enjoy high visibility via television ministries — state unequivocally that Christians and Muslims are not talking about the same God since Muslims reject the divinity of Jesus. Unless one's understanding of God includes the divinity of Jesus, the argument goes, you are talking about a different God. While the reasoning may make sense at first, it quickly breaks down. This perspective would require a corollary: Jews and Christians are not talking about the same God since Jews do not accept the divinity of Jesus. Very few Christians who denounce Islam and Allah without hesitation seem willing to follow their logic and apply the same principle to Jews and Judaism. Why? Because it is obvious to everyone that Jews and Christians *are* talking about the same God.

Do Jews and Christians and Muslims have different understandings about God? Of course they do. Understandings about God vary dramatically between each of the Abrahamic traditions. This is hardly shocking news. Understandings about God vary widely within particular Christian denominations, within particular churches, and within particular individuals over time. Who among us has not changed her or his understandings about God from those of childhood? While some people in all traditions cling to anthropomorphic images of the Transcendent, many connect better with more abstract pointers such as those found in the New Testament where God is described as "light," "love," and "spirit."[9]

A Human View of Religious Truth

By definition, human beings are on precarious ground when talking about absolute truth. We have a difficult time discerning the truth about events unfolding before us, events recorded by the unblinking eye of television cameras. It is all the more challenging when separated by centuries from foundational events or teachings. Study the history of understanding among Christians wrestling with foundational doctrines (e.g., the Incarnation, the Atonement, the Trinity,

Eschatology, etc.), and one quickly discovers why theology is an ongoing discipline.

However profound one's religious insight or experience might be, as human beings we are limited by time, space, mental capacities, experience, and many other factors. The apostle Paul reminded the Christians in Corinth that human limitations are real:

> Love never ends. But as for prophecies, they will come to an end; as for tongues, they will cease; as for knowledge, it will come to an end. For we know only in part; but when the complete comes, the partial will come to an end. When I was a child, I spoke like a child, I thought like a child, I reasoned like a child; when I became an adult, I put an end to childish ways. For now, we see in a mirror, dimly, but then we will see face to face. Now I know only in part; then I will know fully, even as I have been fully known. (1 Cor. 13:8–12)

It is much easier to know the truth than it is to seek it. While people in all religious traditions may wish to know all of God's truth, none of us can make such a claim. We do not possess the mind of God. None of us has everything locked down. On the contrary, we are all on a journey that includes learning, unlearning, growing, and changing. With a moment's reflection, this is obvious in even the most conservative or fundamentalist religious settings. Normal activities in every Christian community include Bible study, educational programs, sermons, retreats, and the like. All of this suggests there is more to learn. If one is reading, thinking, watching the news, experiencing the joys and sorrows of life, and talking with others, one is constantly in a process of learning, unlearning, growing, and changing. The same holds true for religious leaders, even those who pontificate via the media or write best-selling books that detail impending Armageddon scenarios.[10] A simple question illustrates the point. Ask any priest, rabbi, or minister how often he or she rereads his or her sermons from five or ten years ago. Most clergy will acknowledge it is often a disquieting, if not outright painful experience; most readily admit that they would certainly frame some things differently today.

This is not to say that all religious truth is relative or that it does not matter what you think or believe. On the contrary, it matters a great deal — not only to people individually, but also to entire communities. The deep convictions and actions of Mahatma Gandhi and Martin Luther King Jr. helped change the world. The deep convictions and actions of the September 11 hijackers also changed the world.

In addition to being horrified and offended by the violent extremists, many Muslims with whom I have spoken in recent years have also talked about the arrogance of claiming the status of martyr. God alone is judge. I have never met a thoughtful Muslim who claimed with certainty that he or she knew that heaven would be their reward. Rather, Muslims speak of seeking to know and follow the path God has revealed for humankind. The most pious Muslims I have known over the years express their hope that God will find them worthy on the Day of Judgment. Judgment belongs to God, not human beings. Such humility and awareness of human limitations is little understood or even known when headlines focus on an extremist fringe claiming a heavenly reward for perpetrating violence in God's name.[11]

Can we speak of absolute truth in the realm of religion? This question invites an intriguing debate where a range of nuanced perspectives could be advanced. Personally, I believe that absolute truth exists. I believe it rests with God, however, and not with human beings. At best, human beings have a treasure in earthen vessels. People in various traditions — Hindu, Buddhist, Jewish, Christian, and Islamic, as well as native traditions worldwide — speak of religious experiences and insights too deep and powerful for words. A Buddhist may speak of experiencing enlightenment, but cannot neatly articulate the reality; many Hindus refer to the Ultimate Reality that is beyond all names and forms; the apostle Paul refers to a mystical experience of Paradise where he "heard things that are not to be told, that no mortal is permitted to repeat" (2 Cor. 12:4).

The effort to articulate religious truth within different traditions necessarily involves language. But language itself is a large symbol system. Ten or fifty people can read the same text or hear the same speech and come away with distinctly different understandings. The meaning mediated through language, art, or ritual can and does vary significantly, in part because of what the individual or group brings to the process. As human beings, we are all conditioned in ways that we do not always perceive. Sincere and intelligent people perceive and process information and experiences differently. As a middle-aged, Protestant (Baptist), Caucasian male baby-boomer in the United States, my understandings and experiences within the Christian tradition are demonstrably different from a Quaker, Palestinian mother of four in Ramallah or a priest serving an Assyrian church community in Baghdad. This does not mean my understandings or experiences of God or religious truths are wrong. However powerful and life-changing my understandings have been, I must acknowledge that my particular experiences of God and religious truth do not exhaust all the possibilities. Religious traditions and cultural contexts do not determine who we are, but they do frame and shape significantly the worldview of most people.

It is helpful to think of a human view of religious truth as dynamic and relational. It is possible for people of faith to embrace and affirm religious truth without defining truth for others. Wesley Ariarajah, a United Methodist minister from Sri Lanka, illustrates this approach with a profoundly simple example:

> When my daughter tells me I'm the best daddy in the world, and there can be no other father like me, she is speaking the truth, for this comes out of her experience. She is honest about it; she knows no other person in the role of her father. But of course it is not true in another sense. For one thing, I myself know friends who, I think, are better fathers than I am. Even more importantly, one should be aware that in the next house there is another little girl who also thinks her daddy is the best father in the world. And she too is right. In fact at the level of the way the two children relate to their two fathers, no one can compare the truth content of the statements of the two girls. For here we are not dealing with the absolute truths, but with the language of faith and love.... The language of the Bible is also the language of faith and love.... The problem begins when we begin to take these confessions in the language of faith and love and turn them into absolute truths. It becomes much more serious when we turn them into truths on the basis of which we begin to measure the truth or otherwise of other faith claims. My daughter cannot say to her little friend in the next house that there is no way she can have the best father, for the best

one is right there in her house. If she does, we'll have to dismiss it as child-talk![12]

An Inclusive Approach to Religious Truth

Wesley Ariarajah's example suggests the need to move beyond "child-talk" in our theological understanding. The health of the different religions requires such maturation. The future of the planet is also at stake. The world of the twenty-first century is interconnected and interdependent in unprecedented ways. Economic, ecological, military, social, and political systems and problems are global. Religion is often a central and complicating component in the volatile mix, serving as a key motivation for peace or violence. Albert Einstein once noted, "The significant problems we face cannot be solved at the same level of thinking we were at when we created them."[13] For Christians and Muslims, this observation is an invitation to explore new paradigms for understanding particularity and pluralism within the respective religions and an imperative at the interfaith level. In the decades ahead, the ways in which Christians and Muslims understand and relate to people outside their communities of faith will have profound consequences for both religions — and for peace in the world.

Although many Muslims and Christians proclaim a narrow exclusivism, both traditions offer frameworks for more inclusive understandings of religious truth. At the heart of Islam one finds an inclusive message: God's revelation has come through many prophets and messengers worldwide. As noted above, many prominent biblical figures appear in the Qur'an; Jews and Christians constitute legitimate communities of faith whose books — the Torah and the Gospel — come from Moses and Jesus. Many passages in the Qur'an are positive and affirming, including the promise of paradise for "People of the Book." Jews, Christians, and others are limited by presumed distortions or teachings that have obscured the revelation given through their prophets. So, the Qur'an also includes many passages warning against dangerous distortions — most notably the divinity of Jesus and the doctrine of the Trinity — urging believers to unite in Islam.

Under Islamic rule, Jews and Christians who did not embrace Islam freely were to be treated as "protected people" (*dhimmis*). The actual experience of protected people varied from time to time and place to place, but the principle is important: Jews, Christians, and others are considered legitimate communities deserving protection under Islamic authority. This paradigm for an inclusive approach could become a significant basis for religious dialogue aimed at peace instead of violence, as predominantly Muslim countries seek self-determination in religiously diverse lands. Support for this inclusive approach is found in streams of traditions within the Qur'an that indicate that different communities are part of God's plan and that different responses to various prophets who are believed to have brought the same revelation are valid. The different communities are explained as a test for people of faith. The emphasis falls on responsible behavior here in this life, in the context of pluralism:

> If God had so willed, He would have made you one community, but (He has not done so) that He may test you in what He has given you; therefore compete with one another in good works. To God you shall all return and He will tell you (the truth) about that which you have been disputing. (Qur'an 5:48)

Significant shifts have been taking place among Christians during the past century as many people have developed more nuanced and appreciative awareness of other religious traditions. In addition to traditional exclusivist approaches — some of which have softer edges than others — more inclusive and pluralist models are coming into view. Four decades ago, the Second Vatican Council dealt directly with fresh approaches to non-Christian religions and interfaith relationships. Three of the sixteen official documents approached interfaith issues in ways that shifted the traditional doctrine of "no salvation outside the church." A brief quotation from one Vatican II document, "Light to the Gentiles" (*Lumen Gentium*), addresses the possibility of salvation for people outside the church:

Those, who through no fault of their own, do not know Christ or his Church, but who nevertheless see God with a sincere heart, and moved by grace, try in their actions to do his will as they know it through the dictates of their conscience — those too may achieve eternal salvation.[14]

In the four decades since Vatican II, the Catholic Church has pursued a wide variety of programs designed to implement the spirit of this affirmation. Through statements by the pontiff, international meetings, stimulating a "dialogue of life" in local communities, publications on interreligious dialogue and understanding, and cooperative mission activities, the Catholic Church leadership has endeavored to work out the implications of an inclusive theology. Pope John Paul II, often cited for his traditional, conservative positions on celibacy for priests, women in ministry, birth control, and abortion, has been very progressive in pursuing an inclusive interfaith theology. These seismic shifts in the largest Christian community on earth could become increasingly important for dialogue between the religions of the world.[15]

Another type of nonexclusive approach is often described as "pluralism." In recent decades, a number of thoughtful Christian pluralists have articulated theological frameworks that affirm the validity of various paths, understanding Christianity as neither the only means to salvation nor the fulfillment of other religious traditions. Diana Eck, a Methodist from Montana who teaches comparative religion at Harvard University, writes eloquently of ways her theological perspectives have been shaped by the study of other religions as well as by her personal encounters with Hindus, Buddhists, Muslims, Sikhs, Jews, and others:

Through the years I have found my own faith not threatened, but broadened and deepened by the study of Hindu, Buddhist, Muslim, and Sikh traditions of faith. And I have found that only as a Christian pluralist could I be faithful to the mystery and the presence of the one I call God. Being a Christian pluralist means daring to encounter people of different faith traditions and defining my faith not by its borders but by its roots.[16]

Diana Eck reflects a growing pattern of inner dialogue and theological introspection sparked by daily encounter with people of faith in various religious traditions. Increasingly, the practical and theological challenges posed globally by pluralism and interdependence are being manifest in local settings. The United States is now the most religiously diverse country in the world. Many communities reflect the diversity of the world in microcosm. The coming decades will no doubt include a rich variety of religious understandings and truth claims in more inclusive ways.

Exclusivism still remains the most widespread response to religious diversity among Christians. An exclusivist approach often has hard edges defined by rigid absolutism and supported by biblical passages, most notably John 14:6 where Jesus is depicted as saying, "I am the way, the truth and the life. No one comes to the Father except through me."[17] Even within the exclusivist model, however, there are softer, more open forms of traditional truth claims that provide opportunities for religious dialogue to serve peaceful means.

I first discovered the range of options among Christian exclusivists in 1971 while working as a summer youth minister at a Southern Baptist church in Tulsa. In a conversation in the home of the minister, I expressed my strong desire to study world religions in seminary. This minister, a stereotypical Southern Baptist preacher-evangelist, responded very favorably to my interest in studying comparative religion. I asked him to what extent he thought God was at work in the world beyond the walls of the church. He pointed out that the Bible is not a book about comparative religion, but that there were many hints and clues throughout the Bible making clear that God is the God of all creation and that God's love extends to all creation. He pointed out various instances in the Hebrew Bible where God is depicted as actively engaging people outside of Israel—including Job, the most righteous man on earth. He spoke eloquently of the Cornelius story in Acts 10, a powerful story revealing Peter's eye-opening theological discoveries about God's activity in the world. He looked me in the eye and said, "I am 95 percent sure that God is doing all kinds of things that we do not begin to understand, relating to people in different religions and cultures." He expected there would be many surprises in heaven. He went on to say that he was 100 percent sure about the truth of what God had done in Christ. So, whatever else God is doing with and through creation, his responsibility was to proclaim the Good News as he understood it.

The minister concluded by reminding me that the book of Job ends with a clear reminder that human beings do not even begin to understand or grasp the mind of God. It was a wonderfully liberating moment, an affirmation that one can be anchored by life-changing experiences and understandings of God's truth without necessarily framing those understandings in absolute truth claims. This is a powerful and cogent message in a dangerous, interdependent world where conflicting religious truth claims abound. As the Qur'an suggests, the full clarification of disputed truth claims awaits the heavenly realm. In the meantime, people of faith and goodwill should focus their competition on good works: "... compete with one another in good works. To God you shall all return and He will tell you the truth about that which you have been disputing" (Qur'an 5:48).

Seven

Is the Empowered Woman a Warrior or a Dove?

The Enigma of Feminism, Religion, Peace, and Violence

VALARIE H. ZIEGLER

Valarie Ziegler's essay establishes a historical base from which we can better appreciate the crucial role of women in religious dialogue on peace and violence. She shows that women have contributed much of the leading energy to the peace movements in the history of the United States. This strong historical connection to peace through nonviolent action has led to what Ziegler calls an essentialist perception, that women are innately more peaceful than men — a perception that Ziegler rejects. Rather, women have been socialized to give peace and not violence priority. Kimball's argument that religious claims to absolute truth hinder meaningful dialogue takes on a specific face in Ziegler's article. Women have been victimized in almost every religion. Sexism takes a myriad of forms in the world's religions, but in the end, they all spell injustice.

Ziegler's account of women's role in peace movements in the United States forms a foundation for addressing injustices done to women in most religions. She contends that as a result, women have been forced into a world that demands warriors, not doves. We need to learn about women models as peacemakers in order for religious dialogue not to shipwreck on the rocks of sexism. This essay provides such a positive model.

How can religious dialogue talk about common options for peace and at the same time continue to treat women as second-class humans? Ziegler's essay provides a starting point for a new appreciation for the positive force of women's voices in the much-needed dialogue.

Provocations for Dialogue

1. *How can religions confront sexism in all its forms? Why does the subordination and subjugation of women persist within many religious traditions?*

2. *How do scriptural and historical traditions of sexism within religions have any credibility in today's world? Do such views aid or hinder peaceful ends among religions and nations?*

3. *What alternative, more peace-oriented visions of human relationships exist within religious traditions? Why not explore their credibility in the name of peace and justice?*

• • •

I WOULD LIKE to address two questions. The first focuses on the relationship of violence and nonviolence to gender; the second focuses on possible relationships between violence and power, nonviolence, and lack of power. Specifically, the questions I want to pose are these: Is preferring peace to war something intrinsic to women, and alien to men? Or is the celebration of nonviolence attractive only to those who lack the power to enact a political agenda through coercive means? Is the empowered person, in short, a warrior or a dove?

American culture has typically made two claims about peace and war. First, Americans have traditionally argued that women are less prone to and less effective at wielding violence than men. That is one reason that women have never been drafted to serve in American armed forces. Second, Americans have for the most part never doubted the necessity of militarism. For most Americans, it is simply common sense that to be secure in the community of nations we need a strong military, and few Americans deny that at times national security can only be served by going to war.

Historically, Christian theology has produced a number of reactions to war. Christianity has at times provided rich justifications for violence, as we are reminded so often by references to the Crusades. It also espouses a just war tradition which provides specific guidelines and limitations for Christians engaged in military actions, and which has been analyzed insightfully in reference to terrorism earlier in this volume. Certainly in the United States, where each branch of the military employs Christian pastors to minister to Christian soldiers, cooperation between Christianity and militarism has been institutionalized. But Christianity is not necessarily amenable to militarism. There are also significant elements of pacifism within the Christian tradition, and in American history women especially have been noteworthy not only in embracing nonviolence, but also in laboring to convince others to do so as well.

In working for peace, American women have had to address two strategic issues. The first poses the question of *essentialism*: Is there something about being a woman that naturally inclines one to detest violence and embrace harmony? In particular, does woman's biological role as mother predispose her toward pacifism? Or do men and women share a common nature, so that neither is innately more pacifist than the other?

The second strategic issue that has marked women's involvement in peace movements poses the question of *efficacy*. How can women effectively campaign for peace? Given the militarism that has marked American culture and the institutionalized sexism that denied women even the elementary civil right of suffrage for most of our history, finding effective ways to campaign for peace has presented an enormous challenge. Simply campaigning publicly for peace has invariably obliged women to defend their right to a life and a voice outside the domestic sphere of home and family. Thus, working for peace historically has prompted women also to work for political equality with men.

Ironically, however, working for women's political rights is not necessarily tied to working for peace. Contemporary women who have sought equal opportunity within the armed forces have found militarism a venue for seeking their political rights. If we deny the essentialist claim that the "mother half" of humanity has a unique capacity for nonviolence, then the notion that women have a special moral obligation to work for peace falls by the wayside. If women share a common nature with men, they have no intrinsic insight into the things that make for peace, and it is not clear that a politically empowered woman, any more than a politically empowered man, will be a peace reformer. For years the armed forces have urged American men to "pick a service, pick a challenge, set yourself apart," and maybe in the twenty-first century women will find that the best way to "be all that you can be" will be as warriors, not as doves.

Peace Reform in Antebellum America

Organized peace movements in North America began in 1815 as a reaction to the War of 1812. Prior to that, pacifism was most famously associated with several Protestant groups. Those of Anabaptist origin, such as the Mennonites, the Dunkers, and the Brethren, were historic peace churches that eschewed involvement with government. They believed that Christians were called to live according to the nonresistant love ethic outlined by Jesus in the Sermon on the Mount ("love your enemies; pray for those who persecute you; do not return evil for evil; if any one strikes you on the cheek, turn the other cheek to them as well"). Anabaptists assumed that governments, based as they were upon the coercive threat innate to the state's police and military forces, were of necessity violent. Known as "the quiet in the land," these Anabaptist groups withdrew from the larger culture insofar as they could.

Far more influential were the Quakers, a British Christian pacifist group instrumental in the founding of Pennsylvania. Quakers believed in a source of inspiration they called "the inner light." Convinced that women as well as men had access to this inner light, when they gathered to worship, Quakers encouraged one another to speak as God's spirit led them. By inviting women to speak with authority before "promiscuous" audiences that contained men as well as women, Quakers were for their time astonishingly egalitarian. They were also notable for their early and persistent opposition to African American slavery. As a result, Quaker men and women would play important roles in abolitionist, peace, and women's rights movements in the nineteenth century.

In 1815, David Low Dodge and Noah Worcester founded the first formal peace societies in American history (called, respectively, the New York Peace Society and the Massachusetts Peace Society). They had no intention of opening the cause of peace to women advocates. Rather, they were convinced that obedience to the Sermon on the Mount was critical to Christianity, and they hoped to persuade a wide range of Christian men that the cause of international peace demanded their immediate attention. In 1828, under the leadership of William Ladd, a national organization dubbed "The American Peace Society" was formed.

Like most other reform organizations of its day, the American Peace Society enlisted only male members, but it eagerly solicited donations from women, and it also encouraged women to form auxiliary peace societies. The *Journal of the American Peace Society* ran frequent articles reminding women that as mothers they held the key to peace education. In 1836, William Ladd argued that the "subject of peace is particularly adapted to the female mind." He urged women to pray for peace, to refuse to attend military balls and reviews, to teach their children to reject military displays, and to use their talents in writing poetry, music, and tracts for the cause of peace.[1]

Ladd's belief that women were by nature peaceful was thoroughly essentialist. In confining membership to men and in exiling women to auxiliary organizations, the American Peace Society ensured women's tangential status and left little room for them to develop a distinctive voice. Through the cause of abolitionism, however, women would go beyond the stereotypical roles of wife and mother to pioneer a new kind of peace advocacy. They were led by Angelina and Sarah

Grimké, sisters who had moved from South Carolina to Pennsylvania where they became become Quakers and joined other reformers in the emerging abolitionist movement.

"Immediatist abolitionism" (that is, antislavery efforts that demanded an immediate end to slavery) had begun in the early 1830s. It was marked by a commitment to nonviolence, to the Sermon on the Mount as the Christian statement of nonviolence par excellence, and to defining slavery as a form of coercive violence. In 1837 the Grimké sisters traveled to New England on an antislavery lecture tour. Although they had intended to honor the nineteenth-century convention that prohibited women from addressing audiences of such suspicious motives, the Grimkés proved to be such powerful speakers that men began sneaking into their lectures. The Congregational clergy of Connecticut issued a pastoral letter condemning the Grimké sisters, and they were forced to defend their right to speak on behalf of slaves.

Many abolitionists feared that the Grimké sisters, by introducing the "extraneous" question of women's rights into the antislavery cause, would divert abolitionists from their main goal. The Grimkés disagreed vigorously. "*We* will settle *this right before* we go one step further," Angelina insisted, asking, "What *then* can *woman* do for the slave when she is herself under the feet of man and shamed in *silence?*" Indeed, she concluded, woman's right to speak publicly "*must* be firmly established ... on the only firm basis of human rights, the Bible."[2] Sarah agreed: "I ask no favors for my sex. I surrender not our claim to equality. All I ask of our brethren is, that they will take their feet from off our backs and permit us to stand upright on that ground which God has designed us to occupy."[3]

Such claims predicated women's commitment to peace, not to their femininity, but to their humanity — to the God-given nature they shared with men as part of a common humanity. Most American pacifists disagreed with that egalitarian stance and preferred the essentialist arguments typical of the American Peace Society. But a few reformers were delighted to welcome the Grimkés into their midst.

The abolitionists led by William Lloyd Garrison were radical pacifists; terming themselves "nonresistants," they were dedicated to the immediate abolition of slavery, the equality of men and women, and the absolute rejection of all governments that fell below the perfection of the Sermon on the Mount.

By 1838, Garrison's nonresistants had founded their own peace society, the New England Non-Resistance Society. Women joined as full members and were elected as officers. A number of women, such as Lydia Maria Child, Abby Kelley, and Lucretia Mott, became prominent public figures on behalf of nonresistant abolitionism. Younger women such as Lucy Stone, Antoinette Brown Blackwell, Susan B. Anthony, and Elizabeth Cady Stanton received training that prepared them to become prominent leaders in the women's rights movement. The Seneca Falls Convention in 1848 — the first great gathering on behalf of women's rights — thus was directly dependent on nonviolent abolitionism.

These women faced great opposition, even from other abolitionists. Catharine Beecher chastised the Grimkés for operating outside of the domestic sphere she believed appropriate to women, and a minister who belonged to the Connecticut Anti-Slavery Society was so distraught at the prospect of listening to a speech by the nonresistant Abby Kelley that he announced, "I will not sit in a meeting where the sorcery of a woman's tongue is thrown around my heart. I will not submit to PETTICOAT GOVERNMENT. No woman shall ever lord it over me."[4] Within their own community, however, egalitarian abolitionists celebrated women's freedom to speak. As one fan of Abby Kelley and Galatians 3:28 put it:

> Miss Kelley of Lynn,
> Some esteem it a sin
> And a shame that thou darest to speak;
> Quite forgetting that mind
> Is to sex unconfined.
> That in Christ is nor Gentile nor Greek,
> Abby K!
> That in Christ is nor Gentile nor Greek![5]

In these ways, abolitionism, women's rights, and pacifism intertwined. Women who labored on behalf of one cause might easily work for all three. Ultimately, of course, political events drove a wedge into that alliance. The slaves would be freed not through peaceful means, but through a devastating civil war. And with the passage of the Thirteenth Amendment after the war, freed male slaves would receive (at least in theory if not necessarily in practice) full citizenship rights, while the women who had dedicated themselves to the antislavery cause would remain disenfranchised.

After the war, the cause of peace became even more strongly linked to woman suffrage, as well as to other reform efforts, such as temperance and the woman's club movement. By the end of the nineteenth century, hundreds of thousands of American women would be pledged to the cause of peace.

From the Gilded Age to World War I

In the era following the Civil War we find that, unlike the Grimkés, the most prominent women reformers used essentialist arguments as a platform for advocating pacifism and women's rights. If it was the case, as most Victorian Americans assumed, that women were by nature less aggressive, more godly, and more inclined to self-sacrifice than men, then confining women to the domestic sphere meant that Americans' public life would be bereft of the leavening effect of women's pacific spirit. This argument set the notion of separate spheres on its head and made essentialism an argument for efficacy: Because women were more peaceful than men, they owed it to men to enter the public realm. In particular, these reformers believed, women must win the right to suffrage to effectively champion peace reform. The doctrines of essentialism, peace, and woman suffrage thus became linked.

Women peace reformers used a theory of the origins of human civilization popularized by sociologist Lester Ward to bolster their work. Ward argued that human civilization's earliest forms were matriarchal and the current rule of men represented *de*volution, not progress.

Human culture, he said, would remain skewed and underdeveloped so long as men alone controlled the public spheres of work, education, industry, literary arts, and government. Without women to balance men's natural aggression and selfishness, human civilization could never realize its full potential.

The woman who most prominently developed the theological implications of this theory for peace advocacy was an unlikely candidate: Julia Ward Howe, the author of the "Battle Hymn of the Republic." Howe became interested in woman suffrage in the late 1860s, and in 1870, as the Franco-Prussian War was under way in Europe, Howe pondered what she might do to make a witness for peace. Why, she wondered, did men persist in settling their political disagreements violently? And what could she, as a woman lacking even the right to vote, do about it? Feeling both politically marginal and morally outraged, she began to rethink what it meant to be a woman. She explained:

> During the first two thirds of my life . . . I looked to the masculine ideal of character as the only true one. . . . In an unexpected hour a new light came to me, showing me a world of thought and of character quite beyond the limits within which I had hitherto been content to abide. The new domain now made clear to me was that of true womanhood — woman no longer in her ancillary relation to her opposite, man, but in her direct relation to the divine plan and purpose, as a free agent, fully sharing with man every human right and every human responsibility.[6]

Borrowing from the evolutionary language popular in her time, Howe proposed that human development after the original matriarchy consisted of three stages. The first stage was that of primitive animal nature, in which individual men rose to power by brute force. The next stage was that of organized power, in which the "war-ideal, with its rules of loyalty and honor" surpassed the "savagery of primitive man." Thus, she claimed, "the savage individual gives way to the father-ideal, just and noble." Nevertheless, the age of the father-ideal celebrated masculine violence, and needed to give way to divine love. "Now where," she asked, "do we find provided in Nature a counter-influence, a passion and power which shall be as conservative of human life as masculine influence is destructive of it?" The answer, of course, was in motherhood, "which gives...life through months of weariness, through hours of anguish and through years of labor—an organization in which suffering is the parent of love, and all that is endured receives its final crown in the life and love of something other than itself."[7] In short, Howe concluded, "The womanly power is that which links the divine to the human soul."[8]

Having discovered these new ways of defining womanhood and motherhood, Howe quickly put them into practice. In 1870 she called for mothers around the world to organize a crusade on behalf of peace. "My dream," she said, "was of a mighty and august Congress of Mothers, which should constitute a new point of departure for the regeneration of society."[9] She held two well-attended meetings in New York City in 1870 to publicize the cause, and then traveled to England in 1872 where she organized the first woman's peace congress. In 1873 she established the tradition of observing a Mothers' Day of Peace in early June. The first Mothers' Day was celebrated in eighteen American cities, as well as in Rome and Constantinople, and friends of peace in Philadelphia continued to observe her mothers' day for over fifty years.

Howe did not labor alone. Rather, she worked in cooperation with other women to develop a common rhetoric about peace, so that it became second nature to argue that women's higher ethical sensibilities could take hold in American culture only if women were given equal political and social rights with men. Virtually every major reformer in the women's movement, such as Charlotte Perkins Gilman, Jane Addams, Frances Willard, Carrie Chapman Catt, or Anna Howard Shaw, used such language to create an essentialist feminist rhetoric that linked the causes of peace and woman's suffrage.

Women's organizations responded in droves to the call. The Women's Christian Temperance Union (WCTU) alone published two monthly peace journals and also had its own Department of Peace and Arbitration. By 1914 the 800,000 members of the Federation of Women's Clubs, plus the 100,000 women in the Council of Mothers, the 325,000 in the WCTU, the 161,000 in the Woman's Relief Corps, and hundreds of thousands in the National Council of Women were all officially committed to promoting peace. Even the Daughters of the American Revolution (DAR) joined the cause.

As women began to create their own powerful reform organizations, they also began to find places alongside men in the more traditional peace societies. The American Peace Society not only began to admit women as members, but as early as 1871 allowed women to become officers. The Universal Peace Union, founded by Alfred Love at the conclusion of the Civil War, welcomed women as members and officers, so much so that by the 1890s half of the membership and one-third of the executive committee were women. Lucia Ames Mead became an important leader in the American Peace Society, and Belva Lockwood (now famous as the first woman to argue a case before the U.S. Supreme Court) served as a lobbyist for the Universal Peace Union. Fanny Fern Andrews, capitalizing on the common perception that the best way to convert people to the cause of peace was to train them in childhood, helped found the American School Peace League in 1908 and developed an extensive curriculum for grades one through twelve that allowed teachers in social studies and the humanities to incorporate peace studies into their everyday teaching.

There were other ways to crusade for peace as well. American women pacifists actively opposed imperialism and spoke out against the Spanish American War and the U.S. annexation of the Philippines in the late 1890s. A conference on world peace at The Hague in 1899 sparked a plethora of responses from women reformers, as committees from suffrage groups, women's clubs, and even religious clubs sought to educate the American public about peace. Also in 1899, a suffrage organization called the International Council of Women (ICW) convened women from around the globe to focus on issues of peace, violence, and woman suffrage. In 1906 the internationally famous social worker Jane Addams published *Newer Ideals of Peace*, in which she argued that "more strenuous forces" must be applied to create a "newer patriotism" that would impel people to unite across national borders in a heroic struggle for peace and social justice. What people needed, in short, was to crusade for peace as vigorously as they were accustomed to waging war.[10] Addams believed that women would be in the vanguard of that movement since they were the nurturers of every new generation, as well as naturally inclined to cooperate with others for good, rather than to compete against them.

The outbreak of World War I in 1914 presented unique challenges and opportunities. American women's opposition to the war was vigorous; they held dramatic parades and formed the Woman's Peace Party, and women from both the Allied and Central powers met to create "The Women's International Committee for Permanent Peace." But reaction in the United States was not favorable. Theodore Roosevelt denounced the women's peace movement as "both silly and base," and the *New York Times* warned that this "mad plan" could only hurt the cause of woman suffrage.[11] Finally, in April 1917 (despite the negative vote of the only congresswoman, Jeannette Rankin of Montana), Congress declared war on Germany. Now the causes of peace and suffrage came into conflict with one another. For some suffrage pacifists, it made sense to emphasize and even celebrate the important contributions that women could make to the war effort. If the American public believed that supporting woman suffrage meant supporting a strong national defense, then they would be inclined favorably toward extending to women the right to vote. In spite of opposition from more radical suffrage workers, as well as the pleas from her sister members of the Woman's Peace Party, Carrie Chapman Catt, leader of the National American Woman Suffrage Association (NAWSA), declared NAWSA's support for the war and told the nation that the passage of woman suffrage would increase the morale of the hundreds of thousands of American women loyal to the war effort.

Women and men who resisted the war faced great public opposition. Nevertheless, after the armistice in November 1918 women around the globe returned to their efforts to sustain an international organization of women devoted to peace. In May 1919 women from the United States, France, Great Britain, Germany, and other Central Powers nations, as well as women from neutral countries, met in Zürich to establish the Women's International League for Peace and Freedom (WILPF). In 1920 woman suffrage became a reality in the United States, and women peace reformers embarked upon a new stage of peace advocacy.

From One Great War to the Next

Thoroughly disillusioned by the futility of the Great War, U.S. peace activism hit a boom in the 1920–30s as unprecedented numbers of women as well as men committed themselves to work for peace. Historian Charles Chatfield has calculated that by 1933 there were 12 international, 28 national, and 37 local peace societies in the United States, with another 2 international, 56 national, and 51 local groups promoting internationalism, and still another 120 organizations related to peace advocacy.[12] Women were involved at every level, from organizing Pan American conferences with women peace advocates from Latin America, to serving as heads of major agencies that worked in coordination with agencies headed by men, to serving as volunteers in the task of education and war relief efforts. In short, whether women pacifists believed that they had unique gifts to offer the cause as women, or whether they simply saw themselves as colleagues working alongside male pacifists, there had never been so many opportunities to labor on behalf of peace.

Ultimately, however, the biggest challenge facing pacifists in this period was that of efficacy: Would peace reformers have the political acumen to create and sustain just social orders, or would they be at the mercy of military aggressors? For many pacifists the answer to that question would be a sorrowful one. Faced with the rise of European fascism and the Japanese invasion of Manchuria in the 1930s, they would sadly conclude that only military might could resist aggressor nations. Others were not convinced. They still believed it would be possible to labor for both peace and justice simultaneously. In the 1950s the civil rights movement would employ just such tactics in its efforts to fight institutionalized racism. But for most American pacifists World War II marked an unanswerable challenge to their peace convictions. Most Americans saw the Allied war efforts as just and necessary, and even though Congresswoman Jeanette Rankin once again voted against American entry into war, most Americans agreed with President Roosevelt when he asked Congress to declare war in December 1941.

Just as in World War I, moreover, women were offered noteworthy opportunities for social and political advancement if they supported the national war effort. Not only were jobs in industry opened to women in unprecedented numbers (so that "Rosie the Riveter" entered into the national consciousness), but access to female corps in every major military branch was also available. The chance to do work previously reserved exclusively for men promised significant economic and social improvements for women. Gender empowerment and militarism seemed to go hand in hand. But pacifists like Dorothy Day (who founded the Catholic Worker in 1933) urged American women to see the new jobs in industry as a government scheme to enslave women to "work in the factories throughout the land to make the bombers, the torpedoes, the explosives, the tools of war."[13]

When World War II ended with the atomic conflagrations at Hiroshima and Nagasaki, it was predictable that women pacifists would protest the unthinkable destruction of nuclear warfare and that they would commit themselves to offering relief to the many victims of the world's most extensive war. What remained to be seen was how women would find new techniques to work effectively for peace and social justice.

The Fifties and Beyond

The decade following the end of World War II was extraordinarily difficult for American pacifists. Continuing Cold War pressures to build up the military, the outbreak of the Korean War in 1950, plus widespread suspicions encouraged by McCarthyism that peace activism was pro-Communist, combined to discourage peace advocacy.

For pacifism, however, the burgeoning civil rights movement provided the clearest example in American history of the power of nonviolence to effect political and social change. Proclaiming biblical principles of justice and love, and assuming that both men and women could embrace the Sermon on the Mount and eschew violence, hundreds of thousands of Americans marched, protested, boycotted, and worked in voter registration campaigns to extend full citizenship to African Americans. Though the most public figures in the civil rights movement were men — particularly clergy — the backbone consisted of women. From the working-class women who filled the ranks of marchers, to the female students brave enough to integrate public schools, to the professional women of the Montgomery Women's Political Counsel who acted as "trailblazers" for the celebrated bus boycott of 1955–56, to articulate college women like Diane Nash, whose work was critical in desegregating southern lunch counters and buses, women were absolutely pivotal in the work of what participants would come to call "The Movement."

The Student Nonviolent Coordinating Committee (SNCC) was the civil rights organization in which it was easiest for women to assume positions of leadership, but by 1965 tensions in the group were high. As early as 1964, Mary King and Casey Hayden (two white female SNCC staffers) had written that SNCC women were denied equal power with men. "The woman in SNCC," they argued, "is often in the same position as that token Negro hired in a corporation. The management thinks that it has done its bit. Yet, every day the Negro bears an atmosphere, attitudes and actions which are tinged with condescension and paternalism."[14] By 1965, burned out by grueling work and unsure that The Movement was still effecting progress, SNCC staffers evidenced racial tensions too, and it was no longer clear to all that nonviolent direct action was the best strategy for black liberation. In time, both in SNCC and in the larger civil rights movement, the coalition that had united whites and blacks in common cause fell apart. African American reform was headed in the direction of black nationalism and black power, and white civil rights workers transferred their commitment to nonviolent social change to another target, the war in Vietnam.

Women in the mid-1960s who turned their attention to the war discovered that women peace activists before them had prepared the ground well. In November 1961, long before U.S. troop acceleration in Vietnam, fifty thousand American women belonging to an organization called Women Strike for Peace had walked out of their jobs and their homes to demand nuclear disarmament. The 1963 Soviet/American test-ban treaty was in part an answer to the fears expressed in that walkout. Once American involvement in Vietnam became heated, Women Strike for Peace as well as other traditional women's pacifist groups like the Women's International League for Peace and Freedom protested American involvement in a variety of ways, organizing opposition to the draft as well as to the war itself. In this most unpopular of American conflicts, organized protests against war (at least against *this* war, if not all wars) reached a zenith.

One of the results was an abiding suspicion of what President Eisenhower had earlier coined "the military-industrial complex." Even after the end of the war in Vietnam, many women peace activists wanted to continue their witness for peace. By now, women's studies and peace studies were coming into their own as academic disciplines, and it was possible to talk more broadly about the relationship between gender and militarism. The innate hierarchy of the military, the phallocentric language used to describe its weaponry, its goals of mastery and domination, its celebration of violence — all of those factors characterized what many women pacifists came to call "patriarchy." For them, patriarchy described the reality of male dominated cultures and institutions; militarism was just one example. Other examples included domestic violence against women, racial and gender discrimination, and the industrial abuse of the natural world. Simply to be a woman in the United States was to be subject to constant institutionalized violence. So long as patriarchy ruled, violence would thrive.

It was natural for such analysis to prompt women peace activists to turn to the arms race and to "ecofeminism," a convergence of feminism, ecology, and peace. By the 1980s women in both religious and secular organizations were pushing hard for a nuclear freeze. These efforts were most spectacularly visible in the Women's Pentagon Action, a gathering of thousands of women who encircled the Pentagon in 1980. They issued a statement of purpose, which said:

> We are gathering at the Pentagon on Nov. 16 because we fear for our lives. We fear for the life of this planet, our Earth, and the life of the children who are our human future.... We have come to mourn and rage and defy the Pentagon because it is the workplace of the imperial power which threatens us all.... We want to know what anger in these men, what fear, which can only be satisfied by destruction, what coldness of heart and ambition drives their days. We want to know because we do not want that dominance which is exploitative and murderous in international relations, and so dangerous to women and children at home — we do not want that sickness transferred by this violent society through the fathers to the sons.[15]

Opposition to the arms race was furthered by a pastoral letter critical of militarism and condemnatory of nuclear war issued by the Catholic bishops of the United States in 1983. Bishops in the United Methodist Church also wrote a pastoral letter sympathetic to the theological analysis of the Catholic bishops' letter. In some ways, it seemed as though the United States had never been so open to critique of the war system.

But other developments weakened those hopes. The end of the Cold War was credited not to the efforts of peace advocates, but to President Reagan's extraordinary military expenditures; ironically, the standoff between the United States and the USSR was resolved because the USSR ruined its economy trying to keep pace in its arms race with the United States. Moreover, developing feminist theory did not always push women in peaceful directions. For some women who wished to achieve political equality with men, enhanced opportunity for military careers was one of the welcome developments of the 1980s and 1990s. The National Organization for Women (NOW), one of the most powerful women's groups, proclaimed its support for women in the military, and from time to time discussions arose about compulsory military service for women if the draft were ever reintroduced. By the end of the twentieth century, seeking equality with men could lead women to war as well as to peace.

Clearly, the final story on women and peace movements in North America has not been written. Nevertheless, a consistent pattern has emerged. From the start, women peace activists used a variety of arguments against war. Often they argued as women and particularly as mothers, keeping alive the essentialist notion that, unlike men, women innately were pacific. At other times, women reformers abandoned essentialist notions and described peace as a universal human possibility, not as a unique temperament peculiar to females. No matter what strategies women used, they faced a reality that emerged early on with the Grimké sisters — that is, that even in a democracy they were second-class citizens. If women wished to be heard, certainly, if they wished to be taken seriously, they would have to find ways to empower themselves politically so that their voices mattered. In a nation that assumed a strong military was crucial to prosperity, voices to the contrary, particularly if they were women's voices, would always have to struggle to be heard, perhaps never more so than at the beginning of the twenty-first century, when the model of women as warriors threatens to supersede the model of women as the peaceful mother half of humanity.

I once thought that essentialism was a hopeless dead end. As Anne Sisson Runyan noted in a fine dissertation on feminism and peace, as long as we think of women as "mothering humanity towards peace, they will not present a threat to politics-as-usual, for they will be continually expected to provide support services in the absence of any real distribution of economic and political power."[16] Given recent trends, however, I wonder if it does not make more sense to argue that, theologically, the mother half of humanity *is* innately more peaceful.

In the end, however, I do not think the essentialist case is convincing; I do not think we have any idea what women — or men — innately are. We only know how we have been socialized. Ultimately, if we are to think in new ways about what it means to be human and to imagine new possibilities of social harmony, we must move beyond the gender stereotypes of both patriarchy and matriarchy. We do have places to look for those new visions, and here I would cite writers like Charlotte Perkins Gilman and Jane Addams, who realized a century ago that the place to begin is not at the international level, which none of us controls, but rather at the place we actually live — in our neighborhoods and in our families.

Addams, for example, concluded that the way to avoid war was to pioneer methods of establishing harmony between divergent social groups. Obviously, the task of establishing world peace was daunting. But Addams argued that laboratories in which to experiment on a smaller scale were readily available, and that the new discipline of social work was the means to realizing peace. Cities like Chicago, where impoverished immigrant groups were thrown up against one another, provided the perfect microcosm for developing strategies conducive to peace. Precisely because the living conditions in these neighborhoods were so intolerable, she explained, the inhabitants had to consider the demands of social justice, if for no other reason than to escape being crushed to death. Because a city like Chicago was so crowded, it was there that progress could occur most rapidly. As Addams noted,

> We are often told that...[people] under pressure of life become callous and cynical, whereas anyone who lives with them knows that they are sentimental and compassionate. It is possible that we shall be saved from warfare by the "fighting rabble" itself, by the "quarrelsome mob" turned into kindly citizens of the world through the pressure of a cosmopolitan neighborhood.[17]

Addams saw in Chicago's desperately poor immigrants, loyal both to their homeland and to their adopted country, a "newer patriotism" that could save the world. "There arises the hope," she contended, "that when this newer patriotism becomes large enough, it will overcome arbitrary boundaries and soak up the notion of nationalism."[18] At universities we call this something else: celebrating diversity.

I also believe that rethinking of American history in a way that does not celebrate and assume the necessity of militarism is necessary if Americans are ever to give peace a chance. The old curricula of Fanny Fern Andrews's American School Peace League were excellent at this, as is the writing of Carol Hunter, a Quaker historian at Earlham College. If women are to be doves, they must immerse themselves in theological cultures that embrace peace. Mennonites and Quakers are thriving peace communities, and for years they have held conferences, written important studies, and pioneered practical alternatives to militarism. We need to know these materials. We need to read the Mennonite historian John Howard Yoder as well as collections like Louise Hawkley and James Juhnke's *Nonviolent America: History Through the Eyes of Peace* (North Newton, Kans.: Bethel College, 1993) and Theron Schlabach and Richard Hughes's *Proclaim Peace: Christian Pacifism from Unexpected Quarters* (Urbana: University of Illinois Press, 1997).

The only way to be doves in a militarized culture is to join a counterculture. A powerful culture of Christian pacifism that sees the world through different eyes exists in American Christianity and in the history of American women, but in the end, I suspect that most politically empowered women, unless a new world dawns, will be warriors, not doves.

Eight

Latin American Liberation Theology and the Dialogue for Peace

DANIEL M. BELL JR.

Latin American liberation theology is a theology of justice, and its vision of justice transcends the limits of sovereign nations. It seeks justice for all people regardless of ethnic, national, or religious status.

Daniel M. Bell Jr. approaches the "wars of religion" of Western history in a way that denies that most religious wars were "religious," caused by adversarial relations between Protestants and Catholics. Rather, he alleges that they were political, the result of a struggle between church authority and emerging national and personal rights.

"These wars," he says, "were not about religious violence but about the displacement of a public, political church by a sovereign state."

Although many have claimed that liberation theology includes the advocacy of violent acts, he finds little evidence to support this claim. In contrast to the claim that America is an "unjust" state and thus deserving of destruction (see Kelsay's essay), or the inherent violence in dispensationalism (see Musser et al.), or the bellicose possibilities of religious dogmatism (see Kimball's article), Bell finds the reason for violence in "dominion." "The real issue," Bell contends, is "the challenge that the liberationists present to the reigning political order," especially "the empire of capitalism."

The root of modern violence, according to liberationists, is found in an unbridled capitalism that sacrifices the human good for material gain. The war on terrorism is nothing less than a "cover" to advance capitalist ends.

Liberationalists find in Christianity a God who sides with the oppressed. They claim to unmask the root of social conflict — the oppression of the poor. The solution is the "reign of God," which is both the path and instrument toward any lasting peace.

Provocations for Dialogue

1. *Is peace on earth possible? On what terms? Whose peace?*

2. *In what ways is the United States, as the premier capitalist nation, culpable for global violence?*

3. *What are alternative economic systems to capitalism?*

4. *What can churches do locally to curb violence and live peaceably?*

• • •

PRESENTING WHAT Latin American liberation theology has to say about peace, violence, and religion is deceptively straightforward. It is so not because liberation theology's friends and foes both reach the same uncomplicated and incorrect conclusion about liberation theology and violence, but because this presentation of Latin American liberationists' treatment of violence occurs after, and thus in inescapable proximity to, the horrific events of September 11, 2001.

In the aftermath of that day, the question of peace and violence put to religion is unmistakably accusatory. How could religion be implicated in such atrocities? How can religion mix such an unholy cocktail of unbridled rage and nihilistic devastation? From truck bombs to snipers and nail-filled backpacks, to suicide bombers, poison gas attacks, and machine-gun-toting, knife-wielding militias, this is a question that confronts us with nerve-racking frequency. Religion is clearly in the dock, on the defensive. What is it that enables religion to sanction and even encourage such heinous acts? In an effort to probe an answer, we round up suspects for questioning. A prime suspect is Latin American liberation theology.

The Question Posed

As the invited counsel for the Latin American liberationists, I will begin their defense by interrogating the question. The way that the question is typically posed, as well as the very fact that the question is even put to the liberationists in the first place, actually serves to illuminate what it is that the liberationists say about violence and peace.

...Once Before: The "Wars of Religion"

If we jog our collective memory, we will recall that this is a question that has been asked before. Once before we have recoiled in horror and revulsion at the shocking brutality and bloodlust unleashed by religion. That time is remembered as the "wars of religion" — that period spanning roughly the mid-sixteenth through the mid-seventeenth century, when Protestants and Catholics were locked in mortal combat that submerged much of Europe with blood. The story of these wars and their aftermath is told and retold in countless texts. Whatever the nuances, the basic storyline is always the same, reflected in the following editorial:

> Centuries of bloody religious wars and persecutions finally convinced Christians that there must be a better way to organize society, a way that did not involve quite so many burning bodies, human charnel houses and corpse-strewn battlefields.... The forces of the Enlightenment that exalted tolerance in the West were given their impetus by the European wars of the 16th and 17th centuries in which Christian was pitted against Christian — wars over points of doctrine that must have looked exceedingly abstruse, even absurd, to non-Christians, who could see only similarities between the warring systems.[1]

According to the standard account, the revulsion universally elicited by this tide of religiously inspired violence led to the establishment of a political order that, while it could not eliminate doctrinal differences, nevertheless might ensure that religions no longer had the political presence to back up arcane and inane doctrinal disputes with the edge of a sword. The solution to the problem of religious terror was the advancement of the liberal political order of toleration. In the words of Judith Shklar, "Liberalism...was born out of the cruelties of the religious civil wars, which forever rendered the claims of Christian charity a rebuke to all religious institutions and parties. If the faith was to survive at all, it would do so privately."[2] Or in the words of Jeffery Stout, "Liberal principles were the right ones to adopt when competing religious beliefs and divergent conceptions of the good embroiled Europe in the religious wars.... Our early modern ancestors were right to secularize public discourse in the interest of minimizing the ill effects of religious disagreement."[3]

The solution to the question of religious violence then was the depoliticization of religion, the privatization of faith. No longer would religion be permitted to take political form; instead it would be tucked neatly into the realm of culture, where it would be permitted to traffic in abstract values and dispense therapeutic meaning. Thus could religion be denied access to the weapons with which it had worked such bloody woe.

Of course, the corollary of this effort to protect us from the depredations of unbridled religion was that the state necessarily moved to the center of social and political life. With the exodus of the church from politics, the state stepped forward to assume the role of the sole overseer of social-political space. With the church safely sequestered in the private sphere of the human soul, the state could exercise sovereignty over bodies. And, as Max Weber pointed out, it exercised this sovereignty by means of a monopoly on the use of violence.[4]

At this point, one may be tempted to ask, What has this to do with the Latin American liberationists on peace and violence? How does this historical detour shed light on the question at hand? An answer requires that we continue a moment longer on this detour.

The standard story of the wars of religion and the birth of liberalism is a lie. For all of its popularity in intellectual circles (including theological circles), the tale is a myth. The so-called wars of religion were not wars fought over religious differences of opinion; the axis of conflict in the wars that rent sixteenth- and seventeenth-century Europe is not accurately drawn along confessional-doctrinal lines:

Catholic versus Protestant, transubstantiation versus consubstantia-
tion, and so forth. In contrast to received opinion, a careful examination of the historical record suggests that in these wars, Catholics and
Protestants often fought on the same side, and frequently Protestants
fought Protestants and Catholics fought Catholics.[5]

That the battle lines do not correlate in any straightforward manner with confessional identities and differences suggests that the
retreat of the church into the private recesses of the heart and the
emergence of a sovereign state governing a secular *socius* was about
more than an aversion to bloodshed. It was more than a reaction to
an alleged penchant of religion to punctuate its disagreements with
the point of a sword. Read rightly, the historical record reveals that
the violent convulsions of the sixteenth and seventeenth century were
in fact the birth pangs of Leviathan, of the modern state. These wars
were not primarily the doing of clerics and theologians, but the labor of secular princes as they struggled to shed the last remnants
of the medieval ecclesial order, as they strove to establish their sovereignty over a bounded geographical space by subsuming all other
social groupings and formations under their (coercive) authority. Far
from being the product of religious incivility (although unquestion-
ably encouraged by the church's tragic division), these wars were
the culmination of almost a millennium-long struggle between prince
and pope over the lines and forms of political authority. These wars
were not about religious violence but about the displacement of a
public, political church by a sovereign state exercising unchallenged
authority over the bodies of its subjects.

We are now ready to return to the issue at hand: what does this
historical critique of the "wars of religion" have to do with the question put to the liberationists about the use of violence? To be blunt,
the question put to the liberationists is a thinly veiled indictment that
condemns them as fomenters of violence. The question put to the liberationists today is put in the same spirit as the question was put to
religion in the aftermath of the so-called wars of religion. It is also
put in anticipation of the same answer. The same feigned sense of
incredulity and alarm is presumed in the face of violence, and the

solution proffered is the same — the domestication of faith to the service of the sovereign liberal state.

...Once Again: God, Terror, and Ambiguity

The claim that I have made is a strong one, and it demands support. Because it is crucial to appreciating what the liberationists have to say about peace and violence, it is worthwhile to consider briefly two popular contemporary treatments of the question of religion and violence for evidence of the accuracy of my claim.

The first to be considered is Mark Juergensmeyer's *Terror in the Mind of God: The Global Rise of Religious Violence.*[6] Although Juergensmeyer does not directly address Latin American liberationists, anyone familiar with their thought will immediately perceive the aptness of his analysis to their work. Indeed, as an admirer of the liberationists and as one intimately acquainted with their work, on several occasions I found myself nodding in recognition and, with more frequency than I care to admit, shuddering at the striking similarities between much liberationist thought and several of the terrorist movements Juergensmeyer considered. Thus, it is not surprising that many have charged Latin American liberationists with serving as "apologists for terrorism."[7]

Juergensmeyer's analysis concludes that what distinguishes advocates of religious violence is the constitution of their religious imaginations, the constellation of concepts and symbols that shape their worldview. In particular, he highlights a tendency to cast history as the stage for a cosmic war between the forces of good and evil, where the line between ally and enemy, as well as the permissible solutions, are drawn absolutely. The terrorist imagination, Juergensmeyer suggests, is one that has little room for the compromise and accommodation that characterizes life in the modern world. He concludes:

> The radical religious movements that emerged from these cultures of violence throughout the world are remarkably similar, be they Christian, Jewish, Muslim, Buddhist, or Sikh. What they have in common

are three things. First, they have rejected the compromises with liberal values and secular institutions that were made by most mainstream religious leaders and organizations. Second, they refuse to observe the boundaries that secular society has imposed around religion — keeping it private rather than allowing it to intrude into public spaces. And third, they have replaced what they regard as weak modern substitutes with the more vibrant and demanding forms of religion that they imagine to be a part of their tradition's beginnings.[8]

At this point it is worthwhile asking, what is missing from Juergensmeyer's analysis? Or, more accurately, what has disappeared? Ironically, violence has disappeared. As his argument unfolds, the issue becomes not violence but the challenge that some ideas present to the modern liberal political order. Thus, as the passage above indicates, he creates the impression that certain ideas inevitably and inextricably lead to violence. Granted, perpetrators of religious violence may well share certain ideas, but that itself is not sufficient to forge a necessary link between those ideas and violence. In this regard, Juergensmeyer simply ignores religious actors and movements that may be drawn to apocalyptic imagery and reject certain ideological commitments of modernity but who steadfastly refuse recourse to violence.

Likewise, Juergensmeyer ignores religious movements that are thoroughly accommodated to modernity and endorse terrorism. Such neglect may be understandable insofar as such parties have accommodated to liberal modernity and thus are virtually indistinguishable from the prototypical secular Western individuals (and therefore easily overlooked). After all, one of the precepts of modernity is the concealment of religious identity behind the veil of the personal, the private. Nevertheless, it might prove fruitful in this regard to consider adherents of "mainline" religions whose support for the nation-state's use of military force is indiscriminate, who justify terrorist practices like indiscriminate and disproportionate bombing, the use of torture, and various forms of "low-intensity conflict" that target civilian populations in ways that transgress the boundaries of the just war tradition and therefore can be considered forms of terrorism.[9]

That there are many apocalyptic antimodernists who are deeply committed to nonviolence and renounce terror, and many modern religionists who endorse terror, significantly reduces the power of Juergensmeyer's analysis. At the very least, it redirects the cutting power of his judgments. Singling out antimodernist ideas may not shed much light on the riddle of religious violence, but it does bring into the light of day the real issue driving the question of violence that is commonly put to religion. The issue is not violence, but the challenge that the embodiment of particular ideas presents to the dominant, liberal political order. The subtext of Juergensmeyer's work is a critique not of violence but of certain values, whose adherents may or may not embrace violence.

This narrowing of focus to illiberal values, instead of following violence and terror wherever it leads, permits other values that give rise to violence and terror — namely, political liberalism — to escape interrogation. The result is an unexamined liberalism arrayed against an intrinsically violent god. And the question becomes, what can be done to contain this god?

The result is a superficial solution: Temper religion, Juergensmeyer says, with enlightenment. Reject cosmic war and absolutism (said with no apparent recognition of the incongruity of the exhortation, "absolutely reject absolutism").[10] But there is little evidence that enlightened religion leaves the world less bloody. Surveying the course of Western history since the Enlightenment, one could be forgiven for concluding that enlightened religion only delivers us to another, evidently more brutal executioner. It only relinquishes the sword to another, equally adept hand. One could easily conclude that emptying the heavens (banishing the cosmic horizon of history) only paves the way for merely human crusades (wars to end war; wars to rid the world of evil; in pursuit of infinite justice, and so on) by undermining the one and only check on human vindictiveness.

In the end, Juergensmeyer's putting the question of violence to religion is but another instance of the age-old effort to domesticate transcendence, to displace the public, political presence of the church.

R. Scott Appleby begins on a very different note in his *The Ambiva-lence of the Sacred: Religion, Violence, and Reconciliation.*[11] Instead of simply plumbing the terror in God's mind, Appleby is forthright in his desire to encourage the proliferation of public religion that pro-motes peace and justice. Thus the title of the book. Appleby begins with the recognition that religious commitment with regard to vio-lence is ambivalent, that religious militancy is not synonymous with violence but can indeed sow seeds of peace and reconciliation. Several chapters of the book are devoted to the analysis of militant religious peacemaking. Thus, unlike Juergensmeyer, Appleby recognizes that it is not enough to consider ideas; instead, one must attend to how ideas acquire violent sanction. The issue is not simply militancy, but violence. How do the two become connected? Appleby's analysis fo-cuses on matters of leadership, religious literacy (formation), and values.

Unfortunately, as his work unfolds, the initial nuance dissolves. After examining various militant religious movements, Appleby con-cludes that neither types of leadership nor levels of literacy provide clear-cut indicators of whether militancy will issue in violence or peace building. Thus, the question ends up turning on the issue of val-ues. Once again, a study that purports to be about the link between ideas and violence is transposed into a battle of ideas, a critique of values, with similar results — the effacing of militant religious move-ments that challenge modernity's hegemony while rejecting terror, coupled with the not-so-subtle endorsement of the dominant political order's domestication and manipulation of faith.

While Appleby notes that there are substantive and not merely cosmetic differences between the various forms of violent religious militancy, the common thread that appears to unite them is a negative reaction to modern secularization. In particular, Appleby observes that extremists (his name for violent religious militants) tend to hold an apocalyptic and dualist vision of the world that prevents them from engaging in the compromise necessary to engage "outsiders" in a pluralistic world in a spirit of tolerance. The unmistakable message is that antimodernist and illiberal commitments unleash violence.[12]

His treatment of the Latin American liberationists is exemplary in this regard. Mirroring the rhetorical strategy of his larger project, Appleby begins by noting that many liberationists renounce violence, but then he proceeds immediately to ignore this point and cast the liberationists as just another instance of violent religious militancy. Indeed, with a sleight of hand worthy of the liberationists' most uncharitable critics, Appleby concludes his treatment with a blatant misquotation that has a prominent liberationist defend sacred violence on the grounds that one must slaughter or be slaughtered.[13]

Unsurprisingly, this collision of ideas is adjudicated in favor of Western liberal notions of pluralism, tolerance, and inclusiveness. We should foster those strands of religious traditions, Appleby argues, that cultivate tolerance and openness.[14] By this he means we should encourage those faiths that gladly accept their assigned role as a "religion" in the social cartography of the hegemonic liberal order. Obviously, when he writes of tolerance and openness he does not mean that we should tolerate and be open to extremists. Moreover, Appleby suggests that this goal should be pursued by purging religion of its sectarian, exclusivistic, and particularistic elements. He even goes so far as to disparage "first order" religious practice.[15] (I suppose that we should all become urbane, sophisticated university-trained "religionists," who set foot in a sanctuary only out of purely sociological or anthropological interest.)

A Question of Dominion

At this point the correlation between the contemporary treatments of the question of religious violence and the modern effort to safely cordon off the church from independent political power is clear. The issue is not violence, but dominion. Who shall organize social groups and their interaction? The triune God or Leviathan? What is the true configuration of social space? The kingdom of God or Western political liberalism?

Realizing that the question is finally not about violence but dominion proves helpful in our effort to appreciate what the liberationists have to say about peace and violence. To begin with, it helps us to appreciate why it is that the suspicion of "terror" continues to haunt the liberationists. Why is this? Why is it that when the question of religion and violence surfaces, the Latin American liberationists inevitably appear in the lineup of suspected terrorists and their accomplices? Why are they so identified when even the most cursory study of their work reveals that such a suspicion is utterly groundless? Indeed, it would make much more sense to place members of the United Methodist Church on a terrorist watch list, given that the typical United Methodist's reflection on violence is much less disciplined and therefore much more prone to conspire with terror than the liberationists.

Many liberationists hold a principled commitment to nonviolence;[16] many more are pacifist on pragmatic grounds. Most adhere to the just war tradition, which, as it has developed, permits armed conflict within very narrow parameters encompassing both cause (*jus ad bellum*) and effect (*jus in bello*).[17]

Therefore, that the liberationists would be placed on the docket can only be accounted for in light of the preceding discussion. The real issue is not violence or terrorism, but the challenge that the liberationists present to the reigning political order. The issue is not the scale or even the form of violence; after all, as the recent history of Latin America makes agonizingly clear, states regularly engage in terror, torturing, and murdering tens of thousands of people. The issue is the liberationists' bold confrontation with the empire of capitalism. To this challenge we now turn.

The Challenge to Empire

Latin American liberation theology emerged in the late 1960s as a critique of a model of the church that emphasized spiritual verities, while ignoring the material plight of the poor. Over against this spiritualized model of the church, liberationists championed a "church of the poor," a church that promoted the revolutionary cause of justice and the rights of the poor. Although it was a theological movement that addressed distinctly theological topics like models of the church, the person and work of Christ, how to read the Bible, and theological methodology, liberationists are quick to point out that the precipitating factor was not intratheological or intrareligious disputes. Rather, they insist, what prompted this theological revisioning was "the irruption of the poor." Latin America in the 1960s, like much of the world, was immersed in a vortex of anticolonial agitation, and it was the voice of the poor masses, crying out against the dismal poverty that submerged them in inhumane wretchedness and subjected them to premature death, that set the stage for the development of liberation theology. Thus, Gustavo Gutiérrez begins what would become the founding text of the movement, *A Theology of Liberation*, with the statement: "This book is an attempt at reflection, based on the gospel and the experiences of men and women committed to the process of liberation in the oppressed and exploited land of Latin America."[18] Elsewhere, he writes of this irruption of the poor: "The poor, the wretched of the earth, are not in the first instance, questioning the religious world or its philosophical presuppositions. They are calling into question first of all the economic, social, and political order that oppresses and marginalizes them, and of course the ideology that is brought in to justify this domination," and he declares that "this is the context in which the theology of liberation was born and grew."[19]

This introduction to the origins of liberation theology is important for two reasons. First, it reminds us that what put liberation theology on the map was not primarily what it said or did not say about the church (although some liberationists have run into trouble in that regard[20]) or violence (in fact, it says very little). What drew attention to liberation theology was its forthright challenge to the dominant economic, social, and political order of capitalist democracy. Second, it calls our attention to the importance of contextualizing, of locating what the liberationists say within their particular social setting, within their particular historical context.

Three Kinds of Violence

The importance given to contextualizing theology is one of the widely recognized hallmarks and most enduring contributions of Latin American liberation theology. It is particularly evident in liberationists' treatment of violence, inasmuch as they refuse to begin with abstract discussions, instead insisting that the point of departure be the reality of the terrible violence in which the continent is already immersed. As Jon Sobrino states emphatically:

> Speaking of the violence unleashed in Central America in the form of repression, wars and revolutions, we need to make one thing clear at the outset: in these countries, it is not religion that has been at the origin of violence, but injustice, the fruit of capitalism. Religion has therefore found itself caught up in a violence that it has not generated.[21]

Liberationists quickly recognized that violence takes many different forms. "In my own country," writes Gutiérrez, "life nowadays is marked by a hellish cycle of different kinds of violence, each giving rise to the next with increasing rapidity."[22] In a similar vein, Ignacio Martín-Baró characterizes Central America as a crossroads of violence that is conflicted at all levels of life: "Conflict defines our society in all its strata and levels and in all its aspects."[23]

Recognizing the many forms of violence in their context, the liberationists develop a typology of three kinds of violence.[24] The first is the violence identified by the Latin American bishops at Medellín in 1968 as "institutionalized violence." This is the violence of a political and economic order (both national and international) that sacrifices the human rights of the many for the sake of the privileges of the few. It is the violence of a system, of poverty and social injustice accepted under the guise of "law and order," or neoliberal economic programs of structural adjustment.[25] Ellacuría suggests that institutional violence is the "original violence, the root and beginning of all other forms of violence in society," and according to Gutiérrez, institutionalized violence is the most pernicious form of violence because it kills the most young children.[26] Likewise, Sobrino contends that whereas wars and armed struggles are the most obvious forms of violence in Latin America, "the most flagrant violence, which explains almost all the rest, is unjust poverty."[27]

The second type of violence, which is intimately related to the first, is repressive violence. This is the violence of the military and paramilitary groups such as death squads that operate in defense of the oppressive status quo. Often hiding behind the rhetoric of "national security," this violence, Ellacuría suggests, amounts to a legalized or state-sponsored terrorism that hunts down and destroys popular movements.[28]

The first two types, according to liberationists, give rise to the third — revolutionary violence. "What gives rise to the violence of revolutions," observes Franz Hinkelammert, "is the violence involved in putting off solutions to real problems in the old regime.... [T]he violence comes not from the revolution but from the prerevolutionary society."[29] Liberationists describe the goal of revolutionary violence as survival in the face of the empire of death and liberation from what prevents the achievement of a minimum level of human life.[30] This violence is fundamentally different from the types that precede and provoke it because it attempts to affirm the life of the poor, martyred majorities instead of denying life. It differs from institutionalized and repressive violence in its essentially defensive posture — defending instead of attacking basic human rights.[31]

It is difficult to overstate the importance of this typology in the liberationists' discussion of violence. On the one hand, it subverts the double standard that is often at work in discussions of revolutionary violence — a double standard that leads to cries of outrage in the face of armed insurrection and relative silence in the face of repressive regimes whose violence takes institutional and "plausibly deniable" forms such as covert and paramilitary action. As Gutiérrez writes, "This view allows for a study of the complex problems of counterviolence without falling into the pitfalls of a double standard which assumes that violence is acceptable when the oppressor uses it to maintain 'order,' and it is bad when the oppressed invoke it to change this order."[32] On the other hand, the typology provides a foundation for their critique of capitalism, to which we now turn.

The Terror of Capital

By broadening the understanding of the manifold forms that violence takes, particularly institutional and repressive forms, the liberationists create a space for naming and thereby exposing the brutality of the economic order that crushes the poor masses of Latin America. Contrary to the impression created by their critics when liberationists speak about violence, they are not justifying violence, not even within the parameters of the just war tradition, and especially not terrorism. In fact, their overwhelming concern, one could even say preoccupation, is to denounce violence. Specifically, they seek to expose and denounce the violence of an economic order that consigns so many to premature death.

In the early years, this critique of the violence of capitalism proceeded in terms of what is known as dependency theory. According to dependency theory, poverty and underdevelopment are not the result of a region's failure to rationalize its economy in accord with the dictates of liberal capitalism. The inhumane wretchedness of much of Latin America is not the consequence of the persistence of traditional forms of life and passive, static habits of mind and character. Widespread misery and malnutrition is not a product of a country's stubborn failure to follow the path of developed nations. On the contrary, the devastating and persistent poverty is a consequence of the advance of capitalism; it is the result of the way countries on the periphery of the global capitalist economy are dominated and exploited by those at the center. More plainly, poverty persists in Latin America because it has been subsumed by the global capitalist order in ways that its wealth does not nourish its own people, but instead feeds and fuels and clothes the prosperity of others.

Dependency theory has undergone serious critique, principally for the way simplistic proponents focused too narrowly on external forms of dominion to the exclusion of internal factors. Liberationists, however, largely avoided the force of this critique because, oriented as they were by class analysis, they always considered internal actors in their analysis of capitalist violence. Indeed, over the years their denunciation of the violence of capitalism has neither wavered nor weakened. If anything it has intensified.

The critique of Franz Hinkelammert offered after the collapse of global socialism in 1989 is a prime example. Even when socialism had fallen, he prophetically condemned what he calls the advent of a new era of "savage capitalism."[33] His critique proceeded in the form of three theses.

The first thesis is nothing less than a concession of defeat. Hinkelammert acknowledges capitalism's victory. Capitalism has won. Its rivals have been soundly defeated:

> The world that now appears and announces itself is a world in which there exists only one lord and master, and only one system.... [T]here no longer remains any place of asylum.... The empire is everywhere. It has total power and it knows it.... The consciousness that an alternative exists is lost. It seems there are no longer alternatives.[34]

For the Third World, this amounts to being severed from even the minimal assistance it had previously received. With the ascendancy of the capitalist order, with the extension of its empire, Third World countries lost the strategic importance they once possessed as pawns that the competing superpowers would often pit against each other.

The Third World now finds itself adrift in the midst of what Hinkelammert calls "wild" or "savage" capitalism.[35] In the 1950s and 1960s capitalism was tempered by a reformist current that went by the name of "developmentalism." At that time, even as the capitalist market was acknowledged to be largely self-regulating, it was nevertheless recognized that the market, left to its own devices, was unable to assure development and solve the grave social-economic problems that afflicted Latin America. Consequently, the welfare state, public investment, and industrialization by means of import substitution were all accepted components of this "capitalism with a human face."[36] The 1970s, however, marked a shift toward a more extreme, unfettered capitalism. This was the beginning of the era of Milton Friedman's "total capitalism," of neoliberal economics, and "structural adjustment." This is the capitalism of the era for which Ronald Reagan and Margaret Thatcher are icons: anti-interventionist, antireformist, antipopulist. In short, capitalism without its human face.

One of the central precepts of this naked capitalism is an aggressive antistatism. In contrast to the earlier phase of capitalism, which conceded a necessary regulatory role to the state, savage capitalism denounces all state intervention in the market and sets about dismantling the welfare state and selling off state-owned enterprises. In Latin America this antistatism was incarnate in the national security states that appeared in the seventies and eighties — Chile under Pinochet being the paradigmatic example. This antistatism, however, is deceptive. It amounts to a minimalist state that only renounces its regulatory and welfare role. While savage capitalism's advocates say they are antistatist, in truth what they favor is a "small-state, strong-state."[37] That is, they are advocates of a state that is long on repressive capability and short on social assistance. What is forsaken is not intervention, but intervention that obstructs the free operation of the market. This neoliberal state is a police state, the function of which is essentially negative. It exists as a repressive tool of the market, used to deliver society to the market.

With the advent of savage capitalism, states Hinkelammert's second thesis, the population of the Third World is no longer needed. Production in the Third World has traditionally developed on the basis of its labor force and its raw materials. Today, however, that labor force is increasingly being rendered superfluous because of advances in production technology. "The First World still needs the Third World," Hinkelammert writes, "its seas, its air, its nature, even if only as a garbage dump for the First World's poisonous garbage. Its raw materials continue being needed. What is no longer needed is the greater part of the population of the Third World."[38] The market's logic of maximum efficiency entails the sacrifice of the redundant populations. Hence, with the arrival of savage capitalism, it becomes a privilege to be exploited. Hinkelammert cites a Latin American saying, "It is bad to be exploited by the multinationals. It is worse, however, not to be exploited by them."[39] Third World countries increasingly find themselves competing with one another for limited openings in the international capitalist market, with the consequence that more and more people are not even able to find a place on the margins of this system. They are excluded, discarded to wander outside the production system, foraging in the garbage dumps and making newspaper cakes for their children.[40]

Hinkelammert's third thesis is that in this situation development is not possible for Third World countries. Indeed, the controlling countries consider Third World development on the basis of industrial integration into the world market a threat.[41] Third World development is perceived no longer as a goal to be attained, but as a threat to be squelched. With its arrival in the 1970s, savage capitalism did not establish industry that could competitively enter the world market. Rather, it renounced industrialization and silenced the masses with the terrorism of the national security state. Instead of fostering efficient enterprise, it reduced Latin America, once again, to the exportation of raw materials and agricultural products. Instead of overcoming underdevelopment, an efficient underdevelopment was pursued.[42] Even if a few small countries have escaped the First World's grip, the visible tendency in the Third World is away from self-sustainable industrialization. Even those industries that were established in prior decades have been targeted for destruction or stagnation. The First World countries no longer see any advantage to be gained from allowing and encouraging this kind of development. Accordingly, savage capitalism opts for the maximization of profit over development. Perhaps the clearest example of this policy is the collection of the Third World's foreign debt. The debt is the primary tool with which Third World development is suppressed. The structural adjustment policies that are part and parcel of that debt ensure that the debtor country will be unable to develop in a manner that would allow it to achieve any possibility of repaying the debt. In this way, Hinkelammert argues, the West has found a method of shedding blood that easily allows it to wash any stain off its hands.[43]

Such was the critique leveled in the aftermath of the downfall of socialism. Since the collapse of the World Trade Centers, the critique of the empire has continued unabated. Liberationists persist in denouncing the violence of the capitalist order. They point out the ways the war on terrorism is being used as a cover for advancing capitalist ends, whether by bringing the threat of force to bear on negotiations concerning Latin America's continual exposure to capitalist exploitation via the Free Trade Area of the Americas,[44] or eroding human rights, thereby hastening the transformation of the human being into mere human capital.[45] Adapting the rhetoric of the day, they now speak of the "terrorism of the market" and of capitalist fundamentalism.[46]

In the light of this relentless denunciation of the capitalist order, it is unsurprising that the liberationists find themselves in the dock. In a world where "those who are not with us are with the terrorists," it can hardly be unexpected that the liberationists would be lumped together with terrorists and violent militants. After all, the real issue is dominion, and the liberationists clearly do not ally themselves with the capitalist fundamentalists who seek to strengthen and extend the empire of capital. More than this, they want to see the dominant capitalist order overturned. Does this mean that they do indeed side with terrorists? What form does this resistance to empire take?

The God Who Takes Sides

The liberationists are forthright that Christians should take sides in the struggles of history. However, the liberationists are sometimes portrayed as if they were really just garden-variety Marxists cynically using religion as a cover for the promotion of class warfare, envy, and hatred of the rich. From this caricature, it is but a small step to hijacking planes, terrorism, and the second September 11 (the first being September 11, 1973, when Pinochet initiated his bloody coup in Chile).[47] Such a caricature, however, could hardly be further from the truth. For the challenge that they present wells up from their faith, from their reading of scripture, and from their living out the Christian life in the midst of profound and enduring misery. As Gutiérrez writes, "The ultimate reason for a commitment to the poor and oppressed does not lie in the social analysis that we employ, or in our human compassion, or in the direct experience we may have of poverty.... [A]s Christians, we base that commitment fundamentally on the God of our faith."[48]

To many such a claim sounds hollow, incomprehensible, and incoherent. After all, is not the Christian God one of boundless love, of gentle faith, of the sweet hope that binds us all — rich and poor, gringo and Hispanic, citizens of the First World and Third World — together? Does not God love universally, which is to say, does not God love everyone the same? Not according to the liberationists. According to their understanding of the faith, God unequivocally takes sides. This recognition is captured in the well-known phrase, "preferential option for the poor." God is not neutral with regard to the divisions that rend this world; God is not enthroned in the transcendent heavens, wistfully wringing sweaty hands and shaking a sorrowful head, but finally doing nothing as we squabble below. On the contrary, God is partisan. The Bible is the story of God's intervention on behalf of justice for the weak, the poor, the widow, the orphan. The Incarnation was a partisan act: God taking sides by taking on poor flesh. From this it follows that God loves in a partisan manner. God's love is not some sweet sentimentality, but conflictive. To speak of God's love is to speak of how God entered into the struggles of this world in order to liberate the oppressed and establish justice. And this in no way undercuts the breadth of God's love. God does love everyone universally, but, the liberationists argue, God does not love everyone in the same way. Thus, writes Sobrino, "Jesus acted out of love and was for all human beings. But he was for them in different ways. Out of love for the poor, he took his stand *with* them; out of love for the rich, he took his stand *against* them."[49]

From the recognition that God is partisan springs one of the more controversial elements of the liberationists' work, namely, the emphasis placed on social conflict. As Hugo Assmann notes, social conflict is "a constant rather than occasional theme" in the liberationists' work.[50] In accord with their vision of a God who takes sides, who seeks justice, the liberationists insist that Christians cannot ignore conflict or attempt to remain above conflict in a stance of pseudo-neutrality. The God who does justice demands that one enter the fray by choosing sides for some and against others. As Gutiérrez observes, those who seek justice cannot avoid conflict, because in a society scarred by injustice and the exploitation of one social class by another, the proclamation of justice will transform history into something challenging and conflictual.[51]

This association of the pursuit of justice with social conflict has spurred a host of allegations about the liberationists' proclivity toward violence, from making class struggle the engine of history to being apologists for terrorism. Such charges, however, miss the mark. Far from being a call to arms, the liberationists understand the recognition of social conflict to be nothing more than the acknowledgment of a painful historical fact. Gutiérrez states:

> No one agrees with a situation in which human beings come into conflict. And in fact the situation is not "acceptable," either humanly or in a Christian perspective. Conflict is undoubtedly one of the most painful phenomena in human life. We should like things to be different, and we ought to look for ways of getting rid of these oppositions, but on the other hand — and this is the point I want to make — we cannot avoid facing up to the situation as it actually is, nor can we disregard the causes that produce it.[52]

Social conflict is a reality that the liberationists, as long as they do not avert their eyes from the squalor that surrounds them and maintain their commitment to the God who does justice, cannot escape.

Thus, when the liberationists give a prominent place to social conflict in their work, they are neither asserting the ontological necessity of violence nor establishing conflict as a law of history.[53] On the contrary, far from blessing conflict, they are critical of any theology that would baptize revolution or promote conflict.[54] They do not believe that the juxtaposition of oppressors and oppressed is inevitable and that justice can come only at the point of a sword or through the barrel of a gun. On the contrary, social conflict is ultimately the product of sin; it is the historical consequence of collective sin.[55] As such, liberationists understand it to be a contingent historical reality. Humanity need not live in conflict; persons do not need to oppress their sisters and brothers. Conflict can be resolved. The resolution of social conflict, in fact, is precisely why the liberationists give conflict such a visible position. They seek to resolve it by uncovering it and then eliminating its cause, injustice. The alternative to uncovering and resolving conflict is resignation, despair, and finally death.

Martyrdom and the Crucified Peoples

Following Christ the liberator, Christians enter into a conflicted history that is already crossed by institutional and repressive forms of violence. And it is true, as noted previously, that most liberationists who have addressed the issue do not renounce all recourse to violence. Most are not pacifists. Yet, as I have suggested here, all denounce terrorism, and those who do admit the possibility of legitimate revolutionary violence do so only within the disciplined restraint of the just war tradition. This having been said, the heart of the liberationists' vision of resistance to the violence of capital is not fomenting just, revolutionary counterviolence. Although they affirm the possibility, they do not encourage its enactment in reality. Instead, the heart of their vision, in the words of Ellacuría, is the Christian's "clear vocation to peace," a vocation that "points to a preference for unarmed struggle against injustice."[56]

Thus, a far more accurate description of the liberationists than the patently absurd label, "apologists for terror," might be "companions of the martyrs."[57] Indeed, it has even been suggested in recent years that the designation "theology of liberation" ought to be broadened to a "theology of martyrdom."[58] Such a move would be appropriate,

Sobrino explains, because "martyrdom...is the fullest, most integral expression of the incarnation that takes place in concrete Latin American reality."[59]

Martyrdom certainly comes closer than "terror" to the spirit of the liberationists' work and its impact. The spirituality of liberation, and the political holiness it calls forth, finds its center not in the avenger's sword but in Christ's cross and the promise of his resurrection. A spirituality of liberation does not nurture a "mysticism of violence," which, like far too many movies and politicians, insists that violence redeems, that violence can deliver us from evil. Instead, it fosters a cruciform love. The spirituality of liberation arises out of the christological insight that sin, and the unjust suffering that is a consequence of sin, is defeated precisely by its being borne. Reflecting on the cross, Sobrino observes that "what God's suffering makes clear in a history of suffering is that between the alternatives of accepting suffering by sublimating it and eliminating it from the outside we can and must introduce a new course, bearing it."[60] Liberationists point to the truth of the cross and resurrection: that Christ liberates us from the sin of capitalism not simply by opposing its destructive force with an equally destructive force but rather by countering it with a love that bears its violence in the hope of bearing it away.[61]

Thus, the icon of liberation theology is not Che Guevara fighting in the jungle, but Archbishop Oscar Romero, murdered while celebrating the Eucharist. And the ranks of this movement are not filled by wild-eyed guerrillas and shifty terrorists, but by those whom Ellacuría has poignantly called "the crucified peoples." The crucified peoples are the ones who bear the sins of the (developed, first, capitalist) world in the faith and hope of God's promised deliverance. They are the ones who have been gathered by the Spirit into the church of the poor, and it is they who, according to the liberationists, embody the suffering servant today (see Isaiah). "In Latin America," writes Sobrino, "the crucified people are the actualization of Christ crucified, the true servant of Yahweh."[62] As such, the crucified church of the poor is the vehicle of salvation insofar as, like the servant of Isaiah, it is the chosen mediator of God's good news to all of humanity. The crucified people are bearers of salvation insofar as it is precisely in and through them that God confronts oppressors with the good news of salvation.

The End of All Struggle

It is time to draw this defense to a close. The liberationists confront the empire of capital not with a crusade of envious and bloodthirsty rabble but with the long-suffering faith of the crucified. And when this confrontation is finally ended, when the powers and principalities finally realize that their cause is lost (indeed, was never worth winning in the first place), this world will not look like the silent fields of El Mozote, the day after hundreds of campesinos — men, women, and children — were cut down in cold blood by a battalion specially armed and trained by an administration determined to crush resistance to the advance of capital by any means necessary.[63] Nor will this world be covered with the fine gray ash of death spewed from a furnace of nihilistic rage, like that which blanketed not only the streets of New York City but the very soul of North America on September 11, 2001.

When the struggle has ended, the peace that descends upon us will not be a morbid one, like that which lingers over the graves of one's defeated and destroyed foes. The end of the struggle that the liberationists enjoin is not destruction, but peace — the true peace that is (and can only be) the fruit of forgiveness and reconciliation.[64] The liberationists recognize that at the root of all sin lies a breach of communion, a rupture of the bonds of fraternal love. Hence, the liberation they herald is nothing less than the renewal of the communion of all in the circle of charity that is the blessed Trinity,[65] where every tear is wiped away, where all thirst is slaked and hunger satisfied, where everyone belongs, and death is no more. Is this a terrifying outcome?

Latin American liberation theology is in the dock, not because it remotely sanctions terrorism, but because it challenges the empire, because it announces the appearance of a social, political, personal, spiritual kingdom ("integral liberation") that cannot be marketed,

structurally adjusted, sanctioned, privatized, liberalized, commodi-
fied, outsourced, downsized, or finally even bombed to make it fit
like another consumer good on the shelf allotted for it at Wal-Mart
by the empire. It announces the One who can indeed put a hook in
Leviathan's mouth (Job 41:1) and bring every empire to its knees
(Phil. 2:5–11). To the empire of capital, this is truly terrifying.

Nine

Revitalization Movements and Violence

JOHN MOHAWK

The tone of the next essay is different than previous ones. John Mohawk speaks from his Native American heritage combined with his training as an American historian. This gives Mohawk a distinctive insight into the relationships between religion and culture and subtle ways that religion might work in behalf of violence or peace.

Mohawk had rather not talk about institutional religion, but speaks of "revitalization movements," which are often sustained by religious traditions or integral to particular religions. From his perspective, revitalization ideology is the element within religious traditions that usually creates a mammoth obstacle for religious dialogue to take place. These movements are most often started by a group who feel disenfranchised and who take action to restore their lost identity by seeking a "paradise regained," returning to an idealized past and creating an idealized future. They tend to reflect attitudes of inflexibility toward other religions rather than dialogue.

Speaking almost prophetically, Mohawk warns his readers that revitalization movements have historically spawned much violence in the world. From the Crusades to Nazism to Marxism, the quest for the Ideal was combined with the call to restore the lost rights and privileges of those who felt they had been cheated — by another political system or religion. Mohawk argues that the agenda of Usama bin Laden also fits into the blueprint of revitalization movements. With equal soberness Mohawk warns that America's own national psyche includes the same delusion in a different format. The mythic ideal of a global economy that siphons nature's last remaining resources with the United States in military control portends violence, not peace.

This perspective is especially relevant in relation to two previous essays, "Dangerous Faith" and "Latin American Liberation Theology." The Christian tradition that influences President Bush's thinking about the world and the future includes many strands of revitalization thinking. On the other hand, the same strands of thinking are at work in many of the critiques of Latin American theologies. Mohawk stimulates us to be cautious about motivations that are tremendously intertwined with religious convictions but function in the psyche of an entire culture.

Provocations for Dialogue

1. *Does the philosophical concept of "the Ideal" hinder or help religious dialogue for peace? Are there alternatives to this Aristotelian model within religious traditions?*

2. *Should religions attempt to "purify" cultures by means of religious convictions? Is there any validity in speaking about "a Christian America" or "a Muslim nation"?*

3. *Are there alternatives for religions than to seek a "paradise regained" that would promote peace instead of violence?*

• • •

THE LATVIAN PHILOSOPHER Isaiah Berlin, more than anybody I have read, illumines the meaning of the idea of the "pursuit of the Ideal" of Western culture. I propose that when one attempts to assess a culture at any given time, the key question is the one that Berlin asked: How are people thinking, and how has their thinking shaped their culture? Berlin also understood the divide between philosophy and history. At one point in his book *The Crooked Timber of Humanity*, he describes how historians and philosophers do not get along because philosophers have one expectation of history and historians record a different one.[1]

A second thinker who has influenced me is Anthony F. C. Wallace, a premiere American anthropologist in the 1950s. He wrote an article entitled "Revitalization Movements," which was published in the *American Anthropologist*. It has become one of the foundation articles of contemporary anthropology.[2] Subsequently, he wrote a book, *The Death and Rebirth of a Seneca*, which is a recounting of the career of the native Seneca prophet Handsome Lake.[3] I suppose that is how I came under his influence, because I grew up in the community of native people who practice the religion of Handsome Lake. Throughout my career I have been keenly interested in what Wallace had to say about understanding how cultures function. As I read Wallace, the disconnection between what I had been taught about my culture and what other people thought about it became increasingly clear.

Critical to my thinking is his contention that two kinds of revitalization movements — progressive and regressive revitalization movements — have been present throughout history. Wallace proposed that revitalization movements are very common. At any given moment, hundreds of them are happening throughout the world, yet, they are usually not recognized as revitalization movements. In fact, we do not even have language outside of anthropology to talk about them. My thesis is that we need to evoke a language to talk about them that is multidisciplinary.

A revitalization movement happens when a people within a cultural group determine that they are being denied the full benefits of their culture. This situation rises often when someone perceives that they are being repressed or exploited. It is not difficult to grasp why non-Western tribal cultures might feel that way, especially when they are confronted with some element of Western culture. I would propose that the most famous revitalization movement for many native people is the Ghost Dance ritual that took place in the northern Great Plains during the latter part of the nineteenth century. Let us consider this ritual in order to clarify some of the most important elements of a revitalization movement.

The Indians in the northern Great Plains had suffered a calamity in the 1870s. Across the northern Great Plains one of the most violent ecological and human changes to take place in history occurred. In that period the American invasion westward confronted a west populated by an estimated 73 million buffalos. In the course of about six years, a giant buffalo hunt resulted in a slaughter that nearly drove the buffalo to extinction. When the buffalos disappeared, the Indians who depended on the buffalos were left in a very serious quandary. Angie Debo's *A History of the Indians of the United States* recounts the consequences. Without the resource of buffalo and the vegetation that was lost, most of the people who lived in that area disappeared within about a decade. One would be hard pressed to find another place that large with that much change that fast. It left people utterly stunned, without a food supply and without control of their territory. Often they were driven onto reservations, which were to the Native American psyche much like concentration camps. They were told they could not leave. People were disarmed, and their means of transportation were taken from them. It is hard to imagine what it was like psychologically. During this ordeal, one of the people had a vision. He told the people that the answer to their problem would be found in embracing some of the cultural traditions of their past. He focused on a dance, and he said that if the people were to dance they could dance until the buffalo would be reborn and the people who had died from diseases and wars would be replaced and life would return the way it was before the calamity happened.[4]

This story of the beginning of the Ghost Dance is typical of how a revitalization movement works. Some group really feels that it is threatened with extinction or it has been robbed. In desperation the group decides to recover the lost remnants of its culture, and so it focuses on an answer that leads it to reclaim its culture.

Revitalization movements tend to take groups in two directions. On the one hand, people who have discovered something that they feel can revive them from the depths of chaos to restoration often focus all their energy on a plan to initiate that revival. They embrace that plan with an enthusiasm that is quite astonishing. A revitalization movement is not a revitalization movement until there is an enthusiasm for something that will actually bring restoration. If a revitalization movement is nothing more than an enthusiastic embrace of an idea to restore some people's dignity by coming out of their distress, then there are literally hundreds of them going on in any given moment. Some of them are quite innocent, harmless, or even productive. American culture is particularly filled with them. Anybody who lives in central New York knows that there was a moment when the Erie Canal met the immigrants. And then there was the entire Industrial Revolution. In those moments, revitalization movements were the business of the day. All along that canal route there are evidences of that, and many of them still survive. Revitalization movements, however, encompass another distinguishing factor, one that is negative. Those who are enthusiastic because they believe they have discovered a way to correct the wrongs done against them tend to pursue this with an enthusiasm that can end in one of two results: (1) It can either take them into harm's way, or (2) it can carry them into a movement that puts other people's well-being in jeopardy.

This leads revitalization movements in the second direction. Arriving at a solution to solve all of your problems at one time leads people to envision a state of utopia. The concept of utopia is a very interesting idea that has a long life span in Western culture. A utopia refers to a place and time that does not actually exist. Nevertheless, humans have dreamed of utopias as far back as historical memory has existed. Further, the Western idea of utopia is heavily dependent on the biblical narrative about the Garden of Eden. It was a perfect place. Life was wonderful. But problems arose, and so people have a story to tell about their trek. In a way, you could say that the origins of the Judeo-Christian tradition are about the adventures of a group that had been expelled from utopia. Beyond that there are many times when people imagine that they have a plan or a place that would have been perfect and that it is their rightful inheritance. For the most part, however, there exists a kind of intense desire of some group, and then, after the movement runs through a course of intensive and extreme enthusiasm, it is taken over by waiting and waiting and waiting for something to happen. If it does not happen after a while, the group has to accommodate, so it changes over time. Revitalization movements do not stay the same, therefore, since nobody can achieve utopia. The movement tends to evolve, maturing and becoming less intense.[5]

Until the nineteenth century, probably the most intensive kinds of revitalization movements had religious associations. Their utopian vision provided popular visionary glue, imagining some sort of divine or supernatural intervention that would come and rescue the group that was under distress, re-creating Eden.

In the nineteenth century, we start seeing utopian ideologies arise that were secular in nature, one of the most prominent being Marxist utopianism. Here was an idea that history was on the side of the workers. They would overthrow the ruling class and would take over and create a utopian society of workers. The Marxist ideology moved along with a more or less academic fervor for years until the Russian Revolution in 1917, when this idea became embodied in a military dictatorship. When it had the state behind it, the Marxist ideology became a full-fledged revitalization movement. Laborers who worked all day in a shoe factory demanded better working conditions. They solidified their solidarity in cell group meetings. It was at heart an intellectual utopian movement. They had no access to the vast resources of their country, but nonetheless they mobilized around utopian ideas in ways that most of us would consider not very realistic. The most powerful part of this movement was the idea that you could transform a peasant society into a modern-state farm society. The revolutionary Soviet leaders basically dismantled what was probably the most successful peasant society in the world and replaced it with a communal agriculture society. Millions of people actually died as a result of this effort.

The most important revitalization movement to study is undoubtedly Nazism. Nazism is a classic revitalization movement in that it begins with those Germans who felt that they had been denied their natural inheritance. After being devastated in World War I, they did not want to blame themselves. A group arose that tried to identify the problem which had caused their defeat. They concluded that someone else must have been responsible for their trauma. The Jews became their scapegoat, taking away responsibility from Germany for its own difficulties. The Nazi movement identified the Jews as being the people who had double-crossed them during the war, causing the defeat of Germany.

All of Germany's problems flowed out of that premise. There are a few other things about the German revitalization movement, however, that are important to note. One is the level of enthusiasm with which the German people embraced the ideology that was brought to them by a small group of intensive ideologues. The intensity of that emotional embrace is very important. Some readers may remember how often the Nazis showed films of Adolf Hitler speaking to huge throngs of the German people. These films are fascinating on two levels; first, because of the intensity of Hitler's presentation, and second, because of the intense reaction of the crowd. Throngs of people cheered. Columns of pageantry that could have been from a Cecil B. DeMille movie marched before the cameras. There were flags, uniforms, and everybody marched in lockstep. The participants were practically ecstatic. Watching the films with the sound muted, you would wonder what he was saying to so electrify a crowd that way.

Over the years I have studied Hitler's speeches. In print they are not that exciting. Why the excitement then? I think the key is that Hitler addressed a people who had been both defeated in war and also relegated by other Europeans to a second-class status. Furthermore, the Allies did themselves no favor by demanding punitive damages from Germany after the war. Some punishment involved the transfer of land and people, that is, deportation. When Germany could not pay their debts, areas were seized from Germany. In this seemingly hopeless situation the people sank into a state of desperation. Hitler had an answer for that hopelessness: first, to declare that the German people had been cheated not only out of their inheritance at the moment, but out of their inheritance throughout history. He pointed to an idealized moment in the German past where he imagined the Germans as an ideal people, a perfect people. The moment he pointed to was a moment he described as being the period of *Das Volk*, a time just prior to the Roman conquest. In this mythic, utopian beginning, the people were depicted as industrious and creative. Nazism was actually a movement to return to this idyllic past. For Hitler, the first step required the conviction that others had stripped Germany of its rightful past. Germany could rise out of this victimization only if it could muster enough people inside contemporary German culture to reverse their fortunes.

A second step was to use science to this end. Central to this concentration on science was the application of genetics to create a perfect human person, a perfect human race — an *Übermensch*. A perfect being, Hitler surmised, would have the capacity to create a perfect nation and a perfect world. Of course, this strategy to recover Germany's mythic past also led to the question of why an ideal world would need other lesser humans who were consuming resources and land that these superior beings could be using.

An ideal people required a "place" to live and from which to expand. They needed room to live — a *Lebensraum*. Yet surprisingly the Nazis were not interested in conquering overseas empires. They wanted a European empire controlled by Germany. They aimed to move into Eastern Europe to create a "Third Reich" in that space. The war that Germany launched, then, was not exactly a war of conquest, but a war to make space for an idyllic people and nation. It has a kind of logic all to itself. If you embrace the logic, it makes the rest of the movement make sense. Hitler knew that if the rest of the industrialized world in 1940 opposed Germany, then Germany would probably lose the war. At one point he wrote that if they lost the war, the Jews still would not win. It is widely believed that he ordered the murder of the Jews in retaliation for the loss of World War I on the one hand, and the probable loss of the war he was waging at that moment on the other. It is very likely that those were connected.

Sadly, violent consequences often follow imagined utopias. If you believe fervently that you have a plan to restore your originally perfect state, you also believe that all of your cultures' problems can be solved. On the way to this utopia, however, you tend to give yourself permission to do things that in other moments in history you would not have done. You tend to release yourself from the common moral boundaries of human behavior. What is it that should not be paid in order to solve all your problems? What price would there be? First, throughout history people have concluded that no price is too dear to pay if you can solve those problems. The utopian end allows for any and all means. Second, quite often the group that does this decides that some other group should pay the price. A utopia requires some unpleasant side effects. As the saying goes, if you are going to make an omelet, you have to break a few eggs. In the case of Germany, the unpleasant thing was that they believed that they had to eliminate large populations of people who were occupying the land that they desired to possess. Among many studies in recent years, perhaps the most interesting is Daniel Goldhagen's *Hitler's Willing Executioners*, in which he asks, "How could anyone, any nation, actually do the things the Nazis did?"[6] When Germans entered the small towns in Eastern Europe in 1941 and 1942 they targeted specific populations for elimination. German soldiers marched into an elementary school, rounded up all the fourth graders, and marched to a ditch outside of town and shot them dead. You wonder, What kind of people could do that? What kind of people could shoot little kids? The chilling reality is not that it was a group of crazed Nazis that did it. It was not the Waffen SS or some motorcycle soldiers inside of Germany. Everyday, ordinary soldiers did it. These soldiers had been shopkeepers, high school teachers, and social workers. Yet they killed innocent children, and they went on and on doing it. Then German leaders turned to their medical profession and asked the doctors what would be the best way to kill large numbers of people. The medical profession responded with gas chambers. The soldiers built camps, trained executioners, and devised elaborate schemes of gathering victims and transporting them to the death camps. Thus, in the death camps the mechanism of death was transformed into an academic endeavor.

A tremendous cry was heard at the end of the war when people became conscious that one of the most savage instances of human behavior in human society was perpetrated not by a stone-age people living in the backwaters, not by cannibals on some remote island, but by the Germans, a developed society at the heart of European culture.

In almost every case of genocide this kind of ideology underlies a movement. The vision of an idealized society is promoted, and the group seeks the ideal murder if it believes that it can be triumphant and achieve its goal, albeit through such atrocities. It is no accident that when the recent war broke out in Serbia the revitalization of some very ancient ideas about Serbia emerged. Promoters of the reestablishment of Serbia called it "heavenly Serbia." The pattern is common. Idealized aims enable people to commit terrible acts of horror and sometimes put themselves in perilous straits.

Many Germans today are fascinated by the conditions that allowed them as a people to behave in the way they did. The Germans who were born after Nazism look back at their culture and wonder how that could have happened to them. Yet the history of Germany is not unique. The Germans are very much like all of us. Nazism is remarkable only because of its almost universal condemnation; other people have done similar things and they were not as universally condemned as was Nazism. Many times in history we have seen people who set off on a path intended to be a corrective and yet that ended up as a kind of total disaster.

Consider how much Germany put itself in harm's way. Here was a leader who carried people into a war that was devastating to his country. Large numbers of its people were killed. There was hardly an undamaged building in all of Germany by the end of the war. Cities were leveled, and the amount of cost that Hitler brought upon them is incalculable. Even if we do not look at the damage Hitler did to other nations and peoples, consider what damage Hitler did to Germany. Yet, all of these facts notwithstanding, it is absolutely remarkable that one of the most popular politicians in the twentieth century was none other than Adolf Hitler. Why? Not because Adolf

Hitler offered people a plan. He did not have a blueprint. He had a kind of mythological idealism.

We would like to think that the darkest people in history were actually monsters. You can see a monster and know it is evil. Surely you would know evil when you see it, would you not? On the contrary, people do not know evil when they see it, because evil comes wrapped in a promising idealism. It is a person who is offering a desperate people a plan to get to a better place if only they are willing to suffer and sacrifice. The atmosphere is created where people are doing some things you would not normally do. Much enthusiasm exists for ideas that could put other people into great danger. When this formula is invoked, you will find a guy at a podium with two hundred thousand people in uniform, all screaming in unison "Heil Hitler!" Of course, today we would not have that, would we? You would not even be able really to grasp it. However, people have a great deal of trouble sorting out when their enthusiasm is in a good place or a bad one, morally upright or subtly twisted. People glibly accept enthusiasm as a good thing in and of itself.

At this point we need to acknowledge the double-edged sword of religion. Religion can mitigate a response against such irrational exuberance. It may serve as a self-critical balance for uncritical enthusiasm because it has always been very aware about the subtleness of radical evil. But the other edge of the sword spells trouble. Most revitalization movements either founded a religion or used religion for their own purposes. Many religious movements and revitalization movements have been tied together. Even a pope started one. The "peasant's crusade" actually followed the pattern of a revitalization movement. It began in the despair and anger that their "promised land" had been illegally taken from them. Christian peasants mobilized with great enthusiasm. Unarmed and untrained in military operations they crossed the Bosporus and marched toward the Holy Land. They relied on a promise from the pope that once they reclaimed the Holy Land, they would end up rich. Anyone who died along the way would go straight to heaven. Later, a whole army of children marched a similar march under the same motivations. I hear you can still find their bones in Anatolia.

Revitalization movements are movements that generate great enthusiasm, and usually the participants follow their leaders to disaster. How does this relate to our world today? We are faced with some contemporary issues that involve revitalization movements, especially in the worldwide movement of militant Islam. The work of Usama bin Laden is a mini-revitalization movement. As a charismatic leader he has convinced many Muslims that America has illegally taken control of Muslim nations. He thought that if he could get the Americans to invade Afghanistan, the Taliban would defeat the Americans, and thus lead militant Muslims to the overthrow of all the Islamic governments who have cooperated with America and replace them with militant regimes. He actually hopes some day to have one unified Islamic empire. The enthusiasm we have seen already among bin Laden's recruits has been extraordinarily destructive. When young Muslims have been willing to sacrifice their lives in pursuit of an ideology of which no one can tell you the end game, or whose end game sounds extremely suspicious, you have established the ground on which to build a revitalization movement.

Who could possibly believe that a few thousand Afghan fighters would defeat the U.S. military? If you could believe they could do that and could enlist millions of enthusiastic followers in pursuit of a plan that any rational person knows is deranged, then you become a vital part of a revitalization movement. Some appear less caustic than others, but in the end, they all follow essentially the same path. When they become irrationally militant, they leave a wake of destruction behind. They are willing to inflict great destruction in order to get to that place that they think needs to be gotten to. They will embark on this course, however, almost always without a clear end or a clear plan. That was true of Hitler and it was true of the people who led the peasants' and children's crusades. They marched across Europe sixty thousand strong. At Constantinople they stopped. The people in Constantinople asked them, "Okay, what's the plan?" and the leaders said, "When we get there, we are going to liberate Jerusalem and prepare for the Second Coming." So they ferried across the river and marched across Anatolia through some of the most horrible military campaigns in world history. Only twenty thousand of them made it; forty thousand of them died. In Lebanon they were so hungry they committed acts of cannibalism in their campaign against small cities. But they were eventually successful. They broke down the gates of Jerusalem and they murdered everybody in it. They threw up their flag, and then they started to carve the place into Crusader states. At last, the people in that part of the world said, "No more," and re-volted. Some people are still fighting that war. It would have been nice to grab one of those Crusaders on their way into Lebanon and ask them, "What happens when you get to Lebanon, guys?" Of course, their answer was that all of their dreams would be fulfilled. That is a pretty hard thing — to counter people who are willing to march on the basis of a dream, even if the dream really is not very realistic, even if the dream could end up with very, very negative consequences.

A quite different yet similarly frightening prospect beyond the global threat of al-Qaeda resides subtly in our homeland, America. It has to do with Isaiah Berlin's very poignant analysis of what he saw in Western culture's pursuit of "the Ideal." A great ecological disaster looms on the horizon. Fish in all the great oceans of the world are declining dramatically, and we are seeing shifts in agricultural pro-duction that we should be worrying about. The world is running out of water. Humans currently envision a mythic ideal that allows us to pump the last gallon of water from the earth, to catch the last fish in the sea, and cut down the last tree in the forests. We must ask: "We set up the world economy — what now? We got the last fish, the last tree, and the last gallon of water. What's next?" Quite frankly, when you are pursuing an ideal to globalize the world's economies as a solution to all our problems and make a perfect world, you do not have to answer questions like that. As a matter of fact, as I under-stand the plan, you do not answer any questions at all. Yet, this type of idealistic thinking that currently consumes Western global revital-ization thinkers is in the end delusional. Once militarized, if history is any key to truth, this utopian dream portends radical violence on a global scale. If the quest for the Ideal is motivated by religious zeal, as may be true with some of our top government leaders now, then the violence becomes self-righteous and even more dangerous. Then the massive destruction is justified by the delusion that our country is actually carrying out God's will.

Conclusion

I have made two basic points that I want people to consider. First, revitalization movements are common throughout all cultures. I have summarized two of the major movements that functioned to proliferate radical violence in Western culture, Nazism and the Crusades. Second, a revitalization movement at some point in our lives will touch most of us, no matter how stubborn and careful we are. They are just irresistible. We will see more and more revitalization movements, and they will represent great danger to the future of humanity and our earth. It is one of the most significant dangers of violence that humanity faces. Religions must be cognizant of this danger in their own tradition, and warn of its implications within other religious traditions. One of the largest fears that haunt thinking people is the possibility that some movement is going to take root in some part of a country where people already have nuclear weapons. They might seize those nuclear weapons. The rest is not hard to imagine.

Part III

MOVING TOWARD DIALOGUE

Ten

Reconciliation

An Intrinsic Element of Peace and Justice

ADA MARÍA ISASI-DÍAZ

*One of the elements of the "reign of God" (see Daniel Bell's essay)
is the kindred spirit that people of peace have for one another. Just
social and economic conditions contribute to a sense of peaceable
community.*

*Ada María Isasi-Díaz presents "a theo-ethics of reconciliation that
will contribute to make justice a reality." (John Dominic Crossan's
essay which follows on the justice of God is fitting as a complement
to the current essay and a conclusion to this volume.)*

*Like the liberationists, Isasi-Díaz finds the oppressed who suffer
injustice as the place to begin to see how justice and reconciliation
begin and progress. Emphasizing that justice is a process is central
to her argument, especially since two-thirds of humanity "lives in
poverty and/or is oppressed." She points out that reconciliation is
possible only when persons recognize that they have been unjustly
oppressed and also that they have been unjust oppressors.*

*In confession persons must realize this two-edged sword and
humbly choose to be reconciled to self and others. Reconciliation is
both a religious and civil virtue because it derives from God's desire
to be reconciled to all people. A sense of human interdependence that
transcends religious and national identity comes when reconciliation
becomes our moral choice.*

*Isasi-Díaz concludes, "I believe the future of the United States
and of the whole world depends on our human ability to develop
a spirituality, a culture, a mystique of reconciliation that will make*

it possible for us to practice reconciliation as a religious, social, and civic virtue."

Provocations for Dialogue

1. *Is reconciliation possible without reparations to oppressed victims?*

2. *How does capitalism encourage or discourage reconciliation between people?*

3. *How can the author's hope for reconciliation be applied in a religiously diverse world?*

• • •

"THAT THEY ALL may be one so that the world may believe" are words placed on the lips of Jesus by John the evangelist (John 17:21). The context of these words is important: Jesus wants the world to believe that he is one with God and that God sent him. Jesus knows that his mission, to reveal and begin to establish the kin-dom[1] of God, will be fruitful only if the world believes in him. Furthermore, Jesus knows that whether the world does or does not believe in him and his mission depends on his followers living according to what he has taught them. The world will not believe unless his followers live according to the truths Jesus taught — unless Christians are indeed one in body, soul, mind, and heart. The parable of the last judgment in Matthew 25:31–46 contains the clearest explanation of what Jesus meant by being "one." In this parable one finds a stark picture of reality: some are hungry, some have food; some are homeless while others have shelter; some are naked, some have clothing; some are prisoners while others are free; some are sick, and others are healthy. There is a rift between different groups in the community. The teaching of the parable is that the rift has to be healed and that only those who work to heal it will belong to the family of God. The healing of what splits humanity, of what separates one from the other, is the authentic meaning of reconciliation. If what separates us is not bridged, justice will not be able to triumph and the kin-dom of God will not become a reality in our midst.

At the beginning of the twenty-first century the many divisions that exist in our world make it obvious that a central element of the Christian understanding of justice and of work on behalf of justice is reconciliation. Justice is not only "a constitutive dimension of the preaching of the Gospel,"[2] but it is essential to the meaning and mission of the church today. The Bible, as well as a wide variety of documents produced by different Christian churches in the last forty years, makes it clear that the work of justice is a religious practice. By extension then, since reconciliation is an element of justice, the work of reconciliation is a religious obligation for all Christians. "All Christians can agree in saying that reconciliation is an essential mission of the Church, that is, that one cannot be a true Christian if one is not motivated permanently by a preoccupation for reconciliation."[3]

Very simply said, it is not possible to conceptualize reconciliation apart from justice, and one cannot be a justice-seeking person without the ongoing practice of reconciliation. This is the belief and understanding on which this article is built. In it, I seek to articulate an understanding of reconciliation as a social, political, and theological virtue within the parameters of justice. My intention is to present a theo-ethics of reconciliation that will contribute to make justice a reality, since without justice the kin-dom of God cannot flourish; there can be no fullness of life, no peace.[4]

Reconciliation as an Element of Justice

The mode of divine revelation set forth in the Bible provides the basis for understanding justice as a process. The Bible does not set definitions. It does not offer theories but presents rich narratives about the lived experiences of its people. It is in the midst of their lives that God's revelation happens and that the people of Israel and the followers of Jesus come to understand who God is and the demands God makes on humans. Following this biblical tradition, many systems of Christian ethics and moral theologies today eschew a theoretical approach to justice that focuses on universals apart from any social context or on rational reflections that attempt to demonstrate their validity by being self-enclosed systems. Instead, they embrace justice as a process that starts with the experience of those who suffer injustice, and who, therefore, seek to change present oppressive structures. As a process, justice does not avoid rationality but rather proposes normative reflections that are historic and contextual. To understand justice as a process is to embrace the fact that all "normative reflection must begin from historically specific circumstances because there is nothing but what is, the given, the situated interest in justice from which to start."[5]

Acknowledging justice as a process, however, does not mean that it is only a matter of describing what is. Justice aims to evaluate the actual experience of people as well as their hopes and expectations. This evaluation is also "rooted in experience of and reflection on that very society."[6] It is not a matter of importing from other societies and cultures ideas of "the good" and "the just" to evaluate what is. It is a matter, rather, of listening to the cries of the poor and the oppressed in our midst so as to discover how individually and as a society we fail to make it possible for all to become the persons God created us to be. The norms and ideals used to evaluate the presence of justice in any given situation arise, then, from the yearnings of those who suffer oppression and poverty. They arise from those with whom individually and as a community we have not established right relationships. The desire for right relationships is not an extraneous idea but rather arises out of the desire of the people to have in their lives that love of neighbor that the gospel of Jesus turned into a commandment for Christians. This understanding of the basis for and meaning of justice makes it clear that different elements of justice will need to be emphasized at different times. However, no matter what element of justice is being discussed, like any other norm or principle, justice requires exploration of its various meanings and implications.

In the twenty-first century this means that we have to start with the fact that two-thirds of the world lives in poverty and/or is oppressed, lacking what is needed to develop fully. This condition exists because of personal and systemic violence, exploitation, powerlessness, marginalization, and prejudice. These are not only causes but also mechanisms that operate at many different levels in our world. As mechanisms, they are interconnected and create personal and societal modes of being and doing that maintain a status quo where less than one-third of the world controls, consumes, and enjoys most of the natural and humanly developed resources of our world. Justice requires an in-depth examination of the various causes of oppression so that effective strategies can be developed. As a matter of fact, the lack of serious analysis of the causes of oppression and poverty has led to so few positive results despite the goodwill and untiring commitment of many around the world.

How is power understood and used? Who has it and whom does it benefit? To understand the dynamics of oppression in our world we need to analyze power. Second, we need to examine the distribution of goods, both material goods and other goods such as rights, opportunities, self-respect, participation in decision making, and the power to "define" the symbols, images, meanings, behaviors, and myths that give character to the different societies. Third, we need to examine and reconceive our notions of diversity and differences, for it is precisely our present understanding of differences as what separates, excludes, and places persons in opposition to each other that is at the core of all modes of oppression,[7] causing divisions and brokenness. Such an understanding leads to conceptualizing those who are different as outsiders, with those who have power deciding what is normative — themselves — and what is deviant — others. As long as this is the prevalent understanding of diversity and difference, there is no possibility of having right relationships, and it will be impossible to create just societal structures that are inclusive instead of exclusive.

Although identifying similarity and difference is one way people make sense of their "perceptions, experiences, identities, and human obligations,"[8] it does not necessarily have to lead one to assign consequences to difference and to position one group in relation to another. In other words, most of the time the way differences are currently understood and dealt with includes making moral judgments about them, deciding without much reflection that because

some are different they are better or worse, never just "different."
Society has capitalized on "categories of difference that manifest
social prejudice and misunderstanding,"[9] and has ignored ongoing
relationships among people that are based on similarities. Society
understands boundaries as keeping people away from each other instead of highlighting that "the whole concept of a boundary depends
on relationships: relationships between the two sides drawn by the
boundary, and relationships among the people who recognize and
affirm the boundary."[10] This means that because boundaries do not
exist outside of connections among people, if we are to bring about
a paradigm shift in how we understand differences, we need to emphasize how differences are related to relationships rather than to
distinctions.

How can this be done, and more importantly, why should it be
done? Unless one recognizes differences and deals with them in a
way contrary to the present mode, there is no possibility of healing
the rifts that exist among us; there is no real possibility of solidarity
among people. True solidarity insists on genuine mutuality, which can
be reached only by recognizing the common interests that bind humanity. Unless we embrace differences and diversity as constituents
of relationships instead of seeing them as separating and opposing
elements, we will not be able to heal what divides us. We will not
be able to be reconcilers. In other words, the work of reconciliation
is intrinsic to changing the paradigms that have governed the understanding of differences. The work of reconciliation is a key process in
the struggle to create communities of solidarity committed to building a future together. Therefore, reconciliation and solidarity are key
elements in our work for justice, for a just future, one where no one
is excluded.

Reconciliation as a Moral Choice

The work of reconciliation is a humble process, a road to be traveled together one step at a time, by those seeking to be reconciled.
Reconciliation is not a matter of offering preconceived answers to a

given situation. Instead, the work of reconciliation projects itself into the future, opening up and concentrating on possibilities. It is not a matter of repeating or of limiting oneself to the past. Reconciliation understands that there is a plurality of truths and that this plurality is precisely what creates possibilities, what roots human freedom and makes choices possible. Rich possibilities exist that propose and demand options that make reconciliation a moral virtue, a way of being and acting that requires responsible choice. Responsible choice is not a matter of controlling situations. It is not a matter of being absolutely certain that what one chooses is the most effective possible choice or one that guarantees success. Responsible choice, rather, recognizes that what one chooses is but one way to proceed, and that it is the best possible way to proceed given the present situation and the understanding one has.

Reconciliation makes it all the more obvious that moral responsibility has to focus on responding to others and establishing and maintaining mutuality. This, in turn, redefines the concepts of autonomy, self-reliance, and self-definition. The work of reconciliation focuses on responsibility as "participation in a communal work, laying the groundwork for the creative response of people in the present and the future. Responsible action means changing what can be altered in the present even though a problem is not completely resolved. Responsible action focuses on and respects partial resolutions and the inspiration and conditions for further partial resolutions ... [by ourselves] and by others."[11] The work of reconciliation has to recognize that those who have been apart and opposed to each other need to move together, one step at a time, willing to accept that risk, ambiguity, and uncertainty are part of the process. The work of reconciliation asks above all for a commitment to mutuality, to opening possibilities together even if one might never see them become a reality — this over and above a desire for tangible changes. Reconciliation has to be guided by a sense that the results of much work and commitment may be only a list of shared desires and possibilities, but even such a minimal outcome is the result of mature ethical commitment and work that allows and obliges one to sustain a reconciling attitude and behavior.

Reconciliation is a moral choice because it makes one remember that all persons have themselves been, at some point in their lives, oppressors and exploiters. This makes one understand that good intentions are not enough. Moral action requires the risk of taking steps together, of being accountable to each other, of participating in a process that concentrates on the future precisely by working to alter the present. Reconciliation as moral action makes it clear that healing the rifts that divide people cannot be incidental to one's life — that it is essential to being a human being, a responsible person, a person fully alive.

Reconciliation for any community that is divided — and as long as injustice continues, divisions among people will exist — is the only just way to proceed. It is the only way to embrace the responsibility we all have for our communities and for the country in which we live. The only way to participate effectively, to contribute effectively to the future of our world, is to be people willing to suggest and explore possibilities together with those we have oppressed or who have oppressed us. Reconciliation is the only way to proceed with all sides recognizing that reality is more than what is evident and that the future cannot be a slavish repetition of the present or of the past. Reconciliation is the only way we will all come together to create possibilities for a common, inclusive future that is life-giving for all. Such is the moral responsibility of all those who call themselves Christians. Such is our vocation as a religious people who, while acknowledging our potential for self-deception,[12] believe in eternal possibilities because we believe in an ever-abiding divine presence among us.

Reconciliation: Biblical Basis

The way we understand reconciliation is greatly influenced by the process and elements the churches have historically considered necessary for "the sacrament of penance" or "confession," and now call "the sacrament of reconciliation." From a religious perspective, most people would say that reconciliation requires interior repentance, an attitude that rejects wrongs freely done in the past and at the same time accepts responsibility for them. Interior repentance also requires a firm purpose of amendment; in other words, a staunch resolution not to repeat the errors of the past. The sacrament of reconciliation also entails confessing one's sins as well as offering satisfaction or reparation for the wrong done. This satisfaction or reparation is not made only to God, whom the sinner has offended, but also to the persons who have been "injured by sin, for example, as reparation for injured love, for damage to reputation or property."[13] Only once all these requirements are fulfilled is forgiveness granted.[14]

If we begin to conceive reconciliation, however, as an intrinsic element of justice and ground it in the biblical understanding of the absolute need to heal divisions as described in the parable of the last judgment in Matthew 25, reconciliation becomes different from how it has often been conceived. Reconciliation as an element of justice is an essential way of knowing and healing brokenness in the world. Before one can come to know the reality of brokenness, three requisites need to be fulfilled: First, one has to be in the midst of brokenness, to be touched by it and have one's life impacted by it. Second, one has to take responsibility for it, understanding one's role in it. Third, one has to take action to heal it.[15] Healing brokenness — the work of reconciliation — begins happening the minute one enters into this threefold process of knowing its reality. To take responsibility for and start to work to heal the divisions that exist in a given situation is already to become involved in the process of reconciliation. We simply cannot defer healing. Reconciliation begins to unfold even though only one side is willing to start working to make it happen. Reconciliation cannot be postponed until those on the other side of the rift are willing to enter into this process. Reconciliation cannot be postponed until reparation and restitution are made. The work of healing brokenness should not be withheld for any reason whatsoever.

Perhaps this is nowhere clearer than in the early church's understanding of reconciliation reflected in the epistles of Colossians, 2 Corinthians, and 1 John. The early followers of Jesus understood God's love and reconciliation to be something freely given, something that invited them to respond but was not conditioned by or dependent upon an expected response. The author of 1 John says it succinctly: "We are to love, then, because God loved us first" (1 John 4:19). God loves first and unconditionally, and we should respond by loving others in the same manner and not setting conditions to our love. In Colossians the author talks about Christ's reconciling act which does not depend on who is being reconciled or demand reparations but which calls the other to respond. Reconciliation is presented as a one-sided process on God's part. God knows the reality of brokenness because the rift between God and those created to share in the divine "affects" God, if in no other way than by disrupting God's plans. In 2 Corinthians two ideas about reconciliation are elucidated. First, "It is all God's work" (2 Cor. 5:18). Second, reconciliation happens because God does not hold the faults of humanity against us (v. 19). Nowhere in this text does it say that reconciliation happens on the condition that humanity changes; rather, humanity changes because of the reconciliation that God freely bestows.

For the early church, reconciliation was an intrinsic part of its mission, and mission was considered a constitutive element of the church. The church was to appeal to all to be reconciled to God, but this reconciliation was only a second step. The first step has already been given by God: God already has carried out the work of reconciliation. God's love comes first. The church knew that it could not preach what it did not live, so it had to be a reconciling church, offering reconciliation freely, putting no conditions on it. The church knew that God appealed to all through the church's preaching and, particularly, through its behavior. That appeal was to reconciliation (2 Cor. 5:20).

Based on these gleanings from the New Testament, reconciliation has to be considered an element in the justice-seeking process that focuses not on the past but on the future — a future that starts with the present and takes into consideration the past. In this sense reconciliation is a prophetic action; that is, it has to do with healing people who suffer brokenness and divisions, and it looks for ways to make their hopes and expectations a reality in our world.

Reconciliation as a Religious, Social, and Civic Virtue

From an ethical perspective reconciliation is a virtue. As such, reconciliation is not only a value but also a praxis, a way of acting. One has to work at reconciliation in order to become a good practitioner of it. Virtues are not themes to be elaborated in eloquent speeches but rather a way of living. To be good at the virtue of reconciliation one has not only to understand what it is but also to practice it. Virtues involve the disposition and actual competence to accomplish moral good; the virtue of reconciliation leads to actual reconciling behavior. From an ethical perspective, to practice the virtue of reconciliation one has to work in a practical way to build bridges over the rifts created by prejudices or simply because people have had very different experiences. The virtue of reconciliation, like any other virtue, requires working at it in such a way that it becomes a habit, the regular way of relating to others. In turn, because reconciliation becomes a regular way of relating, it also becomes a stable disposition of the person. This means that one cannot say one is in favor of reconciliation and at the same time work mainly at developing formulas for reconciliation so complex that they are not achievable, or think, for whatever reason, of whole groups of people that are to be excluded from the process. One has to find effective ways of working at reconciliation even if the results are limited, even if it involves only a few people, even if all it accomplishes is strengthening one's resolve and giving one a new perspective on reconciliation. It is obvious, then, that reconciliation does not exist unless one is in the process of reconciling oneself to others, unless one is working for reconciliation among different peoples.

Reconciliation is a religious virtue because its driving force for Christians is precisely the gospel message. It is a religious virtue because Christians believe that this is the kind of behavior that Jesus wants his followers to have. The biblical passages presented above make it clear that reconciliation is an important element in the manner the God of Jesus "behaves," a behavior communicated by God in such a way that makes it possible for human beings to embrace it. As a religious virtue, then, reconciliation is a specific form of love and an act of grace. This means that reconciliation is one of the means used by God to enable human beings not only to relate to the God-self but to participate in divine nature itself.[16] Finally, from a religious perspective, reconciliation, as mentioned above, is not only a matter of personal behavior. It is a matter of the very mission and nature of the church.[17]

Reconciliation is also a social virtue. Human beings are social beings, called to be in relationship and called to live as members of various communities — family, workplace, neighborhood — that come together to form societies. Unfortunately, if it is true that human beings are social beings, it is also true that we fail repeatedly to be in right relationships, that we make mistakes, we create enmities. In this sense human beings live in a tension between depending on others and being responsible to them and at the same time wanting to be self-sufficient even to the point of becoming selfish and turning against others. Reconciliation as a social virtue imposes the duty to overcome what separates human beings, what turns one against another, in order to be able to live the sociability that is an intrinsic characteristic of humanity. Not to do so, not to work at overcoming what creates rifts among human beings, is a betrayal of what is a fundamental human characteristic. To create or maintain divisions among persons and peoples is detrimental to all of humanity. This is precisely why reconciliation is a much-needed social virtue.

Finally, in the specific case of the United States at the beginning of the twenty-first century, when this country has waged war as the aggressor, reconciliation is a civic virtue. It is a disposition and a practice that committed and faithful citizens of the United States have to embrace if they believe that this country can flourish only with justice. A true commitment to reconciliation will bring about a revival of this country's moral commitment to respect differences. The "American way of life" — that is, the way the United States is politically, economically, and socially organized, and its secular and religion mores and core values — may be the preferred way for its people. But the "American way" is not the only way of life that is good. It is not, therefore, the way of life that has to be chosen by other nations and other peoples in our world.

Reconciliation as a civic virtue in the United States must necessarily start with sobering humility. The United States must recognize that it needs the rest of the world. It has to search its soul and candidly disclose that it needs others, that it must build common interests with nations and peoples around the world. This country must recognize that without true mutual solidarity with other nations the American way of life is condemned to disappear. Reconciliation as a civic virtue in the United States must recognize that the richness and privileges enjoyed here are, to a great extent, at the expense of others. The exploitation that makes possible the richness and privileges enjoyed in the United States has created the rift between the United States and other countries and peoples. The need to heal that rift for the sake of the future of the world — that is what reconciliation as a civic virtue aims to accomplish.

Reconciliation: Building a Common Future for All

Reconciliation necessitates that people come together and agree on a common future for our world. True reconciling praxis will arouse shared feelings and lead to joint action. Reconciliation involves building a common programmatic vision about our world, and this cannot be done outside of a process of dialogue. In dialogue the parties involved seek not to convince one another or move the other to one's own perspective but rather seek to move all those involved to a point of view and a program of action that has been forged together. The kind of dialogue needed for reconciliation to happen demands that we embrace a way of understanding differences that does not focus on what separates, excludes, and sets us in opposition, but rather recognizes that differences presume boundaries that enable people to make connections and come together. Dialogue cannot happen unless we recognize differences and diversity not as what separates us but as resources in the process of reconciliation from which each of us can draw to conceptualize the future and begin to create it.

Yet a call to reconciling dialogue is not a call to betray one's values, for in fact, different values or shared values can be actualized differently in diverse circumstances. Sometimes, through the process of dialogue one realizes that what originally were thought to be values contrary to ours are simply other values, not necessarily values opposed to ours. Personal insecurity often makes us incapable of seeing what we could well consider positive in the values held by others. Yet to be sure, some values directly oppose or work to diminish the ones we hold. This is important and should not be minimized. However, there are more areas of similarities than of dissimilarities among the values that people hold. Commitment to dialogue makes us adept at finding these similarities, these areas of agreement, these joint understandings, and common visions about the future of our world, our future as a people and a nation.

Understanding, appreciating, and learning from realities, experiences, and worldviews of people who are quite different from us are essential to the process of dialogue and reconciliation. We are inescapably linked to them, for today no country can consider itself isolated from others. Common interests pervade our world. We do not need to invent them. However, we do need to consciously recognize those common interests, to embrace the infinite number of ways in which we are as interconnected with people who live far away as we are with people nearby.

The first realization in this part of dialogue is the acceptance that we all have something to contribute to a common future. Second, we are called to see reality from the point of view of others. We are called to decentralize ourselves and not only to dispassionately understand the perspective of others but also to appreciate what is positive in their understandings, how their understandings can enrich us. It is not an easy process. After all, it entails building a programmatic worldview that uses a shared understanding of history, the experiences of the everyday life of people who live in very different circumstances, and our own dreams and expectations about our world. A programmatic worldview has to remain open to developments because it is not about an absolute future but about a historical future and because it must not impose an ideology but rather must respond to the needs of the people and be intentional about being open to different possibilities.[18] Therefore, no matter where we live, we need to realize that getting to know each other and learning about the many interconnections that exist among people all over the world are viable and important first steps in the process of reconciliation. We are the poorer when we forget how we need each other, how we are related to each other, for then we ignore what gives all humans meaning: friendship, love, and relationships.[19] Without a strong appreciation of our interdependence we begin to lose the sociability that is characteristic of the human species.

This will not happen easily. Often, it seems almost impossible to come to the table with those with whom we seek to be reconciled. And, though the gratuitousness of God's reconciliation demands of us to be reconciling persons, the process of reconciliation involves more than one party. Therefore, those with whom we are trying to be reconciled also have to recognize that reconciliation is needed. Perhaps the key is to make those with whom we need to be reconciled understand that what we seek is not to convince them that they are wrong or to win them to our side. Rather, we seek mutual dialogue that will move us jointly to a place we have created together. Reconciliation is a process; the dialogue that is central to this process has to start as soon as possible, at whatever level is possible, in whatever circumstances exist. In this case, dialogue is a practice of reconciliation which needs to be sustained and enriched by the common experiences of coming together, of getting to know each other and understanding each other for the sake of a common future.

Reconciliation: Dealing with the Past, Rooted in the Present, in View of the Future

The process of becoming acquainted in new and better ways and of building a programmatic worldview together is but one of the elements of reconciliation. Undoubtedly and necessarily we also have to deal with the wrongs that have been committed on all sides that cause many pain and suffering. This makes the process of reconciliation both taxing and difficult, yet also more demanding and urgent. Suffering is not the prerogative of any one side. Suffering abounds everywhere. There is no easy way through this rough and dangerous part of the path to reconciliation. However, even when it comes to wrongs committed and suffering inflicted, we have to keep in mind that reconciliation is first of all about the future and not about the past. In looking at the past, we therefore keep in mind that the passing of time makes retrieving it impossible, that who we are today is different from who we were in the past, who we were even in the recent past, even yesterday. This is why "any return is not a return: it is coming into a new place."[20] This is why looking at the past only makes sense if it is part of constructing the future.

The second thing to keep in mind is that in the process of reconciliation, dealing with the past, dealing with the wrongs we have done and the pain we have caused each other, has no room for revenge.[21] Revenge is destructive; in its wake follows a never-ending and ever-widening spiral of violence. Revenge is a stagnating force that makes future-oriented movement impossible. Revenge is antithetical to reconciliation because it capitalizes on what separates us; it insists on payment for what simply cannot be paid for.[22] Revenge refuses to recognize that wrongs have been committed and suffering has been caused on all sides. Revenge does not make right what was wrong or restore the value of what was lost. Most often revenge stems from attempts to assuage guilt for what we did or allowed to happen, guilt we feel but will not admit. Revenge promotes a self-centeredness that makes any attempt to build common interests and actions impossible.[23]

In dealing with the past we often talk about restitution and retribution. When we claim retribution for those who suffered and are no longer with us, is it not our own needs and expectations that motivate us? Just as we say that the dead demand restitution and retribution, we can say that they pardon those who harmed them and that their memory pleads for reconciliation. Those of us living now are the ones who decide how to appropriate and use what has happened in the past. We do indeed choose how to read into the present and future the sufferings of the past. Those who are alive today, not those who have died, are the ones who will benefit from any restitution and retribution. Therefore, those who are alive today can also move beyond restitution and retribution, which focuses on the past, and embrace reconciliation, with their eyes fixed in the future.[24]

What can we say about those who are still alive who have been personally wronged, who have endured pain and suffering, who can point to specific individuals who have exploited and abused them? This is a most delicate and personal matter but not a private one. Personal forgiveness or nonforgiveness is something in which we are all involved. Any attempt to hide or ignore the pain and suffering inflicted will be devastating for the creation of a common future. But how we deal with that pain and suffering cannot be left in the hands of individuals, for what they do becomes part of how we all facilitate or impede reconciliation. Though we need to acknowledge and give a public hearing to the voices of those who have suffered, reconciliation must prevail instead of the demand for retribution or the decision not to forgive.[25]

If we do not make public the memories of those who suffered personally, individual and national healing will not be possible. However, without reconciliation we cannot move on to build the future together.[26] Those who have suffered need to tell their stories, need to have others witness to the horror that has been inflicted on them in order to have their memories respected, to find a way of dealing with what they have endured, to regain their wholeness as human beings. Unless those who have suffered can be healed, the nation will suffer by not being able to benefit from what they can contribute to the building of our common future. Yet the process of personal healing has to happen within the national process of reconciliation and in no way can it militate against it.[27] Those who for many reasons find it difficult to embrace reconciliation, given what they have personally suffered, might do well to take seriously the many who have been at each other's throats, who have been enemies, and yet want to live together in peace in the future

A Spirituality, a Culture, a Mystique of Reconciliation

At the beginning of the twenty-first century I believe the future of the United States and of the whole world depends on our human ability to develop a spirituality, a culture, a mystique of reconciliation that will make it possible for us to practice reconciliation as a religious, social, and civic virtue. To embrace a spirituality of reconciliation is to understand that for Christians there can be no possibility of relating to God unless we have a reconciling attitude and practice toward each other. Because our relationship with God is intrinsically linked to the way we relate to each other, a reconciling God cannot but ask of those who believe to have a reconciling attitude toward each other. To relate to God is not something apart from how we live our daily lives. Therefore, our response to a reconciling God has to be a reconciling day-to-day living without exception and without conditions.

Culture includes all that we humans have cultivated and created to deal with the world: tools, customs, societal structures, ideas about reality, and representations of ideas. A culture of reconciliation, therefore, requires us not only to counter in every way possible enmity, opposition, and alienation, but actually to nurture and foster openness, dialogue, and a dynamic understanding of differences not based on exclusion and confrontation. A culture of reconciliation is key in this whole process because all nations have a cultural origin before they have a political one. A culture of reconciliation is important for the United States because the way it has dealt and still deals with many nations and peoples around the globe has resulted in deep-seated mistrust, enmity, and war. Given the primacy of culture in all national identification, reconciliation has to be an option that those of us who live in the United States make for ourselves, a practice that we implement in every aspect of our lives.

Finally, we need a mystique of reconciliation. A mystique is an intangible force that enables those who embrace it to face all reality. It refers to an understanding that provides a social cohesion, enabling participants to do what they have not been able to do alone but what becomes possible when one participates in a shared experience.[28] A mystique of reconciliation, therefore, makes it possible for us, even in the most adverse of circumstances, to practice the virtue of reconciliation as a way — the most needed way — to be truly patriotic, to be truly Christian. A mystique of reconciliation provides for us the strength that we might not have individually to struggle against accepted convictions, convictions such as that we have nothing to repent about, that as a country our motives always are liberty, freedom, and democracy. A mystique of reconciliation will make it possible for us to be open to the dreams and the hopes of people all over the world, particularly the poor and oppressed. It will allow us to welcome other ways of understanding reality and of organizing societies, economies, and governments different from those in the United States. Only then will we have a solid base on which to build peace and justice. Only a mystique of reconciliation will help us create a world in which the main preoccupation is how to stand together, how to recognize the common interests that bind us, how to be inclusive societies that take into consideration the well-being of all peoples.

Eleven

The Justice of God
and the Peace of Earth

JOHN DOMINIC CROSSAN

John Dominic Crossan appropriately concludes this collection of essays with a profound summary of the biblical understanding of justice. If Jewish and Christian scripture provide any key, then we must enter religious dialogue with a clear understanding that the center of God's focus and concern is justice. Biblical justice forces us to be transparent about our own greed and self-interests at the political, economic, and personal expense of others. This is an especially important matter for religions in the United States, since our standard of living is, to a large extent, built off the backs of the rest of the world. When reading Crossan, we cannot help but recall Dan Bell's essay. The critique from Latin America toward the United States is echoed in much of the world. The American empire has supported violence all over the world on behalf of securing and maintaining economic prosperity — if not downright hedonism — at home. This domination has led to what Bell calls "the terror of capitalism." Crossan's study confirms once again what adherents to Judaism and Christianity find hard to accept: Their God is a God who shows preference to the weak and powerless — the victims of the capitalistic structures of domination.

Crossan's essay keeps the target in clear focus. Hope for meaningful dialogue hinges on Christians and Jews rejecting support of political and economic systems that attempt to establish "peace" through violence. Peace can only come through seeking and defending justice. Violence never results in peace. Peace comes through justice. For this reason, the meaning of justice must be at the center of dialogue between religions.

Provocations for Dialogue

1. *Are religions prepared to discuss self-critically how their particular tradition has supported injustice instead of justice toward other religions? What would such a discussion mean to prospects for peace?*

2. *How could the religious concept of repentance advance religious dialogues for peace and against violence?*

3. *Can religions from economically wealthy and politically powerful nations listen carefully to those living in less dominant societies, giving them a "moral preference" that seems evident within biblical traditions of Judaism and Christianity?*

• • •

I BEGIN THIS ESSAY with a confession: Although I have spent most of my professional life working on the first century, down deep I pursue those studies because I am intensely concerned about the twenty-first century. I am interested in the first century with regard to how it reverberates with the issues of our contemporary world. In other words, what has Rome then to do with America *now*? How do the origins of Christianity challenge *today's* Christianity, especially with regard to violence and nonviolent resistance to violence? We are not therefore merely visiting museum artifacts in the first century. It is with intense concern for the culture of violence which now pervades our society and the current global situation that I want to address the subject of justice and injustice — both then and now. Before American Christianity can truly contribute to meaningful dialogue with other religions of the world about peace and justice in the world, it must,

---

This essay is transcribed from a presentation in the Values Council Lecture Series on *Poverty and Wealth* at Stetson University, DeLand, Florida. It has been but minimally edited to retain that original oral register.

in my opinion, understand its own biblical traditions that already suggest an alternative vision of justice and peace.

Let me first be very clear about what I mean when I am talking about justice. Daily local newscasts report on somebody crying out for justice. Perhaps a child has been killed by a drunk driver. Through their tears the victim's parents are asking for the driver to be "brought to justice"; in other words, to be punished. We call this "retributive justice." It is a perfectly acceptable form of justice. We frequently refer to the courts as "the halls of justice," where the most typical form of justice carried out is retributive justice.

There is, however, another kind of justice. Suppose that the drunk driver was an important, rich, and influential person who claims that good reasons exist to reconsider the punishment for vehicular homicide. Now the discussion would shift from retributive justice into a debate over what ethicists call distributive justice. The debate would consist of arguments about how punishments must be distributed equally to everyone involved in the case.

When I use the term "justice" in this essay and when the Bible uses the term "justice," the primary and dominant meaning is distributive justice. Only in a secondary sense does justice focus on retribution. The Bible continually speaks of God as a God of justice and righteousness. The Bible is not asserting that God is an avenging God who is going to punish you, a God who is waiting to strike you with a sword. It means that God is a God of distributive justice, a God who owns the world and who, being just, demands that the world be administered justly. Basic to the biblical meaning of justice is a theology of creation. The Bible is not concerned at all about how God created a world, a matter which we like to argue about because it costs us nothing. The Bible asks who owns the world. The basic biblical affirmation is that God brought the world into being and God therefore owns it. We humans do not own it, although we act and think as though we do. As creator, then, God owns the earth.

Moreover, as part of God's ownership of the creation, God demands just dealings between people. That is what we call social justice. Most of the time, however, we tend to think of justice in individual terms. I should not defraud you; you should not defraud me. That is individual personal justice. Is it legitimate? Of course it is legitimate. But there is also what is called structural or systemic justice. The Bible asserts that God is most interested in a structured world that manifests justice for all. This structural justice is far harder to see. It is that line item in a budget that somebody formulated so that not Group A but Group B will be hurt by its inclusion. And, as it were, nobody did it. That is simply structural injustice. Consider an illustration from the Gospels. Jesus tells the parable of the workers in the vineyard. The vineyard owner sends workers out at 6:00 in the morning, 9:00 in the morning, 12:00 noon, 3:00 in the afternoon, and 5:00 in the afternoon, just before sundown. At the end of the day, he gathers all the laborers in his vineyard, giving everyone a full day's pay. Immediately, we ask along with Matthew and a host of commentators for two thousand years, "Is that right? Should you not give more to the person who has labored longer?" We focus instinctively on personal and individual justice. Jesus' intention in telling the parable, however, was to evoke a different issue. He hoped some listener would ask: "Why at high harvest time in the vineyards are there workers looking for work all day long? Even at 5:00 in the afternoon they are still looking for work. Who set up that system? Did it just happen?" The parable is supposed to raise the listeners' awareness of the difference between personal or individual justice and social or systematic justice. Of course, it did not happen just by coincidence that at the high moment of harvest, when you think you can get top denarius for a day's work, you are still looking for work at 5:00 in the afternoon — exactly what the landowners would want — cheap labor even at high harvest! Thus, when we think of justice in the Bible, we must think primarily of distributive justice, not retributive justice, and we must think of systematic or structural justice and not individual or personal justice.

Justice in the Torah

We catch a glimpse into the character of the God of the Bible when we read the Torah, a glimpse that over and over again shows God to be intensely concerned with distributive justice. God demands the fair, just, and equitable distribution of goods among the inhabitants of the earth. We see it in the law of the Sabbath: six days you should do your work but on the seventh day you should rest. Why should we rest? The answer in Exodus 23:12 is, "so that your ox and your donkey may have relief, and your homeborn slave and the resident alien may be refreshed." The Sabbath has to do with the donkey getting a day off. When we read this, however, most of us think of the Sabbath quite differently. Our popular conception is that the Sabbath rest is for worship. We go to the synagogue or the temple or the church. But, at its core, the Sabbath was to give everyone a day off, even the working animals. Theologically, the Sabbath meant that for one day a week the whole world is reduced to equality. Deuteronomy 5:12–14 agrees: "Observe the sabbath day and keep it holy, as the Lord your God commanded you. Six days you shall labor and do all your work. But the seventh day is a sabbath to the Lord your God; you shall not do any work — you, or your son or your daughter, or your male or female slave, or your ox or your donkey, or any of your livestock, or the resident alien in your towns, so that your male and female slave may rest as well as you." Sabbath rest portrays God's concern for all creation; it is not rest *for* worship, it is rest *as* worship.

The Torah extends this view beyond the Sabbath day to include even a Sabbath year. The land was to be farmed for six years. Then, during the seventh year it was to rest and lay fallow. Today people might say that is a very good policy because it allows the soil to replenish its fertility. But that is not mentioned. The purpose was, according to Exodus 23:11, "so that the poor of your people may eat; and what they leave the wild animals may eat," and it extended to cereals, vines, and olives. But it was also so that the land itself get a rest. As Leviticus 25:4–5 says twice, "There shall be a sabbath of complete rest for the land.... it shall be a year of complete rest for the land." All creation gets the justice of at least some rest. Maybe it's good horticultural and agricultural practice, but theologically the purpose is to provide justice for the poor, the animals, and the land itself.

The key point is that the biblical God is a God of justice and righteousness. God does what is just by doing what is right and does what is right by doing what is just. This is the God who demands justice understood as distribution. Let me draw the picture of the biblical vision of justice one step further. In Leviticus 25:23 there is a very serious statement in which God decrees, "The land shall not be sold in perpetuity, for the land is mine; with me you are but aliens and tenants." If we understand this theological starting point, we can comprehend one of the most central aspects of the Torah — you cannot buy and sell land. You can buy and sell the donkeys and the oxen; you can buy and sell sheep and goats; but you cannot buy and sell land, because land is life itself. Why is the land so essential? The answer is not complicated, but strange to our modern, capitalistic mentality. It is because the land produces food, the material basis of life itself. The land belongs to God. We are not to buy and sell it. This is, in my opinion, one of the most extraordinary declarations in the Bible.

The famous story of Naboth's vineyard in 1 Kings 21:1–15 shows this idea in action. Naboth has a vineyard near the palace. King Ahab wants it and offers to buy it from him or give him another vineyard somewhere else in exchange. Actually, King Ahab was being very reasonable. Most kings would say, "You got it; I want it. Do you have a problem with that?" But Naboth responds, "The Lord forbid that I should give you my ancestral inheritance." He knows he cannot sell his ancestral inheritance because it is against the Law. But the story has a tragic ending. King Ahab has a Canaanite princess, Jezebel. Although she is demonized in Jewish and Christian tradition, she simply comes from a different economic theology. She believes in free trade. She thinks Naboth's refusal is an absolute and calculated insult. How can anyone refuse so fair an offer? So, she has Naboth put to death, and gives her husband the vineyard.

What are we to conclude from this biblical vision? In the Torah, biblical legislation against buying and selling land is an attempt to restrain the growth of inequality. This vision is not some naïve ideal constructed by a people who had no idea about the realities of the world. On the contrary, they knew what happened. If you can buy and sell land, then a few people will own all of it, and most would end up owning none of it. Or, as Isaiah 5:8 put it, "Ah, you who join house to house, who add field to field, until there is room for no one but you, and you are left to live alone in the midst of the land!" The vision is that God gave the land to the tribes and families of Israel. That vision is a practical extension of the biblical theology of creation: God's creation is based in distributive justice. The land belongs to God. Creation will only run correctly if it is run justly. If you try to run it any other way, it will not work. You can't buy and sell land without the danger of compromising divine justice.

Whenever human beings come up against an ideal that is profoundly difficult to live with, the first thing we do is find a way around it. If we had a proposed reform of election finances, the lobbyists would not leave Washington and become theologians. They would just find a different way to deal with election finances. That does not make them monsters. It just makes them human. Basically, the drive of Western civilization throughout history has included the drive to keep my piece of land and take your piece — of course, in your own best interest. Given the biblical ideal, how would we do that? Suppose I gave you a loan and you defaulted on the loan. I, of course, possess the collateral, which was your land. I would not have bought or sold land at all. We would engage in mortgaging and foreclosing. Nowhere in the Law does it say you cannot do that. What does occur is all sorts of laws whose logic is to control the processes of mortgaging and foreclosing. For example, there can be no interest on loans. Suppose you are a poor peasant and reaped a bad harvest. You do not even have enough saved for seed-barley for next year, so you have to get a loan. I would give you a loan, but I cannot charge interest on it. What could I do now? I will give you a loan of 100 dollars onto the next harvest — no interest. But the default penalty is 50 percent. If you do not come up with 100 dollars six months later you now owe me 150 dollars, your land is collateral, and I have just acquired it.

The biblical ideal is aware of the dangers of mortgaging and fore-closing on collateral and especially on land. That is why the Torah specifies a whole series of laws to restrain the growth of inequality through those procedures. First, for example, in Exodus 22:26–27 and Deuteronomy 24:6–11, you cannot take a millstone as pledge, because a millstone is somebody's livelihood. The millstone that grinds the corn and the barley — maybe for the whole village — is not allowed as a pledge. Further, when you take a pledge from your neighbor, you cannot go into the neighbor's house. You must stay outside and let them bring the pledge out to you. In plain language, you may not enter into their private space, their home. Second, every seven years the Sabbath year attempts to clean up the human mess of human inequality. Every seven years, according to Deuteronomy 15:1–11, all loans are liquidated. Of course an obvious problem is that the creditor might try to guard his wealth by not making any loans the sixth year. So God warns, "I'm watching! Be careful!" Third, that Sabbath year's liquidation of debt also applies to slaves in Exodus 21:2–11 and Deuteronomy 15:12–18. All slaves were to be freed. You cannot have permanent slavery. Finally, in the Sabbath of Sabbath years, the fiftieth or Jubilee year, all dispossessed property must go back to its original owner. The land, according to Leviticus 25:8–31, reverts, as it were, to the original equity of its inaugural divine justice.

Many times scholars like myself reach in to put out the fire of such radical thinking. We like to be skeptical about whether or not these things really happened in Israel. But my interest is not there. My point is that this vision is embedded deep in the Law. The very fact that it is deep in the Law tells me much about the character of the Lawgiver. This is a God wrestling with human nature to keep some justice here on earth. The character of this Lawgiver includes a deep and abiding concern for justice understood as distribution of wealth and a minimalization of poverty. An imbalance of this justice results in violence — violence done by humans against humans, as well as violence by humans against the land itself.

The Prophets and Justice

Let us now turn to the prophets. It is common to hear that the prophets concentrate on social justice. We need to strike the word "social" and replace it with "divine." The prophets were concerned with divine justice. I say this because the prophets spend much of their time complaining that Israel was not following the Law. If that were not their concern, I would consider the Law might have been an ideological, utopian window-dressing that nobody ever heeded; a beautiful thing that was written down but for practical matters should be ignored. The fact that the prophets are constantly struggling with it means that they are taking it seriously. Notice what the Hebrew prophets say. God usually is speaking: "I reject your worship because of your lack of justice." The classic examples range from Amos 4:1–5 or 5:21–24; through Hosea 6:6, Isaiah 1:10–17, and Micah 6:6–8; to Jeremiah 7:5–7. Once again we scholars rush in to put out the fires. What God really means, we may assert, is that God wants both worship and justice. Yet, I could give you a dozen examples in the prophets of God saying, "I reject your worship because of your lack of justice," but I cannot cite a single text where God says, "I reject your justice because of your lack of worship." The priorities are quite clear: God is a God of justice. How can you worship a god of justice in the state of injustice?

Perhaps the place where this becomes most clearly evident is in Jeremiah 7:5–7 and 26:2–6. The prophet is told to go and stand in front of the Temple on a festival day and tell the people streaming into it for worship that if they are not maintaining justice in their daily lives their Temple worship is in vain. "Don't come panting," he says, "the Temple, the Temple, the Temple" as if you are now pleasing God. The show of worship in the face of injustice, according to Jeremiah, turns the Temple into "a den of thieves." We should remember that a den of thieves is not where thieves do their thieving, but where they run for refuge. It is a safe house, a hideaway, a refuge. When Jesus quotes Jeremiah years later and symbolically condemns the Temple, he is not cleansing the Temple because it is doing something wrong.

He is not purifying it; he is symbolically destroying it, which is why he cites Jeremiah's "den of thieves" phrase. Jesus, like Jeremiah, was saying that if divine justice is not maintained every day, then worship on special days is worthless. The function of divine worship is to empower you for divine justice.

Justice in the Wisdom Traditions

If we look in the wisdom traditions of the Hebrew Bible, we find justice is a major theme. I will only summarize one poignant statement in Psalm 82 that shows dramatically the centrality of God's justice in a theological understanding of our world. Psalm 82 is a magnificent psalm because it imagines God in heaven surrounded by all the gods who run the world. God has taken the throne in the divine counsel in the midst of the gods, and God holds them in judgment for not maintaining justice. It is like a CEO sitting down with upper management. God accuses: "How long have you judged unjustly and shown partiality to the wicked? Give justice to the weak and the orphan. Maintain the right of the lowly and the destitute. Rescue the weak and the needy. Deliver them from the hand of the wicked." This picture imagines the God of the Bible as a supreme God seated with all the gods who run the world, and their job is to maintain justice. Yet, God laments, "They neither have knowledge nor understanding; they walk around in darkness." They didn't have a clue that their job description was about justice. It is *as if* the gods said (I am not quoting the Psalm), "We are in charge. Our job is about power. Where does justice come in? Our job is to run the world. Whoever brought up this justice stuff?" God answers, "All the foundations of the earth are shaken." In my opinion, this is the scariest statement in the entire Bible, because it says that injustice shakes the very foundations of the earth.

Jesus and God's Justice

How does Jesus plug into this tradition? In the territories of Herod Antipas in lower Galilee during the life of Jesus, what was happening is what I call "Romanization." The result of Romanization was urbanization that served the purpose of commercialization. The way the Roman empire operated was to plant cities. The function of these cities was to commercialize the countryside. They did that primarily by means of loans and foreclosure much in the way already described above. The aristocrats in those cities operated by foreclosing on small peasant farms, accumulating 10- or 20-acre farms together and making little megafarms with 150 or 200 acres. Slowly, the Romans would orchestrate a change in the farming so that the yield of return might result in around 5 percent return on cereals and 7 percent on vineyards. The result for Rome was that Lower Galilee would become part of the economic boom in the first-century empire but built on the back of the region's peasant farmers who were the victims of this economic program.

With this background in mind, I want now to make a comparison between the strategy of John the Baptist and the strategy of Jesus. The two strategies can be compared by use of a modern aphorism: John the Baptist had a monopoly and Jesus had a franchise. We can see this is true simply by remembering that John was "*the* Baptizer." Not only do the Gospels call him that, but the Jewish historian Josephus does as well. He was *the* Baptizer. This meant that when Antipas wanted to execute him and destroy the movement, all he had to do was to kill John. The movement might live on in nostalgia and memory for one or two generations, but it was really finished.

Jesus could have done the same thing as John. He could have settled down at Nazareth and talked about the kingdom of God. His family would have liked that very much. He could have said, "I am the kingdom and I have the kingdom. If you want it, you come to me. You want to be healed, you come to me. You want to be taught, you come to me. I'm here in Nazareth; you come to me." He could have created a kind of "Jesus Center" in Nazareth. Instead, Jesus pointed not toward himself, but toward the kingdom of God.

I used the anachronistic term "franchise" above to describe Jesus' strategy. What I mean by this is that his strategy was completely different from John's. Jesus did not settle down in one place. He keeps telling other people to go and do the same thing that he is doing. Instead of saying, "I've got it, you come to me," he said, "Go do what I'm doing." That strategy functions in the same way as a franchise functions. It is hard to destroy it by simply executing the founder.

Given this strategy, what exactly does he want his followers to do? First, he tells them to heal the sick. Second, his followers should eat with those they heal. Third, they are to announce that the kingdom of God (i.e., the way God wants the world to be run) is already beginning. It is important to understand each of these three actions of Jesus. With regard to healing, we must distinguish our modern conceptions of curing from the theologically complex idea of healing that Jesus is talking about in relationship to the kingdom of God. Curing is straightforward. If you have a certain virus, you see the virus under the microscope, take a prescribed medicine, and when the virus is gone, you are medically cured. Healing is a far more complex thing. What do we mean when we say that, after a certain amount of time, "the healing has begun"? What do we mean when we say people are being healed? This is a much more complicated process than the concept of curing. What Jesus is doing is building a countercommunity in the midst of Roman society, what I call "share-community." A share-community stands against the status quo of Rome as a "greed-community," based on the accepted economic and political orientations not only of first-century Rome, but of twenty-first-century America. The greed-community concept is, "I keep what is mine and take what is yours."

Tied to healing is eating. In the Hebrew Bible, as we noted, the emphasis is on the land. In contrast, we hear almost nothing about the land in the New Testament. Instead, the talk is almost entirely about food. We have to ask, why is there so much emphasis on food? I am convinced that it is very difficult for most of us in the United States to understand, because food is something we take for granted, on the one hand, and possibly have to minimize in consumption, on the other hand. For example, the dominant image of heaven in the New Testament is a great banquet feast. However, this is not the most popular image of heaven in America. Rather, our culture focuses more on images of pearly gates and streets paved with gold. The New Testament image is of well-aged wines and lots of fat, things we associate with high levels of cholesterol. But if you grew up in the impoverished Mediterranean during the time of Jesus, where you are never quite certain if you will eat well from day to day, then heaven is a place where God supplies abundant food. That is a God worth loving. That is a God worth worshiping.

Just as land is essential to God's justice in the Hebrew Bible, so it is with food in the New Testament. Food is the physical basis of life. The peasant who wants the land does not want just fifteen acres of sand and desert. What matters is that the land can produce. So in the end, God's justice is always fundamentally about food, that is, about an equitable access to life itself. When the Bible talks about the fair distribution of the land, it is talking about the fair distribution of food as the basis of life. That concept is hard to understand in a culture where we go through life fairly well fed and spend most of the time thinking about *not* eating too much. Yet, the gospel message makes us remember that throughout most of its human history much of the human race has struggled to find the next meal. That is why it is no coincidence that the central moment in early Christian worship developed as a meal, the Eucharist, the Lord's Supper.

This brings us to the third action of Jesus, announcing that the kingdom of God is already here. It is very hard for us to imagine what Rome would have heard when it heard that expression. Any Roman would have said, "Wait a minute! Kingdom of God? It must be Rome he's talking about." After all, the Roman empire contained all the glory that the gods could have poured on any nation, and it had the power of twenty-five legions of soldiers. We should not overlook the fact that Jesus does not use alternative phrases, such as "community of God" or "people of God." He speaks rather with a phrase that would have been heard in Rome as a direct challenge to the power and authority of Rome: kingdom of God. The content of what Jesus intends by use of this phrase can be seen clearly in Matthew's Gospel. In it Jesus prays, "May your kingdom come, may your will be done, on earth, as in heaven." For Jesus it is the earth that needs reordering. The issue at hand for him is how to make this earth fair and equitable and just for all the people, since it belongs to God. Imagine a Roman aristocrat's response to this: "Wait a minute. This god of yours doesn't own the land. Look around. We took it from you by war. And if you would like to talk theologically, our Jupiter took it from your Yahweh." Kingdom-of-God talk by Jesus is on a collision course with Rome, because it challenges Rome's ideas of justice and peace.

One more thing needs noting about Jesus' mandate that others go announce the kingdom of God. He tells them not to carry a staff. This sounds so inconsequential to us, but it gives us insight into the depths of what Jesus had in mind. In the ancient world, a staff was the one item that anyone traveling would certainly wish to have. Carrying a staff functioned to ward off anything from small-time robbers to prowling dogs. Not carrying one made a person much more vulnerable to attacks. The traveler not only became defenseless, but also would be boldly advertising that vulnerability. Not only would Jesus' followers refuse to strike back, they would also be telling anyone who saw them that they could not do so. Jesus' directive not to carry a staff disassociates his followers from the use of violence, even from defensive or protective violence.

Jesus is organizing an alternative vision of the world right under those Roman noses. Both Jesus and the Roman empire were interested in peace, but their visions of how to achieve it were diametrically opposed. Roman imperial theology rested on one fundamental premise: "Peace comes through victory," a slogan that comes up again and again in their writings and in their poetry, on their images and on their inscriptions. First you get victory, then you establish peace. As we have seen in this short study, however, for Jesus and his Jewish tradition, peace comes through justice.

For me, this vision — and challenge — can best be seen in the story popularly known as "the multiplication of the loaves and fishes" in Mark 6:30–44. I would really like to change that title to "the distribution of the loaves and fishes." I believe it should be read like a parable. Notice what is stressed in the text. The first thing I want you to watch is the situation. Nobody is starving to death. The crowd had just spent the whole day listening to Jesus, and at the end of the day the disciples make an obvious statement: "We are hungry." The solution to this problem for the disciples was simple: send the crowd away so we can get food. Jesus, however has a different solution: he orders his disciples to give the crowd something to eat. When they scoff at Jesus' absurd demand, he makes them go out among the people and find out what food is present, which was five loaves and two fish. After pronouncing a blessing over the food, the disciples passed out the food to the crowd. Amazingly, there is enough to go around with even food left over. Where did the abundance of food come from? Not a few scholars argue that this story has parallels to the tradition of manna that was provided by God to the Hebrews in the wilderness. Maybe. But this story is also very different. The manna came down from heaven. And in this story, Mark probably believed that Jesus could also have brought down manna from heaven. And if Jesus wanted to turn stones into bread, I am sure Mark thought he could. But Jesus does not do either. Rather, Jesus takes what is already there and when it passes through his hands it becomes more than enough for everyone.

It is hard for me to read this story without hearing Mark and his church in the background. The twelve disciples represent the church, the followers of Jesus, as they do consistently throughout Mark's Gospel. Their attitude toward the hungry was, "Not our problem, send them away!" But Jesus says, "No, it is your business to give them food to eat, and the food that is there already is perfectly adequate for everyone when it comes through the hands of divine justice." That is Jesus' message. It is not about proving Jesus was capable of doing this sort of thing. It's about distribution. When the food that is already available comes through the hands of God's justice, it is enough. When the justice of God is understood as the touchstone for how we must relate to the rest of the world, human and non-human, violence is replaced with peace, *Shalom*. The substratum for that model is a fair distribution of the earth and its food.

Conclusion

After September 11, 2001, and the war with Iraq, it should be clear to us that two options are set before us: either *victory for peace* or *justice for peace*. The first model is provided by the Roman empire and the second by the Jewish and Christian traditions found in the Torah, prophets, wisdom, and historical Jesus. Between these two options, it has become clear to me that the violence of victory which establishes peace comes at too high a price because it keeps feeding violence into the process. The second option holds our only promise of a meaningful future. It is a much more radical idea fraught with many pitfalls and dangers. Among them is the danger that we confuse justice with victory. When this happens it is usually because we have forgotten the mold within which God's justice is held — love. Justice without love easily turns into brutality, while love without justice often results in banality. In order for the religions of the world to benefit from any dialogue, or contribute to any efforts for global peace, we must opt for the second option. Lasting peace comes only through justice. Lack of justice shakes the very foundations of the earth.

Notes

One / Küng / Replacing Clashes with Dialogue

1. Participants were: Dr. A. Kamal Aboulmagd, Egypt; Dr. Lourdes Arizpe, Mexico; Dr. Hanan Ashrawi, Palestine; Dr. Ruth Cardoso, Brazil; The Honorable Jacques Delors, France; Dr. Leslie Gelb, United States of America; Nadine Gordimer, South Africa; His Royal Highness Prince El Hassan bin Talal, Jordan; Prof. Sergey Kapitza, Russia; Prof. Hayao Kawai, Japan; Prof. Tommy Koh, Singapore; Prof. Hans Küng, Switzerland; Graça Machel, Mozambique; Prof. Amartya Sen, India; Dr. Song Jian, China; Dick Spring, T. D. (Ireland); Prof. Tu Weiming, China; The Honorable Richard von Weizsäcker, Germany; Dr. Javad Zarif, Iran; Giandomenico Picco, Italy (personal representative of Secretary-General Kofi Annan for the United Nations Year of Dialogue among Civilizations).

2. Avraham Burg, "A Failed Israeli Society Collapses While Its Leaders Remain Silent," *The Forward*, August 29, 2003, www.forward.com/issues.

3. Ibid.

Two / Cook / Ethical Challenges in the "War" on Terrorism

1. Augustine, *City of God*, trans. Marcus Dods (New York: Modern Library, 1950), 19.13.

2. Thomas Hobbes, *Leviathan*, ed. Richard Tuck (Cambridge: Cambridge University Press, 1991), 13.62.

Three / Kelsay / Islam and the Problem of Violence

Some of the material in this essay appears in different form in Paul Robinson, ed., *Just War in Contemporary Perspective* (London: Ashgate, 2003); other portions appear in a different form in connection with my October 2003 Templeton Lecture at the Foreign Policy Research Institute in Philadelphia (see www.fpri.org) and in *Sewanee Theological Review* (December 2003).

1. For a very interesting and readable account of al-Zawahiri's pilgrimage to radicalism, see Lawrence Wright, "The Man behind Bin Laden," *New Yorker*, September 16, 2002.

2. The translation is by the Foreign Broadcast Information Service. I have made some minor alterations to fit my sense of the Arabic original.

3. For many years the standard introductions to Islamic law have been the works of Joseph Schacht. See, for example, his *Introduction to Islamic Law* (Oxford: Clarendon Press, 1964). This and other works by Schacht must now be supplemented by various studies authored by Wael Hallaq. See, for example, *A History of Islamic Legal Theories* (Cambridge: Cambridge University Press, 1997).

4. Here, as elsewhere in the *Declaration*, the authors refer to sources that many Muslim readers will recognize. The notion of a time when the nations will attack Muslims like people fighting over a plate of food refers to a saying of the Prophet which may be found, among other places, in James Robson's translation of the compendium of prophetic sayings known as *Mishkat al-Masabih* (Lahore: Sh. Muhammad Ashraf, 1981), II: 1115, in the "Book of Words Which Soften the Heart." Thanks to Michael Cook and James Pavlin for calling this to my attention.

5. The prime example is that of Ibn Ishaq. See the translation by A. Guillaume as *The Life of Muhammad* (Karachi: Oxford University Press, 1978). Martin Lings combines several traditional biographies for his *Muhammad: His Life Based on the Earliest Sources* (Rochester, Vt.: Inner Traditions International, 1983).

6. When I quote the Qur'an apart from the text of the *Declaration*, I use the translation by Yusuf 'Ali, with my own variations to reflect the sense of the Arabic text.

7. See, for example, the study by Fred Donner, *The Early Muslim Conquests* (Princeton, N.J.: Princeton University Press, 1981); idem, "The Sources of Islamic Conceptions of War," in *Just War and Jihad: Historical and Theoretical Perspectives on War and Peace in Western and Islamic Traditions*, ed. John Kelsay and James Turner Johnson (Westport, Conn.: Greenwood Press, 1991).

8. Here, see John Kelsay, *Islam and War: A Study in Comparative Ethics* (Louisville: Westminster/John Knox Press, 1993), as well as James Turner Johnson, *The Holy War Idea in Western and Islamic Traditions* (University Park: Pennsylvania State University Press, 1997).

9. The quotation appears to be from Ibn Taymiyya's treatise *al-siyasa al-shari'a*, which is translated by Omar A. Farrukh as *Ibn Taimiyya on Public and Private Law in Islam* (Beirut: Khayat's, 1966), as well as by Henri Laoust as *Le traité de droit public d'Ibn Taimiya* (Beirut: Institut Français de Damas, 1948).

10. See Mohammed Hashim Kamali, *Principles of Islamic Jurisprudence* (Cambridge: Islamic Texts Society, 1991).

11. On these points, note the very interesting comments made by Richard Bulliett in "The Crisis within Islam," *Wilson Quarterly* 26, no. 1 (Winter 2002): 11–19.

12. I discuss the reasoning of Hamas and Egyptian Islamic Jihad in Kelsay, *Islam and War*, 77–110. See materials cited there. Gilles Kepel, in *Jihad: The Trail of Political Islam*, trans. Anthony F. Roberts (Cambridge, Mass.: Belknap Press of Harvard University Press, 2002), argues that the Palestinian scholar Abdullah Azzam (d. 1989), who was a noteworthy figure among Arabs who made the journey to fight against Soviet forces in Afghanistan, is the key figure in articulating an "international" vision in which it would be necessary and justified to strike at targets far away from the Islamic "heartland," viz., in Europe and in the United States.

13. In my forthcoming article "Islam and the Justice of War," I show the consistency with which historic interpreters of *Shari'a* insisted on this point, even in the case of fighting classified as an "individual duty."

14. Michael Walzer, *Just and Unjust Wars*, 3rd ed. (New York: Basic Books, 2000).

15. See, for example, the very interesting (though in some ways obtuse) discussion regarding the permissibility of Muslims fighting on the U.S. or allied side in Afghanistan following the September 11, 2001, attacks at www.memri.org, Middle East Media Research Institute "Inquiry and Analysis Series," no. 75, November 6, 2001.

16. For these interviews, see www.pbs.org, where in particular the May 1998 interview with ABC correspondent John Miller is presented.

17. Abu Ghayth's article was originally published at www.alneda.com, which at the time was a frequent location for al Qaeda–related postings. The Web site changes URLs frequently, however, so that it is difficult to locate. A convenient translation of portions of the article is available at the Web site of the Middle East Media Research Institute, www.memri.org, where it is entry No. 388 in the "Special Dispatch Series." I quote from MEMRI's translation, with very slight alterations.

18. Again, a convenient translation of portions of the transcript may be found at www.memri.org, Special Dispatch Series, entry number 400. Quotation are from the MEMRI translation.

19. There is a translation available at www.observer.co.uk/worldview/story/0,11581,845725,00.html. Quotation are from this source.

Four / Jacobs / Jewish-Christian Relations

First presented at the Second International Holocaust Conference, "Remembering for the Future II," Berlin, Germany, March 1994.

1. Manfred R. Lehmann, " 'No' to a Jewish-Christian 'Theological Dialogue'!" *Southern Jewish Weekly* (September 1992): 11–12.

2. Jacob Neusner, "There Has Never Been a Judaeo-Christian Dialogue — But There Can Be One," *Cross Currents* 42, no. 1 (Spring 1992): 3–25. My own response appeared in that same journal, 42, no. 3 (Summer 1992): 424–26.

3. I remain indebted to the writings and teachings of Professors Ellis Rivkin (Emeritus) and the late Samuel Sandmel, *alav hashalom*, both of the Hebrew Union College–Jewish Institute of Religion, Cincinnati, as well as others, for much of my thinking about the New Testament text and the environment of first-century Judaism which produced it.

4. For a full explanation of my position, see Steven L. Jacobs, *Rethinking Jewish Faith: The Child of a Survivor Responds* (Albany: State University of New York Press, 1994), 90. The following discussion of obstacles depends heavily on my treatment here.

5. James H. Charlesworth, "Is the New Testament Anti-Semitic or Anti-Jewish?" *Explorations: Rethinking Relationships among Jews and Christians* 7, no. 2 (1993): 3.

6. Craig A. Evans, "Polemics or Anti-Semitism?" *Explorations: Rethinking Relationships among Jews and Christians* 7, no. 2 (1993): 3.

7. Krister Stendahl, "Anti-Semitism and the New Testament," *Explorations: Rethinking Relationships among Jews and Christians* 7, no. 2 (1993): 7.

8. The writings of James Charlesworth, Paula Frederiksen, John P. Meier, Jacob Neusner, Sharon H. Ringe, E. P. Sanders, Elisabeth Schüssler-Fiorenza, John Townsend, and Clark Williamson, among others, come readily to mind.

9. Blu Greenberg, in her article "The Holocaust and the Gospel of Truth," originally presented at the "Remembering for the Future" Conference, Oxford, England, July 10–13, 1988, offers a somewhat different suggestion:

> The conclusion that I draw from the Holocaust, and from the four decades following it, is that Christianity needs a Talmud and a Midrash that deal with the foundation documents of its faith; that Christians of the next two thousand years ought not to be able to read or teach or understand first-century Christianity without these hermeneutic texts

of quasi-canonical status; that in the year 2500, a Christian child standing at any point along the religious denominational spectrum will not and need not know where Scripture leaves off and quasi-Scripture begins.

Why do I use terms such as Talmud and Midrash, so particular to the Jewish tradition? In order to precisely convey the notions of power, and sacredness, as Talmud and Midrash have done for Jews for so many centuries unto this very day.

Blu Greenberg, "The Holocaust and the Gospel of Truth," *Holocaust and Genocide Studies* 4, no. 3 (1989): 273–74.

10. Following this reasoning, as we move more and more toward a global village, both Jews and Christians need to become conversant with the Qur'an of the Islamic tradition, the *Upanishads* and *Bhagavad Gita* of the Hindu tradition, etc., if we are to engage in dialogue with those of other faith communities. This conclusion is based on my *prejudice* [sic] that the real place to begin such interreligious dialogue in the post-*Shoah* world is with the sacred texts of each other's religious tradition, letting the issues which surface there from an intense examination of those literatures set the agenda.

11. Jacobs, *Rethinking Jewish Faith*, 92–93.

12. Thomas A. Idinopulous, "How the *Shoah* Affects Christian Belief," in *Contemporary Christian Religious Responses to the Shoah*, ed. Steven L. Jacobs (Lanham, Md.: University Press of America, 1993), 113.

13. Matthew 28:18–20, with appropriate parallels to Mark 16:15; Luke 24:47–49; John 20:21–23; and Acts 1:8.

14. That repugnance stems, in large measure, from the *fact* that, although such sharing is to occur out of genuine love and caring for the non-Christian, and a sincere and heartfelt desire for that person to share in the afterlife as Christianity understands it, overzealousness to do so down through the centuries, as well as contemporarily, has, all too often, negated these positive emotions and feelings, and led to further estrangement between Jews and Christians.

15. Huneke is referring here to, what for him, is a cardinal principle of post-*Shoah* Christian theology, that of Irving "Yitz" Greenberg's oft-quoted dictum: "Let us offer, then, as working principle the following: No statement, theological or otherwise, should be made that would not be credible in the presence of burning children." See Irving Greenberg, "Cloud of Smoke, Pillar of Fire: Judaism, Christianity, and Modernity after the Holocaust," in *Auschwitz: Beginning of a New Era? Reflections on the Holocaust*, ed. Eva Fleishner (New York: Ktav Publishing, 1997), 23.

16. Douglas K. Huneke, "In the Presence of Burning Children: The Reformation of Christianity after the *Shoah*," in Jacobs, *Contemporary Christian Religious Responses to the Shoah*, 98.

17. A most interesting exploration of this very topic is contained within the 1994 paper "Mission in a Pluralistic World: Implications for Our Understanding of Mission for Christian-Jewish Dialogue," by Hans Ucko, secretary for Christian-Jewish Relations of the World Council of Churches, Geneva, Switzerland, and delivered at the "Conference on Christian Mission and Jewish-Christian Relations," Center for Christian-Jewish Understanding, Sacred Heart University, Fairfield, Connecticut.

18. Rabbi Dr. Harold Schulweis of Valley Beth Shalom Congregation, Encino, California, was, indeed, correct in a lecture delivered in Birmingham, Alabama, in January 1975 when he stated that "the hardest thing for Jews to realize is that not every Christian is an anti-Semite, and not every German is a Nazi." That understanding on his part led to his creation of the Foundation for Righteous Gentiles, recognizing those who, during the *Shoah*, acquitted themselves honorably on behalf of Jews. The Foundation is now under the auspices of the Anti-Defamation League of B'nai B'rith, New York.

Again, theologically, we Jews must now begin accepting the fact that, during the darkest days of the *Shoah*, there were "Righteous *Christians*" who sought to ally themselves with us and did what they did *because* they were Christians. What will result from such Jewish discussions and perceptions is presently open to conclusion.

19. Raul Hilberg's threefold schema appears relevant in this context: "You have no right to live among us as Jews" to "You have no right to live among us" to "You have no right to live." See his magisterial work *The Destruction of the European Jews*, rev. and definitive edition (New York: Holmes and Meier, 1985), 3 vols., for his presentation of this thesis. Also, one need only read Roman Catholic Father Edward Flannery, *The Anguish of the Jews: Twenty-Three Centuries of Anti-Semitism* (New York: Paulist Press, 1985), among others, to find concrete evidence of this tragic story.

20. Joseph A. Fitzmyer, *Romans: A New Translation with Introduction and Commentary* (New York: Anchor Bible, 1993), 542.

21. Central Conference of American Rabbis, *Sha'arei Tefillah/Gates of Prayer: The New Union Prayerbook — Weekdays, Sabbaths, and Festival Services and Prayers for Synagogue and Home* (New York: CCAR Press, 1975), 221–22.

Five / Musser, Sutherland, Puchalla / Dangerous Faith

1. The term "evangelical Protestants" in this paper refers politically to the religious Right, perhaps the core constituency of George W. Bush. It refers religiously to evangelicals, fundamentalists, and many Pentecostals, and includes persons like Billy Graham, Jerry Falwell, and Pat Robertson. Generally speaking, evangelical Protestants believe that the Bible is without error and that Jesus is the only means to salvation. See Donald G. Bloesch, "Evangelicalism," 181–85, and William Vance Trollinger Jr., "Fundamentalism," 206–9, in *New and Enlarged Handbook of Christian Theology*, ed. Donald W. Musser and Joseph L. Price (Nashville: Abingdon Press, 2003); George M. Marsden, *Understanding Fundamentalism and Evangelicalism* (Grand Rapids: Eerdmans, 2000); "Defining Evangelicalism," *Institute for the Study of American Evangelicals*, October 12, 2001; see www.wheaton.edu/isae/defining_evangelicalism.html.

2. "21st Century Adversaries," www.trbc.org/sermons.

3. www.cnn.com/ELECTION/2000/epolls.

4. George W. Bush, *A Charge to Keep: My Journey to the White House* (New York: HarperCollins, 1999), 136.

5. Howard Fineman et al., "Bush and God," *Newsweek*, March 10, 2003.

6. Bush, *A Charge to Keep*, 137.

7. Ibid., 136.

8. The term "evangelical" has a wide range of meaning in contemporary American religious culture. In general theological terms, evangelicalism places a high priority on the Bible as divinely inspired and truthful; it teaches that salvation came through the grace of Jesus Christ alone; it emphasizes the crucial nature of conversion and thus the urgency of missions. Evangelicalism may be seen as an umbrella for a spectrum of conservative Christianity. On the far right of evangelicalism is fundamentalism. A simple definition for fundamentalism is sometimes given as an evangelical who is angry about something; this hits on the fundamentalist characteristic of militancy in fighting against liberalism in church, society, and politics. The core value of fundamentalism, however, is the view of the Bible as the inerrant, literal, and final authority on all matters. It is from the literal and inerrant reading of the Bible that dispensationalism was first produced.

9. Fineman, "Bush and God."

10. "Inaugural Invocation," www.samaritanspurse.org.

11. Donald W. Musser, "Eternal Life," in *Handbook*, 170–71.

12. Hans Schwarz, "Eschatology," in *Handbook*, 166–70.

13. Timothy P. Weber, "Dispensationalism," in *Handbook*, 129–31.

14. Paul Boyer, *When Time Shall Be No More: Prophesy Belief in Modern American Culture* (Cambridge, Mass.: Belknap Press of Harvard University Press, 1998), 88–89.

15. The belief that the church will be raptured *before* the Tribulation begins is why dispensationalism is also called pretribulational premillennialism. (There are also premillennialists who believe that the church will be raptured during or after the Tribulation, but these have become few and far between.)

16. Boyer, *When Time Shall Be No More*, 315.

17. Bush, *A Charge to Keep*, 6.

18. Quoted by Fineman, "Bush and God."

19. Ibid., quotes an anonymous former Bush staffer as saying, "No one is allowed to second-guess, even when you should."

20. George Bush, *108th Cong., State of the Union* 1st Session (Washington, D.C.: U.S. Government Printing Office, 2003).

21. Billy Graham, *Approaching Hoofbeats: The Four Horsemen of the Apocalypse* (Minneapolis: Grason, 1983), 79.

22. Address to a Joint Session of Congress and the American People, September 20, 2001, www.whitehouse.gov.

23. Bush at a Town Hall Meeting in Ontario, California. Transcript can be found at www.usembassy-israel.org.

24. Mark Juergensmeyer, *Terror in the Mind of God: The Global Rise of Religious Violence* (Berkeley: University of California, 2001), chaps. 8 and 11.

25. Quoted in John Dart, "Bush Religious Rhetoric Riles Critics," *Christian Century* 120, no. 5 (2003): 10–12.

26. Address to a Joint Session of Congress and the American People.

27. Fineman, "Bush and God."

28. Graham, *Approaching Hoofbeats*, 75.

29. Dispensationalists consider the Christian church, with its affirmation of Jesus as the Jewish messiah, as a "parenthesis" in God's covenant with Judaism.

30. Pat Robertson, "On Israel and the Road Map to Peace," online at www.Patrobertson.com/Teaching.

31. See Donald Wagner, *Anxious for Armageddon* (Scottdale, Pa.: Herald Press, 1995).

32. Grace Halsell, *Forcing God's Hand: Why Millions Pray for a Quick Rapture — and Destruction of Planet Earth* (Washington, D.C.: Crossroads International, 1999), 95–96.

33. Grace Halsell, *Prophecy and Politics: The Secret Alliance between Israel and the U.S. Christian Right* (Chicago: Lawrence Hill, 1986), 96–102.

34. Jane Lampman, "New Scrutiny of the Role of Religion in Bush's Policies," *Christian Science Monitor*, March 17, 2003.

35. Jerry Falwell, "Revelation Chapter 11: Hell on Earth," www.trbc.org/ sermons.

36. Proverbs 24:16 states, "For a just man falls seven times, and then he will rise again, but the wicked are overthrown by calamity." See "Ariel Sharon — Lion of God???" *EndTimeInfo*, December 1998.

37. The danger of unintended results that foreign policies are subconsciously determined by a presupposed theological agenda of a "coalition" between Christian dispensationalists and pro-Israeli parties is intensified by the visible presence of vociferous Jewish figures in tremendously powerful positions in the Bush administrations. Among the most influential are Richard Perle, one of Bush's foreign policy advisors and chairman of the Pentagon's Defense Policy Board; Paul Wolfowitz, deputy defense secretary, and member of Perle's Defense Policy Board; Douglas Feith, undersecretary of defense and policy advisor at the Pentagon, who is also closely associated with the extremist Zionist Organization of America, which even attacks Jews that don't agree with its views.

38. Boyer, *When Time Shall Be No More*, 208.

39. Remarks by the President at Multilateral Meeting with Arab Leaders, Sharm el-Sheikh, Egypt, June 3, 2003, www.whitehouse.gov.

40. Bush, State of the Union, 2003.

41. Ibid.

42. Paul Findley, "An Historic Breakthrough?" *Washing Report on Middle East Affairs* 22, no. 6 (July–August 2003), www.epnet.com.

43. "Letter to President Bush," *Institute for Global Engagement*, August 5, 2002, www.globalengagement.org.

44. A complete collection of President Bush's statements about Islam can be found at www.whitehouse.gov/infocus/Ramadan/islam.

45. NBC quoted F. Graham saying this at the dedication of a North Carolina chapel in October 2001. See also www.cnn.com/2003/ALLPOLITICS/ 04/18/graham.pentagon for his Good Friday message at the Pentagon.

46. Pat Robertson, "Bring It On: Are God and Allah the Same?" online at www.cbn.com/700club.

47. Jerry Vines, "Muslims Angered by Baptist Criticism," www.cnn.com/ 2002/ALLPOLITICS.

48. Falwell, "What Is Next in the End Time Drama," September 9, 2001, online at www.trbc.org/sermons.

49. "Revelation Chapter 9: D-Day on Planet Earth," January 4, 1998, online at www.trbc.org/sermon.

50. Ibid. It is also curious that this statement is taken verbatim from a document published by Dr. Edward Hindson, dean of the Institute of Biblical Studies at Falwell's Liberty University. Dr. Hindson's document, "What Will It Be Like to Be Left Behind?" can be found on the Tim LaHaye School of Prophecy Web site at www.schoolofprophecy.com/left-behind.html. The School of Prophecy is also one of Jerry Falwell's ministries.

51. "Revelation, Chapter 8, WWIII" December 14, 1997, www.trbc.org/sermons.

52. Billy Graham, "What Is the Battle of Armageddon?" available online at www.billygraham.com/LFA_Article.asp?ArticleID=27.

53. Boyer, *When Time Shall Be No More*, 145. Robison delivered the invocation at the 1984 Republican Convention. George W. Bush also appeared on Robison's television program, *Life Today*, while Bush was governor of Texas. Bush also invited the televangelist to speak during his second inaugural prayer breakfast. See Molly Ivins and Lou Dubose, *Shrub: The Short but Happy Political Life of George W. Bush* (New York: Random House, 2000), 61.

54. Tim LaHaye and Jerry Jenkins, *Left Behind* (Wheaton, Ill.: Tyndale, 1995).

55. Genesis 19:24.

56. Isaiah 5:24.

57. Amos 7:4.

58. Ezekiel 39:6.

59. Second Peter 3:10 NRSV states that some ancient authorities read "disclosed" instead of "burned up."

60. Revelation 8:7–8.

61. Boyer, *When Time Shall Be No More*, 115.

62. Halsell, *Prophecy and Politics*, 36.

63. Boyer, *When Time Shall Be No More*, 119–20.

64. Ibid., 145.

65. Ibid., 144.

66. Falwell, "Revelation, Chapter 8."

67. Hal Lindsey, *2000 A.D.: Will Mankind Survive?* (Palos Verdes, Calif.: Western Front, 1994), 309. For further examples, see Daniel Wojcik, *The End of the World as We Know It: Faith, Fatalism, and Apocalypse in America* (New York: New York University Press, 1997), 170.

68. Falwell, "Revelation, chapter 1," www.trbc.org/sermons.

69. Glenn Scherer, "Religious Wrong: A Higher Power Informs the Republican Assault on the Environment," *E Magazine* (March–April 2003).

70. Bush, State of the Union, 2003.

71. "Politics," *Ecologist* 33, no. 1 (February 2003), www.epnet.com.

Six / Kimball / Absolute Truth Claims

1. The term "fundamentalist" is used widely by journalists to refer to individuals, groups, and movements within various religious traditions worldwide. Elements linking such groups include claims of strict adherence to literalist interpretation of sacred texts, vehement rejection of elements of modernity deemed to undermine traditional values and religious structures, and a desire to return to a perceived "ideal time." For many scholars, the term produces more confusion than clarity. Since fundamentalism is a term tied to a particular movement among Protestant Christians beginning in the nineteenth century, some suggest it may confuse rather than clarify issues when applied to Muslims, Hindus, et al. The large majority of Muslims worldwide, for instance, are "fundamentalist" in the sense that they affirm the Qur'an to be the literal Word of God, mediated through the prophet Muhammad and without error. Within this framework, however, Muslims have and continue to understand and interpret the sacred text in a wide variety of ways. For an extensive study of this issue and an exploration of movements worldwide, see Martin E. Marty and R. Scott Appleby, eds., *The Fundamentalism Project*, 5 vols. (Chicago: University of Chicago Press, 1991–5).

2. See Charles Kimball, *When Religion Becomes Evil* (San Francisco: HarperSanFrancisco, 2002) for an exploration of five warning signs of corrupted religion, including contemporary and historical examples of major ways adherents in all religious traditions can and do justify violent, destructive behavior in the name of religion. Short portions from chapters 2 and 7 are included in this present article.

3. A comparative study of sacred texts reveals a wide variety of understandings about and approaches to sacred scriptures. One cannot easily compare the appropriation of the Qur'an with the array of sacred texts in the Hindu or Buddhist traditions, for example. While the points of contact and functional similarity with the Bible are more visible with the Qur'an, great differences remain. Catholic, Orthodox, and Protestant Christians, for instance, don't agree on what constitutes the canon or the role of the Bible in setting forth authoritative doctrine. See Wilfred Cantwell Smith, *What Is Scripture?* (Minneapolis: Fortress Press, 1993), for a thoughtful, comparative study of sacred scriptures in the major religious traditions.

4. The Arabic term for "striving" or "struggling in the way of God" is *jihad*. All Muslims are enjoined to engage in *jihad*. The term "holy war," which is widely used in Western media and among some Muslims, includes one of the ways this obligatory duty has been and is being promulgated. The primary meaning of *jihad* for Muslims is the "struggle to do the right thing."

A well-known saying (*hadith*) attributed to Muhammad reminds Muslims that the "lesser *jihad*" is the outward battle in defense of Islam; the "greater *jihad*" is the inner struggle to overcome selfish and sinful desires, the strong tendencies that inhibit human beings from doing what they know to be right. Thus, Muslims speak often of the *jihad* of the heart, of the tongue, and of the hand.

5. Muslim commentators often elaborate on a particular "occasion of revelation." Similar processes of interpretation are employed with the Bible. One cannot read a passage on sacrificial ritual requirements or a Pauline epistle without reference to the particular context. People in both traditions, of course, do draw general teachings from specific circumstances. It is misleading or disingenuous, however, to simply quote a passage without any reference to context and declare, "The Qur'an says . . . " or "The Bible says . . . "

6. See Peter Gomes, *The Good Book: Reading the Bible with Mind and Heart* (New York: William Morrow, 1996), and Marcus J. Borg, *Reading the Bible Again for the First Time: Taking the Bible Seriously but Not Literally* (San Francisco: HarperSanFrancisco, 2001), for a refreshing exploration of the biblical texts. Burton L. Visotzky, *Reading the Book: Marking the Bible a Timeless Text* (New York: Doubleday, 1991), provides a thoughtful introduction to classical Jewish approaches to the Bible.

7. The variations on this theme are many. In November 2002, Jerry Falwell's comment on the CBS program *60 Minutes* was among the most offensive and widely publicized claims repeatedly featured in the worldwide media: "Jesus taught a gospel of love, but Muhammad was a terrorist." In June 2002, a past president of the Southern Baptist Convention, Jerry Vines, was quoted in the worldwide press when he addressed the Pastor's Conference prior to the convention in St. Louis. Vines called Muhammad a "demon-possessed pedophile." Coming in the same week U.S. Catholic bishops were meeting in Dallas to deal with the exceedingly difficult issues surrounding problems of sexual abuse among clergy, Vines took a backhanded slap at Catholicism along with his assault on the prophet of Islam.

8. News stories focused on American Protestant leaders denouncing Islam and Muhammad make headlines for a few days in the United States; they continue to get attention for months in many parts of the world, sometimes fueling violent responses. Muslim extremists have attacked and killed Christian missionaries in Yemen, the Philippines, and India in 2002–3. In an effort to halt irresponsible and incendiary rhetoric, fifty Southern Baptist

missionaries issued a strong statement in 2003, asking U.S. leaders to refrain from derogatory pronouncements about Islam.

9. Two recent award-winning books explore the understandings about God in the Abrahamic tradition. See Karen Armstrong, *A History of God: The 4,000-Year Quest of Judaism, Christianity, and Islam* (New York: Alfred A. Knopf, 1993), and Jack Miles, *God: A Biography* (New York: Alfred A. Knopf, 1995).

10. The pervasive influence of dispensational theology, a version of which suggests we are literally on the verge of cataclysmic events leading to Armageddon, can be seen in the runaway bestselling books in the "Left Behind" series. More than 50 million volumes are currently in print. Untold millions of well-intentioned Christians read and excitedly share these novels as biblical theology.

11. See Jane I. Smith and Yvonne H. Haddad, *The Islamic Understanding of Death and Resurrection* (Albany: SUNY Press, 1982), for a detailed study of Islamic eschatology.

12. Wesley Ariarajah, *The Bible and People of Other Faiths* (Maryknoll, N.Y.: Orbis Books, 1989), 25–26.

13. Several variations of this sentiment are widely attributed to Albert Einstein. See www.giga-usa.com/gigaweb1/quotes2/quateinsteinalbertx005.htm.

14. Austin P. Flannery, ed., *Documents of Vatican II*, 2d ed. (Grand Rapids: Eerdmans, 1980), 367.

15. Paul Knitter, a theologian at Xavier University, has written several books that analyze and interpret a range of nuanced positions within the Christian community of scholars. See, for instance, *No Other Name?* (1985) and *One Earth Many Religions* (1995) and other titles in the "Faith Meet Faith" series published by Orbis Books, Maryknoll, N.Y.

16. Diana L. Eck, *A New Religious America: How a "Christian Country" Has Become the World's Most Religiously Diverse Nation* (San Francisco: HarperSanFrancisco, 2001), 23. John Cobb, Wilfred Cantwell Smith, and Harvey Cox are among the more prominent scholars to articulate a pluralist position. See John Cobb, *God Has Many Names* (London: Macmillan, 1980), for an analysis of the world's religious traditions as different responses to the one divine Reality. A more radical approach is found in Wilfred Cantwell Smith, *Towards a World Theology: Faith and the Comparative History of Religion* (Philadelphia: Westminster Press, 1993). Smith seeks to erase the "we-they" interpretation within the boundaries and self-sufficiency of Christianity. In Harvey Cox, *Many Mansions: A Christian's*

Encounter with Other Faiths (Boston: Beacon Press, 1988), the author offers theological reflection rooted in the personal experience of interfaith dialogue.

17. This passage, together with Acts 4:12 ("There is no other name given under heaven by which you must be saved"), are routinely cited by Christian exclusivists to establish the bottom line: Jesus is the only way to salvation. The official position of the Roman Catholic Church and different forms of inclusive theology affirm the uniqueness of Jesus as the way. Clearly, it is possible to interpret these seemingly narrow statements in broader, more encompassing ways. In the case of John 14:6, it is worth noting that this is one of several "I am" statements attributed to Jesus. Others are clearly metaphorical (e.g., "I am the shepherd, you are the sheep..."; "I am the vine, you are the branches..."; and, "I am the door..."). Why do many people come to this particular verse and insist that it can only be interpreted one way? In the highly charged theological language of John's Gospel, there are several ways to interpret what is being conveyed in John 14:6. The context for the passage is framed by Jesus saying, "In my Father's house there are many dwelling places" and Thomas asking, "Lord, we do not know where you are going. How can we know the way?"

Seven / Ziegler / Is the Empowered Woman a Warrior or a Dove?

1. William Ladd, "On the Duty of Females to Promote the Cause of Peace," *Journal of the American Peace Society* (1836): 6–30, 34–35.

2. *Letters of Theodore Dwight Weld, Angelina Grimké Weld, and Sarah Grimké,* 2 vols., ed. Gilbert H. Barnes and Dwight L. Dumond (New York: D. Appleton-Century, 1934), 1:428.

3. Sarah M. Grimké, *Letters on the Equality of the Sexes and the Condition of Women* (New York: Source Book Press, 1970), 10.

4. Dorothy Sterling, *Ahead of Her Time* (New York: W. W. Norton, 1991), 107–9.

5. Ibid., 124.

6. Julia Ward Howe, *Reminiscences* (Washington, D.C.: Ross & Perry, 2002), 372–73.

7. Julia Ward Howe, "The Woman's Peace Festival — Mrs. Howe's Address," *Woman's Journal* 6, no. 23 (June 5, 1875): 180.

8. Howe Family Papers, Houghton Library, Harvard University, August 27, 1872.

9. Florence Howe Hall, *Julia Ward Howe and the Woman Suffrage Movement* (Boston: D. Estes, 1913; reprint, New York: Arno, 1969), 42.

10. Jane Addams, *Newer Ideals of Peace* (New York: Jerome S. Ozer Publisher, 1972), 16–18, 37.

11. Marie Louise Degen, *The History of the Woman's Peace Party* (Baltimore: Johns Hopkins University Press, 1939), 70, 81.

12. Charles Chatfield, *For Peace and Justice* (Knoxville: University of Tennessee Press, 1971), 95.

13. Rachel Waltner Goossen, *Women against the Good War* (Chapel Hill: University of North Carolina Press, 1997), 4.

14. Sara Evans, *Personal Politics: The Roots of Women's Liberation in the Civil Rights Movement and the Left* (New York: Knopf: 1979), 86.

15. Ynestra King, "If I Can't Dance," in *Rocking the Ship of State: Toward a Feminist Peace Politics*, ed. Adrienne Harris and Ynestra King (Boulder, Colo.: Westview Press, 1991), 284, 287.

16. Anne Sisson Runyan, "Feminism, Peace, and International Politics: An Examination of Women Organizing Internationally for Peace and Security" (Ph.D. dissertation, American University, 1988), 436, 78.

17. Addams, *Newer Ideals of Peace*, 16–18.

18. Ibid., 16–18, 37.

Eight / Bell / Latin American Liberation Theology

1. Thomas Cahill, "The One True Faith: Is It Tolerance?" *New York Times*, February 3, 2002.

2. Judith N. Shklar, *Ordinary Vices* (Cambridge, Mass.: Harvard University Press, 1984), 5.

3. Jeffery Stout, *The Flight from Authority: Religion, Morality, and the Quest for Autonomy* (Notre Dame, Ind.: University of Notre Dame Press, 1981), 241.

4. Max Weber, "Politics as a Vocation," in *From Max Weber*, ed. H. Gerth and C. Mills (New York: Oxford, 1946), 78.

5. William T. Cavanaugh, "A Fire Strong Enough to Consume the House: The Wars of Religion and the Rise of the State," *Modern Theology* 11, no. 4 (October 1995): 397–420. See also William T. Cavanaugh, "The City," in *Radical Orthodoxy*, ed. J. Milbank, C. Pickstock, and G. Ward (New York: Routledge, 1999), 182–200. There he writes, "To cite a few examples: in the French civil wars of the late sixteenth century, the Catholic League was opposed not only by Huguenots, but by another Catholic party, the Politiques; in German territory, Catholic Habsburg wars against Lutherans in both 1547–55 and 1618–48 were opposed by the German Catholic nobility, and in both cases the French Catholic king came to the aid of the Lutherans; the Thirty Years' War — the most notorious of the 'Wars

of Religion' — became a contest between the Habsburgs and the Bourbons, the two great Catholic dynasties of Europe" (190–91).

Note that the character of these conflicts does not immediately suggest that these were wars directly against religion. Instead, they appear to be the wars of princes seizing and consolidating territorial sovereignty. How this is a displacement of the church is seen in precisely the ways princes were able to claim an allegiance that exceeded Christian identity, the way in which the people were mobilized along lines that defied and even ruptured ecclesial-confessional authority. They are "against the church," then, in an indirect sense insofar as they are the culmination of the long struggle of the prince to escape the tutelage and subdue the temporal power of the church.

6. Mark Juergensmeyer, *Terror in the Mind of God: The Global Rise of Religious Violence*, updated ed. (Berkeley: University of California Press, 2000).

7. See, for example, Richard John Neuhaus, *The Catholic Moment* (New York: Harper and Row Publishers, 1987), 171; Neuhaus quoted in Thomas C. Fox, "Group's Statement Describes Conflict of 'Totalitarianism' vs. 'Democracy,'" *National Catholic Reporter*, November 20, 1981, 6. Other examples include John W. Cooper's claim that some forms of liberation theology constitute a threat to human rights. See John W. Cooper, "Liberation Theology, Human Rights, and U.S. Security," in *The Politics of Latin American Liberation Theology*, ed. Richard L. Rubenstein and John K. Roth (Washington, D.C.: Washington Institute Press, 1988), 288. Or Richard C. Brown's statement that liberation theology creates an atmosphere in which terrorism is made to appear morally justifiable. See Richard C. Brown, "Liberation Theology in Latin America: Its Challenge to the United States," *Conflict* 4 (1983): 45. In a related vein, Frederick Sontag suggests that some liberation theology displays a tendency to incite hatred. See Frederick Sontag, "Liberation Theology and the Interpretation of Political Violence," in *The Politics of Latin American Liberation Theology*, ed. Richard L. Rubenstein and John K. Roth (Washington, D.C.: Washington Institute Press, 1988), 109, 112.

8. Juergensmeyer, *Terror in the Mind of God*, 221.

9. Most recently, consider the groundswell of support in North America for the use of torture in the aftermath of September 11, 2001 — whether in popular discourse or in the actual practice of delivering suspects over to foreign governments who practice that form of interrogation. Historical examples abound — from the support for obliteration bombing, including the nuclear incineration of Hiroshima and Nagasaki during the Second World

War to popular support for the various forms of state-terrorism in Latin America garnered during the latter half of the twentieth century.

10. Juergensmeyer, *Terror in the Mind of God*, 243.

11. R. Scott Appleby, *The Ambivalence of the Sacred: Religion, Violence, and Reconciliation* (Lanham, Md.: Rowman and Littlefield, 2000).

12. There is some truth to this assertion — namely, faiths that accept the dominion of the liberal political order do not face the liberal state's wrath, while those that resist such dominion — even by means of a principled commitment to nonviolence — are subject to the terror of low-intensity conflict, death squads, disappearances, and so forth.

13. Appleby, *The Ambivalence of the Sacred*, 117. In the original text, the liberationist Ernesto Cardenal is actually making the opposite point. With reference to the parable of the Good Samaritan, he says that liberationists interpret the gospel as calling Christians to join in solidarity with the slaughtered. See Teófilo Cabastrero, *Ministers of God*, trans. R. Barr (Maryknoll, N.Y.: Orbis Books, 1983), 22–23.

14. Appleby, *The Ambivalence of the Sacred*, 307.

15. Ibid., 280. See also 254, 281.

16. See Philip McManus and Gerald Schlabach, eds., *Relentless Persistence: Nonviolent Action in Latin America* (Santa Cruz, Calif.: New Society Publishers, 1991); Dominique Barbé, *Grace and Power: Base Communities and Nonviolence in Brazil*, trans. J. Brown (Maryknoll, N.Y.: Orbis Books, 1987); Dominique Barbé, *A Theology of Conflict and Other Writings on Nonviolence* (Maryknoll, N.Y.: Orbis Books, 1989); Hélder Câmara, *Revolution through Peace*, trans. A. McLean (New York: Harper & Row, 1971); Adolfo Pérez Esquivel, *Christ in a Poncho: Witnesses to the Nonviolent Struggles in Latin America*, ed. C. Antoine, trans. R. Barr (Maryknoll, N.Y.: Orbis Books, 1983); Leonardo Boff, "Christ's Liberation via Oppression: An Attempt at Theological Construction from the Standpoint of Latin America," in *Frontiers of Theology in Latin America*, ed. R. Gibellini, trans. J. Drury (Maryknoll, N.Y.: Orbis Books, 1979), 120; Segundo Galilea, "Liberation Theology and New Tasks Facing Christians," in *Frontiers of Theology in Latin America*, ed. R. Gibellini, trans. J. Drury (Maryknoll, N.Y.: Orbis Books, 1979), 175.

17. See Daniel M. Bell Jr., "The Violence of Love: Latin American Liberationists in Defense of the Tradition of Revolutionary Violence," *Journal for Peace and Justice Studies* 8 (1997): 17–36.

18. Gustavo Gutiérrez, *A Theology of Liberation*, rev. ed., trans. C. Inda and J. Eagleson (Maryknoll, N.Y.: Orbis Books, 1988), xiii.

19. Gustavo Gutiérrez, *The Power of the Poor in History*, trans. R. Barr (Maryknoll, N.Y.: Orbis Books, 1983), 91.

20. In particular, the events surrounding the publication of Leonardo Boff's *Church: Charism and Power,* trans. J. Diercksmeier (New York: Crossroad, 1990). See also the two Vatican instructions concerning liberation theology found in Alfred T. Hennelly, ed., *Liberation Theology: A Documentary History* (Maryknoll, N.Y.: Orbis Books, 1990), 393–414, 425–30.

21. Jon Sobrino, "Latin America: Guatemala/El Salvador," in *Religion as a Source of Violence?* ed. E. Beuken and K. Kuschel (Maryknoll, N.Y.: Orbis Books, 1997), 38.

22. Gustavo Gutiérrez, *The God of Life*, trans. M. O'Connell (Maryknoll, N.Y.: Orbis Books, 1991), 62.

23. Ignacio Martín-Baró, "Developing a Critical Consciousness through the University Curriculum," in *Towards a Society That Serves Its People: The Intellectual Contribution of El Salvador's Murdered Jesuits*, ed. J. Hassett and H. Lacey (Washington, D.C.: Georgetown University Press, 1991), 221; Martín-Baró, "Violence in Central America: A Social Psychological Perspective," in *Towards a Society That Serves Its People: The Intellectual Contribution of El Salvador's Murdered Jesuits*, ed. J. Hassett and H. Lacey (Washington, D.C.: Georgetown University Press, 1991), 333.

24. Hélder Câmara led the way in this reflection. Note that there is some variation among liberationists with regard to this typology. For example, Câmara distinguished between established, revolutionary, and repressive violence, whereas Martín-Baró distinguished between the violence associated with crime, with sociopolitical repression, and with war. See Câmara, *The Spiral of Violence*, trans. D. Couling (Denville, N.J.: Dimension Books, 1971), 29–34; Martín-Baró, "Violence in Central America," 337.

25. Gustavo Gutiérrez, "How Can God Be Discussed from the Perspective of Ayacucho?" *Concilium* 1 (1990): 112. Liberationists view the external debt of Latin American countries as a weapon of war and instrument of tremendous violence. See Hugo Assmann, "The Improvement of Democracy in Latin America and the Debt Crisis," in *Liberation Theology and the Liberal Society*, ed. M. Novak (Washington, D.C.: American Enterprise Institute, 1987), 44; Franz J. Hinkelammert, *Cultura de la esperanza y sociedad sin exclusión* (San José, Costa Rica: DEI, 1995), 13, 39. It is worth noting that in the *Summa*, Thomas Aquinas equates unjust laws with violence (I–II.96.4).

26. Ignacio Ellacuría, "Violence and Non-violence in the Struggle for Peace and Liberation," *Concilium* 195 (1988): 70; Gutiérrez, "How Can God Be Discussed from the Perspective of Ayacucho?" 112.

27. Jon Sobrino, "Unjust and Violent Poverty in Latin America," *Concilium* 195 (1988): 57.

28. Ellacuría, "Violence and Non-violence in the Struggle for Peace and Liberation," 71.

29. Franz J. Hinkelammert, *The Ideological Weapons of Death*, trans. P. Berryman (Maryknoll, N.Y.: Orbis Books, 1986), 223.

30. Jon Sobrino, *Jesus the Liberator*, trans. P. Burns and F. McDonagh (Maryknoll, N.Y.: Orbis Books, 1993), 213.

31. Liberationists do acknowledge and lament the possibility, indeed the reality in a place like Peru, that revolutionary violence can end up being as vicious and life-denying as the repressive violence that provoked it. In this case it rightfully deserves the label "terrorist" and is denounced. See Gutiérrez, *The God of Life*, 62; Ellacuría, "The Struggle for Peace and Liberation," 71–72; Juan Luis Segundo, *Jesus of Nazareth Yesterday and Today*, vol. 1: *Faith and Ideologies*, trans. J. Drury (Maryknoll, N.Y.: Orbis Books, 1984), 282–303.

32. Gutiérrez, *A Theology of Liberation*, 63–64.

33. This article is found in Franz J. Hinkelammert, *Cultura de la esperanza y sociedad sin exclusión* (San José, Costa Rico: DEI, 1995), 25–38. While I use this article to frame the discussion that follows, I draw from the entire book to unpack the theses. All translations are mine.

34. Ibid., 27–28.

35. Ibid., 92.

36. Ibid., 17.

37. While this phrase accurately portrays Hinkelammert's analysis, I actually take it from Alfred Stepan, "State Power and the Strength of Civil Society in the Southern Cone of Latin America," in *Bringing the State Back In*, ed. P. Evans, D. Rueschemeyer, and T. Skocpol (Cambridge: Cambridge University Press, 1985), 324.

38. Hinkelammert, *Cultura de la esperanza*, 29.

39. Ibid., 319.

40. The reference to foraging in garbage dumps and feeding one's children newspaper is drawn from Susan George's *A Fate Worse Than Debt* (New York: Grove Press, 1988), 137. She recounts the story of a social worker in the Brazilian town of Porto Alegro who, upon approaching a hut near the River Guaibe, was greeted by five young children whose parents were out foraging in the garbage heaps. In response to the social worker's queries

about when they had last eaten, one of the children answered that they had eaten the day before when their mother had kneaded little cakes for them out of wet newspaper.

41. Hinkelammert, *Cultura de la esperanza*, 32.

42. Ibid., 133.

43. Ibid., 39. He also suggests that the collection of the debt amounts to a "genocide without comparison in history" (13).

44. See *Pasos* 98 (November–December 2001): passim.

45. Franz Hinkelammert, "La caída de las torres," *Pasos* 98 (November–December 2001): 48; Hinkelammert, "La proyección del monstruo: La conspiración terrorista mundial," *Pasos* 101 (May–June 2002): 33.

46. The current capitalist formation is identified as "fundamentalist" insofar as it is in a sense as ill-liberal and antimodernist as the movements commonly called fundamentalist. It is a capitalism that has dropped the modern, liberal pretense of concern for the "general interest" or common good of all. This is the capitalism that has no scruples about exposing its greed, its aggressive desire to consume all. It is frequently referred to as "casino capitalism." Germán Gutiérrez, "El ALCA y la guerra antiterrorista de George W. Bush," *Pasos* 98 (November–December 2001): 22–23; Germán Gutiérrez, "Fundamentalismo y sujeto," *Pasos* 103 (September–October 2002): 20–21. See also Sobrino, "Latin America," 42.

47. The U.S.-sponsored coup of Augusto Pinochet in Chile unleashed a wave of terror that not only destroyed liberal democracy in that country but also marked the beginning of the neoliberal model of complete opening to global capital. See Germán Gutiérrez, "Fundamentalismo y sujeto," 20. See also Ariel Dorfman, "I Have Been through This Before," in *Strike Terror No More: Theology, Ethics, and the New War*, ed. J. Berquist (St. Louis: Chalice Press, 2002).

48. Gustavo Gutiérrez, "Option for the Poor," in *Mysterium Liberationis: Fundamental Concepts of Liberation Theology*, ed. I. Ellacuría and J. Sobrino (Maryknoll, N.Y.: Orbis Books, 1993), 240.

49. Jon Sobrino, *Christology at the Crossroads*, trans. J. Drury (Maryknoll, N.Y.: Orbis Books, 1978), 370.

50. Hugo Assmann, *Theology for a Nomad Church*, trans. P. Burns (Maryknoll, N.Y.: Orbis Books, 1976), 65.

51. Gutiérrez, *The Power of the Poor in History*, 207.

52. Gustavo Gutiérrez, *The Truth Shall Make You Free*, trans. M. O'Connell (Maryknoll, N.Y.: Orbis Books, 1990), 67; see also 72–75; Gutiérrez, *A Theology of Liberation*, 157–58; Ricardo Antoncich, *Christians in the*

Face of Injustice: A Latin American Reading of Catholic Social Teaching (Maryknoll, N.Y.: Orbis Books, 1987), 127–28.

53. See Gutiérrez, *The Truth Shall Make You Free*, 38, 131.

54. See Gutiérrez, *A Theology of Liberation*, 274; Gutiérrez, *The Power of the Poor in History*, 43–44.

55. Sobrino, *Christology at the Crossroads*, 54.

56. Ellacuría, "Violence and Non-violence in the Struggle for Peace and Liberation," 73.

57. Note the designation "companion of martyrs" is itself not entirely unproblematic insofar as while many of the liberationists are friends and companions of those martyred in the struggle against the empire, many liberationists have themselves been martyred for their witness.

58. See Jon Sobrino, "De una teología solo de la liberación a una teología del martirio," in *Cambio social y pensamiento cristiano en América Latina*, ed. J. Comblin, J. González Faus, and J. Sobrino (Madrid: Editorial Trotta, 1993), 101–21.

59. Jon Sobrino, "Spirituality and the Following of Jesus," in *Mysterium Liberationis: Fundamental Concepts of Liberation Theology*, ed. I. Ellacuría and J. Sobrino (Maryknoll, N.Y.: Orbis Books, 1993), 695.

60. Sobrino, *Jesus the Liberator*, 245–46.

61. It is worth noting that even as they lift up suffering and the possibility of martyrdom, the liberationists warn against developing a cult of suffering. Gutiérrez, for example, cautions that "amid all our admiration and respect for martyrdom we must not forget the cruelty that marks such an event, the abhorrence that the conditions giving rise to these murders should make us feel. Martyrdom is something that happens but is not sought" (Gutiérrez, *We Drink from Our Own Wells*, trans. M. O'Connell [Maryknoll, N.Y.: Orbis Books, 1984], 116–17). Likewise, Sobrino asserts, "Christian spirituality... is not a spirituality of the cross or of suffering. It is a spirituality of honest, consistent, and faithful love — a wide-awake love that knows the necessary risks it is taking" (Sobrino, "Spirituality and the Following of Jesus," 694).

62. Jon Sobrino, *The Principle of Mercy* (Maryknoll, N.Y.: Orbis Books, 1994), 51. See also Jon Sobrino, "Los pobres: crucificado y salvadores," in María López and Jon Sobrino, *La matanza de los pobres* (Madrid: Ediciones HOAC, 1993), 361.

63. See Mark Danner, *The Massacre at El Mozote* (New York: Vintage Books, 1994).

64. For an extensive treatment of forgiveness and reconciliation in Latin American liberation theology, see Daniel M. Bell Jr., *Liberation Theology*

after the End of History: The Refusal to Cease Suffering (New York: Routledge, 2001). See also Sobrino, *The Principle of Mercy*; Elsa Tamez, *The Amnesty of Grace*, trans. S. Ringe (Nashville: Abingdon, 1993).

65. Gutiérrez, *A Theology of Liberation*, 24.

Nine / Mohawk / Revitalization Movements

1. Isaiah Berlin, *The Crooked Timber of Humanity* (New York: Knopf, 1991).

2. Anthony Wallace, "Revitalization Movements," *American Anthropologist* 58 (April 1958).

3. Anthony Wallace, *The Death and Rebirth of a Seneca* (New York: Vintage Books, 1973).

4. Angie Debo, *A History of the Indians of the United States* (Norman: University of Oklahoma Press, 1970).

5. See my *Utopian Legacies: A History of Conquest and Oppression in the Western World* (Santa Fe, N.Mex.: Clear Lights Publishers, 2000).

6. Daniel Jonah Goldhagen, *Hitler's Willing Executioners: Ordinary Germans and the Holocaust* (New York: Vintage, 1997).

Ten / Isasi Díaz / Reconciliation

1. The use of "kin-dom" instead of "kingdom" or "reign" stems from the desire to use a metaphor that is much more relevant to our world today. From my perspective as a *mujerista* theologian, the point of reference for kin-dom of God is the concept of family and community that is central to my Latina culture. There is also the need to move away from "kingdom" and "reign" that are sexist and hierarchical metaphors.

2. 1971 Synod of Bishops, "Justice in the World," in *The Gospel of Peace and Justice*, ed. Joseph Gremillion (Maryknoll, N.Y.: Orbis Books, 1975), 514.

3. René David Roset, "Para una teología y pastoral de reconciliación desde Cuba" [unpublished article], November 1981, revised in 1982, 3. David Roset (David is the first part of his last name) is an elderly Roman Catholic theologian who has taught for many years at the Catholic seminary in Havana, Cuba, with whom I have visited. Originally he is from Canada.

4. This echoes the well-known quotation of Martin Luther King, "Without justice, there can be no peace." See Martin Luther King Jr., *Stride towards Freedom: The Montgomery Story* (New York: Harper, 1958). This also echoes the thinking of Pope Paul VI. See Pope Paul VI, "Message of His Holiness Pope Paul VI for the Celebration of the 'World

Day of Peace,' January 1, 1972: 'If You Want Peace, Work for Justice,' "
www.fju.edu.tw/homepage2/peace/1972e.htm.

5. Iris Marion Young, *Justice and the Politics of Difference* (Princeton, N.J.: Princeton University Press, 1990), 5.

6. Ibid.

7. Ibid., 169.

8. Ibid., 7.

9. Ibid., 9.

10. Ibid., 10.

11. Sharon Welch, *A Feminist Ethics of Risk* (Minneapolis: Fortress Press, 1990), 68.

12. Stanley Hauerwas, *Truthfulness and Tragedy* (Notre Dame, Ind.: University of Notre Dame Press, 1977), 82–98.

13. Karl Rahner and Herbert Vorgrimler, "Satisfaction," in *Dictionary of Theology* (New York: Crossroad, 1990), 462. See also articles on "Penance," "Penance, Sacrament of," "Contrition," "Metanoia," and "Penalties of Sin."

14. The way these different elements are embodied depends on the different church traditions. For example, in the Roman Catholic tradition, confession of one's sins is to a priest, while in the Protestant traditions, confession is to God.

15. I am applying here Ignacio Ellacuría's understanding of the process of knowing reality to knowing the reality of brokenness and the need for reconciliation. See Ignacio Ellacuría, "Hacia una fundamentación del método teológico latinoamericano," *Estudios centroamericanos* 30, no. 322–23 (August–September 1975): 419.

16. Though the language I use here is the traditional Roman Catholic theological language, this understanding is also embraced by the Protestant tradition, though different terminology is used. See Rahner and Vorgrimler, "Grace," in *Dictionary of Theology*, 196–200.

17. This point is clear in 2 Corinthians 5:18–20. This is also one of the points David Roset makes so clear in his 1981 article.

18. Aloysius Pieris, *An Asian Theology of Liberation* (Maryknoll, N.Y.: Orbis Books, 1988), 24–31.

19. See Antjie Krog, *Country on My Skull* (South Africa: Random House, 1998), particularly chap. 10.

20. Robert J. Schreiter, *Reconciliation — Mission and Ministry in a Changing Social Order* (Maryknoll, N.Y.: Orbis Books, 1992), 11.

21. The violence between the Israelis and the Palestinians rages on while I write this article. Yesterday a Palestinian woman who lives in a border town

in Gaza spoke in her broken English with a U.S. television reporter. "The people who want revenge have a little heart," she said gesturing with her hand to show the tiniest of space between her two fingers. Behind her one could see her children playing with their little friends.

22. The importance of giving up any desire for revenge is striking in the following event. In 1996 the Cuban Air Force shot down two small civilian airplanes belonging to a Cuban exile group, "Brothers to the Rescue." Though the families of the four men killed have pursued action against the Cuban government in the U.S. courts, one of the families has taken the position of not asking for nor accepting any monetary compensation for the death of their son. In part their reason might be not to "put a price" on the life of their dead relative. But part has also to do with the desire not to seek revenge.

23. In the history of my own country, Cuba, there is an important example of the need not to seek revenge. The *"Manifiesto de Montecristi,"* Cuba's declaration of independence from Spain, written by José Martí, "the father of the country," on March 25, 1895, twice speaks against vengeance. The document insists that those declaring war have been cleansed of hatred and have a sense of indulgence regarding Cubans who are timid or who are mistaken. It also mentions that during the war and once it is over they will be merciful with those who repent. See Carlos Ripoll, *José Martí — Antología mayor* (New York: Editorial Dos Ríos, 1995), 59–61.

24. Desmond Tutu, *No Future without Forgiveness* (New York: Doubleday, 1999), 257–82.

25. Sister Helen Prejean, a nun who works with persons on death row and who opposes capital punishment, made this point in a public lecture a few years ago. See Helen Prejean, *Dead Man Walking — An Eyewitness Account of the Death Penalty in the USA* (New York: Random House, Vintage Books, 1994).

26. This is the understanding of Archbishop Tutu that has become entrenched in large areas of South African society and that has guided the work of the South African Truth and Reconciliation Commission.

27. The *Sunday Times* of Cape Town, South Africa, December 6, 1998, carried an article entitled, "Forgive the torturer, not the torture," written by Wilhelm Verwoerd, lecturer in political philosophy and applied ethics at Stellenbosch University. The article talks about Ashley Forbes, a black South African, tortured by Jeffrey Benzien, who before the Truth and Reconciliation Commission of that country had "publicly demonstrated his notorious 'wet-bag' torture technique." The article says that it was "Forbes's choice to put aside legitimate feelings of anger and humiliation and thus, 'get on

with the rest of my life.' " The article goes on to say, "Sometimes victims are asked to forgive for the sake of perpetrators, to release the wrongdoers from their burden of guilt. That is an important part of forgiveness, but not the whole story.... Forbes shows that forgiveness should be encouraged, perhaps in the first place, as an antidote to the poison of unresolved bitterness and repressed resentment, as a call to those violated to liberate themselves from the prison of victimhood — for the sake of themselves, their children and the rest of society.

" ... A powerful emotional reason for resisting forgiveness is because it is seen as diminishing the seriousness of violations. Forgiveness becomes a sign of disrespect to those who have been violated.... Archbishop Desmond Tutu ... is requesting nobody to forgive the gross human-rights violations of the past. It is a call to recognise the humanity of 'perpetrators' even if their humanity is hidden behind a wet-bag.... Those who suffered and continue to suffer are given the moral first place they deserve. The truth commission process flows from that commitment."

28. Renny Golden, *The Hour of the Poor, the Hour of the Women* (New York: Crossroad, 1991), 17.

Contributors

Daniel M. Bell Jr. is Associate Professor of Theological Ethics, Lutheran Theological Southern Seminary.

Martin L. Cook is Professor of Philosophy, United States Air Force Academy.

John Dominic Crossan is Professor Emeritus of Religious Studies, DePaul University.

Ada María Isasi-Díaz is Professor of Ethics and Theology, Drew University.

Steven Leonard Jacobs is Aaron Aronov Professor of Judaic Studies, University of Alabama.

John Kelsay is Richard L. Rubenstein Professor of Religion, Florida State University.

Charles A. Kimball is Professor of Religious Studies, Wake Forest University.

Hans Küng is Director Emeritus of the Institute for Ecumenical Research, University of Tübingen, Germany.

John Mohawk is Professor and Director of Indigenous Studies, Center for the Americas, State University of New York, Buffalo.

Donald W. Musser is Hal S. Marchman Chair of Civic and Social Responsibility, Stetson University.

Daniel A. Puchalla is a graduate student at the University of Chicago Divinity School.

is a recent graduate of Stetson University majoring in Religious Studies.

D. Dixon Sutherland is Professor of Religious Studies and Director of the Institute for Christian Ethics at Stetson University.

Valarie H. Ziegler is Professor of Religious Studies, DePauw University.